Engagement & Wedding Rings

The Definitive Buying Guide For People In Love

Antoinette L. Matlins

Antonio C. Bonanno, F.G.A., A.S.A., M.G.A.

Jane Crystal

GEMSTONE PRESS

South Woodstock, Vermont

Distributed by
Van Nostrand Reinhold
New York, New York

Matlins, Antoinette Leonard.
   Engagement & wedding rings : the definitive
buying guide for people in love / Antoinette L.
Matlins, Antonio C. Bonanno, Jane Crystal.
    p.   cm.
   Includes bibliographical references.
   ISBN 0-943763-05-3 : $14.95
   1. Diamonds—Purchasing.   2. Gems—Purchasing.
3. Rings—Purchasing.   4. Betrothal.
5. Marriage customs and rites.   I. Bonanno, Antonio C.
II. Crystal, Jane, 1950–   .   III. Title.
IV. Title: Engagement and wedding rings.
   HD9677.A2M38   1990   89-77334
   739.27—dc20   CIP

Book design by James F. Brisson
Illustrations by Kathleen Robinson

10 9 8 7 6 5 4 3 2 1

Published by GemStone Press
A Division of LongHill Partners, Inc.
Long Hill Road, P.O. Box 276
South Woodstock, Vermont 05071
Tel: (802) 457-4000
Fax: (802) 457-4004

Distributed to the book trade and libraries by:
Van Nostrand Reinhold
115 Fifth Avenue, New York, NY 10003

Cover
Photography: John William Farrell
Design: Elizabeth Rand Graphics
Gemstones: Courtesy of David S. Kwiat,
      and Maurice Shire, Inc.
Rings: Courtesy of David S. Kwiat, Inc.,
      U. Doppelt & Co., Precious Stones Co.,
      Henry Meyer Inc., and Maurice Shire, Inc.

This book is about Your rings

To be given to

_____ **by** _____

BRIDE   GROOM

and to

_____ **by** _____

GROOM   BRIDE

Who met and fell in Love on

_____

MONTH / DAY / YEAR

Who decided to become engaged to one another on

_____

MONTH / DAY / YEAR

Who celebrate their Wedding on

_____

MONTH / DAY / YEAR

And whose rings will be for all the world to see… the sign of their Love and Commitment to each other.

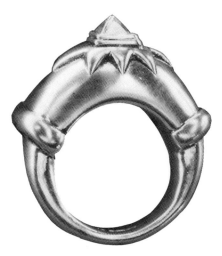

*"Two torches in one ring of burning fire.
Two wills, two hearts, two passions are
bonded in marriage...."*

*Inscription within The
Sforza Marriage Ring, 15th century.*

Photo: Diamond Information Center,
copied by Julie Crossland, London

OTHER BOOKS BY THE AUTHORS:

Gem Identification Made Easy:
A Hands-On Guide to More
Confident Buying & Selling
    GemStone Press, South Woodstock, VT (1989)

Jewelry & Gems: The Buying Guide
    GemStone Press, South Woodstock, VT (1989)

DEDICATION

To my daughter, Dawn, and my sons,
Andrew and Seth,
With the hope that you will each find
that special someone
To surround you in a love that,
Like the rings you will place upon each
other's finger,
knows no beginning and no end.
A love for all eternity.

And to my husband, Stuart,
Who is that special someone for me.

CONTENTS

Acknowledgments

All of the charts that appear here were especially designed and executed for use in this book; however, in some cases, charts from other publications were used as inspiration and reference. Grateful acknowledgment is given to Gemological Institute of America (GIA), for use of the following charts as reference: The charts appearing on pages 53, 54, and 65, from their book, *The Jewelers' Manual.*

Some of the material appearing in this book is condensed from the authors' *Jewelry & Gems: The Buying Guide.*

Grateful acknowledgment is also given to the following for use of their photographs, reports and other invaluable assistance:

Accredited Gemologists Association (AGA),
San Francisco
Ambar Diamonds, Inc., Los Angeles
American Gem Society (AGS), Los Angeles
American Gem Trade Association (AGTA), Dallas
American Gemological Laboratories, Inc. (AGL),
New York
American Society of Appraisers (ASA), Washington, DC
James Breski & Co., Chicago
Barbara Brisson, JB Graphics, Williamsville, VT
Cartier, Inc., New York
Christie's, London and New York
Diamond Information Center, New York and London
Aaron Faber Gallery, New York
The Gold Information Center, New York
Lazare Kaplan, Inc., New York
Richard Kimball (The Goldsmith), Denver
National Gem Appraising Laboratory, Washington, DC
Nova Stylings, Van Nuys, California
Radiant Cut Diamond Corporation, New York
George Sawyer Design, Minneapolis

xii ⓪ *Acknowledgments*

Tiffany & Company, New York
David Tomono Photography, New York
Monica Wilson, GemStone Press
Benjamin Zucker (Precious Stones Company), New York

Special thanks to the Bonanno family for their loving support, encouragement, and professional expertise:
Kathryn Bonanno, F.G.A., P.G.
Kenneth Bonanno, F.G.A., P.G.
Karen Bonanno Ford, F.G.A., P.G.
Ruth Bonanno, Wife and Mother

Introduction

"With this ring, I thee wed."

These were the words my husband and I said to each other, and the words that you, too, will be saying one day soon. Our rings have been symbols of our love and commitment to each other and of our hopes and dreams for the future. Your rings of love will have the same deep meaning.

The purchase of your engagement and wedding rings is one of the most significant purchases you'll ever make, both financially and emotionally. No other single piece of jewelry will ever be as important. No matter how successful you become, no matter how magnificent other jewelry purchases might be, nothing carries with it the same excitement and magic.

Since *Jewelry & Gems: The Buying Guide* was published, clients and readers have urged us to write a book dedicated exclusively to engagement and wedding rings—a book that incorporates our knowledge of gems and jewelry and our own experience in helping couples with this meaningful purchase. After searching the current literature, we were surprised to find that there was nothing that covered what couples really need to know. Given the importance of this purchase, and being the romantics that we are, we agreed that this book had to be written. And, to make it even more useful, Jane Crystal, a journalist who has written extensively on fashion, style and bridal themes, joined our team to add her special perspective.

From our own experience, we know how often the excitement and anticipation you should be feeling is replaced by anxiety. If you feel you don't even know where to begin, you're not alone. Most people feel overwhelmed, intimidated, and confused at the prospect of buying an engagement and wedding ring. This is a shame, but it's no surprise.

Today's couple has many more choices than did couples in earlier generations. To begin with, there are more jewelers than ever before, each anxious for your business. There are more stones than ever before from which to make a selection, and a wider range of sizes, shapes, qualities and prices. And once you've chosen the stone, there's an almost endless variety of ring settings from which to choose. It's easy to feel dazed. But it really doesn't have to be overwhelming, and it won't be if you know how to go about it. More importantly, *knowing how* is the key to experiencing the thrill and excitement that should be part of making this most significant acquisition.

In *Engagement and Wedding Rings*, we share our own and our clients' experiences with you, and provide a practical guide through the entire process. With it, you'll find all the information you need to feel more confident about making the right choice, including:

- Romantic traditions behind engagement and wedding rings
- What factors affect quality differences in diamonds and colored gemstones
- How to spot differences in stones that may appear to be the same quality
- How to compare prices
- How to select the right style and design
- How to get what you want on a budget
- How to select your jeweler, appraiser and insurer
- Types of misrepresentation to guard against, and how to protect yourself
- Questions you need to ask when buying particular stones
- What to get in writing
  . . . And more.

We hope you enjoy *Engagement & Wedding Rings* and find it to be an indispensible guide. Most of all, we hope it will remove your fear and enable you to enjoy this special time to the fullest, to truly experience the wonder, surprise, and romance that should all be part of creating that perfect moment . . . and that perfect ring with which to begin your marriage and life together.

Antoinette Matlins
South Woodstock, Vermont

PART ONE

ENGAGEMENT AND WEDDING RINGS THROUGH THE AGES

A proud Maximilian of Austria gave a sparkling diamond to Mary of Burgundy in 1477, in celebration of their decision to marry.

CHAPTER 1

The Romance of the Ring*

*Just as the blushing dawn gives promise of
the glory of the sunrise, so the betrothal
ring, as the token of a pledge, serves to
herald, as it were, an emblem that denotes
the fulfilment of the vow.*

from a Victorian ladies' magazine

The romantic traditions associated with rings, especially those containing diamonds and precious gems, resound throughout history. In fact, evidence of the engagement tradition dates back as far as the caveman. The Pharaohs of Egypt, however, are credited with being the first to use a ring in the form of a circular band as a symbol of eternity. The Egyptians regarded the circle, a shape that has no beginning and no end, as a heavenly reminder that life, happiness, and love have no beginning and no end.

By Roman times, it was an established tradition to give a ring, a symbol of the cycle of life and eternity, as a public pledge that the marriage contract between a man and woman would be honored. These early rings were made of iron, according to the accounts of Roman historian C. Plinius Secundus. Gold was introduced some time in the second century A.D. Soon, the Christians adopted the custom, and the ring became an integral part of the marriage service.

* Some of the material in Chapter 1 and Chapter 2 has been condensed from *The Power of Love*, copyright © 1988, The Diamond Information Centre, London, England. Reprinted by permission.

5

It wasn't long before the symbolism of the circular ring was further enhanced by the addition of gems. By medieval days, wealthy citizens were married with gem-set rings—diamonds, colored gems, and diamonds combined with colored gems became the fashion. Colored gems were often used because of the symbolism of particular colors. For rings of love, ruby was a particular favorite because it was the color of the heart. Sapphire was also popular since it was the color of the heavens. Other colored gems believed to hold certain magical properties (see Chapter 12) also became popular choices for betrothal rings.

Diamond held a particularly regal position at this time. It was one of the rarest and costliest of gems. And it was prized above other gems for marriage because of its unique properties and the many special powers attributed to it. While reserved for only the most privileged, it became the choice for those fortunate enough—or powerful enough—to acquire one.

❖ *The Allure of Diamond*

Diamond, nature's hardest substance—uniquely able to resist both fire and steel, and therefore all of man's early efforts to alter it—epitomized unyielding power and invincible strength. It seemed truly indestructible. What more natural symbol for the marriage covenant, and for the edict "What God Has Joined Together, Let No Man Put Asunder." If the many properties of diamond and its indestructibility were in fact transferred to the wearer, a marriage sealed with the diamond would certainly last forever.

Indeed, throughout history, the diamond has been one of the most coveted gems. Uncut diamonds adorned the suits of armor of the great knights; cut diamonds have appeared in the crowns of kings and queens all through the ages. Legends of the diamond's mythical properties have been passed along for centuries.

Hundreds of years before Christ, in India, where diamonds were first discovered, the diamond was valued even more for its strength and magic than for its great beauty. The diamond was thought to protect its wearer from snakes, fire, poison, illness, thieves, and all the combined forces of evil. It was a favorite choice for rings given in love, some of which date back to earliest Indian history.

As the gemstone of the zodiac House of Aries, symbolized by

the Ram, the diamond was believed by ancient astrologers to be powerful for people born under the planet Mars. They thought the diamond could provide fortitude, strength of mind, and continued love in marriage, as well as ward off witchcraft, poisons, and nightmares.

Each culture has prized the diamond for its unique properties. The Romans believed a diamond worn against the skin of their left arm would help them remain brave and daring in battle and give them strength over their enemies. An ancient passage reads: "He who carries a diamond on the left side shall be hardy and manly; it will guard him from accidents to the limbs; but nevertheless a good diamond will lose its power and virtue if worn by one who is incontinent, or drunken." Another Roman practice was to set diamonds in fine steel which would then serve as a charm against insanity.

The word diamond derives from the Greek *adamas*, meaning the unconquerable; its Latin equivalent is *diamas*. The diamond has a long and extensive history in books of importance to mankind, with the earliest references occurring in the Bible, Book of Exodus, Chapter 28. Here, in describing the details of the tabernacle and its furnishings, a description is given of the High Priest's breastplate: "And the second row shall be an emerald, a sapphire and a diamond." It was believed that the diamond worn by the Jewish High Priest had special powers to prove innocence or guilt—if the accused was guilty, the stone grew dim; if innocent, it shone more brilliantly than ever . . . and thus diamonds came to be associated with innocence, justice, faith, and strength. Early Christians also endowed the diamond with special powers, believing it to be an antidote against both moral and physical evil.

The Hindus classed diamonds according to the four castes of their social strata. The Brahmin diamond (colorless) gave power, friends, riches, and good luck; the Kshatriya (brown/champagne) prevented old age; Vaisya (the color of a "kodali flower") brought success; and the Sudra (a diamond with the sheen of a polished blade—probably gray or black) brought all types of good fortune. Red and yellow diamonds were exclusively royal gems, for kings alone. The Chinese treasured the diamond as an engraving tool, while the Italians trusted it to protect against poison.

Through the ages, diamonds have been associated with almost everything from sleepwalking to producing invincibility and spiritual ecstasy. In the 1500s it was believed that diamond would enhance the love of a husband for his wife. To dream of diamonds was considered symbolic of success, wealth, happiness, and victory. Even sexual power has been strongly attributed to the diamond. There is a catch, however, to the powers associated with it—some believe that one must find the diamond "naturally" to experience its magic, that it loses its powers if acquired by purchase. However, when offered as a pledge of love or friendship, its powers return!

CHAPTER 2

Engagement and Wedding Ring Traditions*

❖ The Middle Ages Set the Stage for Betrothal Traditions

As early as the fifteenth century, the diamond, although only available to a very few, was prized above all others as the gem for betrothal. It was acknowledged as the ultimate symbol because of its unique properties, especially its ability to resist destructive forces.

In 1477, we find one of the first recorded accounts of the use of diamond in a betrothal ring. Desiring to please his prospective father-in-law, Archduke Maximilian of Austria proposed to Mary of Burgundy, heeding the words of a trusted advisor who wrote:

> At the betrothal your grace must have a ring set with a diamond and also a gold ring.

Maximilian wed his beloved Mary within 24 hours of the betrothal ceremony. Thus began a tradition that has spanned centuries.

At the time of Mary and Maximilian the diamond was used in its natural crystal state. Certainly this was in part because it was the hardest natural substance known and man lacked the

A replica of the diamond betrothal ring given by Maximilian of Austria to Mary of Burgundy in 1477. This is one of the first diamond rings known to have been given to seal an engagement.

Photo: Copy of ring, courtesy Kunsthistoriches Museum, Vienna, Austria, and Diamond Information Center

---

* Some of the material in Chapter 1 and Chapter 2 has been condensed from *The Power of Love*, copyright © 1988, The Diamond Information Centre, London, England. Reprinted with permission.

knowledge and skill to cut it. But perhaps there was more to it than that. Diamond crystals look like two pyramids joined together base-to-base. From the time of the Pharaohs, the shape of the pyramid was identified with power, strength, and mystery, so the "pyramidal" shape of the diamond crystal itself may have added to diamond's allure, to the mystery and power identified with it. The very shape of the natural diamond crystal may have made it all the more attractive as the choice to symbolize the power of love and marriage.

A natural diamond crystal. Notice its resemblance to two pyramids placed together, base-to-base.

Photo: Diamond Information Center

One might think that using an uncut diamond would have detracted from the beauty of these early rings. However, this was not the case. Medieval goldsmiths used imagination and ingenuity to create beautiful mountings to hold the diamond crystal. Ornate and complex settings distinguished by elaborate enamel detail made up for the somewhat crude condition of the rough diamonds they held.

At the same time, the inside of the ring took on added significance as the "posy" ring gained popularity. These rings were known for the little poems and romantic messages inscribed inside the hoop of the ring, a tradition which has continued until today, although with inscriptions somewhat more concise than the poems of old!

The first significant breakthrough in diamond cutting techniques occurred by the end of the fifteenth century, enabling a cutter to apply the first "facet" to the natural diamond crystal. These early cut diamonds were called table-cut because the big, flat facet resembled the top of a table. This was the initial step toward diamond cutting and polishing, and the first step in unlocking the diamond's hidden fire, brilliance, and dazzling beauty.

A 17th century posy ring, engraved on the inside "I doe rejoyce in thee my choyce."

Photo: Christie's

❖ *Sixteenth-Century Craftsmen Reach New Heights*

The table-cut diamond became a great challenge to the goldsmiths of the sixteenth century as they strove to create designs which could exhibit the rare stone to its fullest potential. As they refined their art—with the full support of the royal court—their efforts reached a peak of perfection. The results are masterpieces of delicate design and fine enameling, combined with pointed

or table-cut stones. An impressive example is the wedding ring of Duke Albrecht V of Bavaria, a rosette set with sixteen small diamonds.

Renaissance Jewish Wedding Rings

Some of the most beautiful and intricate rings ever created were those associated with the Jewish wedding ceremony during the Renaissance period. These Jewish wedding rings, however, were used only during the wedding ceremony, as they were far too unwieldy for daily wear. In many of these elaborately ornamented rings, the bezel took the form of a gabled building, a synagogue or Solomon's Temple. They were further enhanced with extensive detailing in enamel, as well as Hebrew inscriptions.

The Gimmel Ring

The increasing technical know-how of Renaissance goldsmiths also created a new style of marriage ring called the gimmel, from the Latin *gemelli*, meaning twins. The gimmel, or twin ring, has two hoops (sometimes three) that fan open from a pivot at the base. When open, they often contained intricately sculptured forms symbolizing eternity in life and death figures. When shut, the hoops slid together so perfectly that only a single ring could be seen. The gimmel ring thus symbolized the coming together of two lives truly as one. When three hoops were used, the third symbolized the presence of God in the marriage. This symbolic allusion to marriage was further emphasized by an inscription on the hoop taken from the marriage service: "Whom God Has Joined Together Let No Man Put Asunder." Martin Luther and Catherine Bora were married in 1525 with an inscribed gimmel ring.

Renaissance Jewish wedding rings representing some of the most beautiful and intricate rings ever made.

Around 1600, the gimmel began to incorporate another romantic symbol—two clasped hands. In the *fede* (Italian for faith) ring, the gimmel hoops ended in hands which, when the ring was closed, joined together.

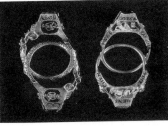

A third symbol was often added—a heart. In some of the more elaborate fede rings, delicately enameled hands embraced a sumptuous diamond heart.

In addition to its prevalence in the fede ring, the symbol of

*This ring is a German **gimmel**-type, dated 1631. It comes apart in the center to reveal two figures symbolizing the life cycle and the unity of the couple's role in it.*

A typical fede betrothal ring showing two clasped hands that symbolize faithfulness. The red ruby was also associated with the heart (late 13th century). Photo: Christie's

the heart was very popular in seventeenth-century rings. This natural symbol of love and romance was often depicted "aflame with desire," incorporating rose- and table-cut diamonds, or colored gems.

At this time we also see a reaction to the increasing use of rings, especially the more elaborate examples. In contrast to an atmosphere in which expensive symbols of romance were fashionable, the Puritans, rebelling against Church ritual, attempted, unsuccessfully, to abolish the wedding ring. This test of tradition ultimately proved that the symbolism surrounding the custom of the wedding ring was too powerful to be destroyed.

*An early 17th century **gimmel-type fede** ring in which the hands clasp a heart, shown here in both the open and closed positions. The heart contains a diamond and ruby, combining the associations of love (identified with ruby) and eternity (symbolized by diamond).* Photo: Christie's

The Tradition of the "Fourth Finger"

Wedding rings of the seventeenth century were frequently worn on the thumb. During the marriage ceremony, however, the fourth finger was most commonly used. There are various origins for the tradition of placing the ring on the fourth finger. According to one source, the custom stems from the Christian wedding service in which the priest arrives at the fourth finger after touching three fingers of the left hand: "In the Name of the Father . . . Son . . . and Holy Ghost." A more romantic legend that harkens back to Egyptian times holds that the third finger of the left hand follows the *vena amoris* (vein of love), a vein that was believed to run from that finger directly to the heart. The more practical explanation is that the fourth finger is the most protected finger, so by placing the ring there, one could best avoid damage to it.

❖ In the Eighteenth Century Diamonds Abound

The eighteenth century produced a sparkling variety of betrothal and wedding rings. The discovery of diamonds in Brazil dramatically increased the supply so that diamond jewelry became more widely available. Simultaneously, improved candle-lighting increased the number of social events held in the evening, when sparkling diamonds could be admired to the fullest. The height of fashion at the time was for a woman to appear with her fingers glittering with diamonds. Pro-viding enough diamond jewelry became the major preoccupa-tion of the eighteenth-century jeweler.

An 18th century ring making use of two diamond hearts.

Photo: Private Collection, courtesy Diamond Information Center

Polishing techniques under-went improvement to meet the demand for glittering stones, and the rose-cut was replaced by an early version of the round, bril-liant-cut. Settings were pared down to show more of the diamond, and silver settings were created to enhance the diamond's white sparkle. Stones also were often backed with metallic foil to add greater brilliance and sparkle, or to emphasize or enhance color— *red foil* to enhance the red of ruby, *green foil* for emerald, and so on.

Mid-eighteenth Century Introduces Diamond "Keeper Ring"

By the mid-eighteenth century, jewelry design began to show the effects of the fanciful rococo spirit. Colored gems (including colored diamonds) were increasingly popular, especially used with white diamonds, and the stones themselves increasingly became the centerpiece of the design. In keeping with its romantic tradition, the heart motif was especially popular, often set with both white and colored diamonds, and colored gems such as ruby. Delicate, feminine jewelry of this kind expressed the elegant and refined taste of the time.

Rings which symbolized love and romance were cherished, particularly the betrothal ring. In 1761, King George III of En-gland started what was to become a popular tradition when he presented Queen Charlotte a diamond *keeper ring* on their wed-ding day. This was a simple diamond hoop worn on the finger next to the engagement ring to *protect* it and, perhaps, the mar-riage itself. The symbolism of the diamond combined with that of the circle was clear—diamond was indestructible and would protect; the unending circle represented eternity. We find a con-temporary version of Queen Charlotte's keeper ring in today's diamond wedding or anniversary band, a band that usually con-tains a single row of diamonds encircling the finger.

❖ The Nineteenth Century: Forerunners of Modern Traditions

A replica of Queen Charlotte's **keeper** *ring—to* **keep** *her engagement ring safe (1761). Today a similar style, a single row of diamonds encircling the finger, is popular as a wedding or anniversary band.*

Copy made by Julie Crossland, London.

Photo: courtesy Diamond Information Center.

At the start of the nineteenth century, the idealized status of women was reflected in the style of their jewelry—pretty, feminine, and sentimental. Symbols of love—hearts, crowns, flowers—followed them from the previous century. But as the century progressed, jewelry began to play a more important role and increasingly became a status symbol in nineteenth-century society. The Industrial Revolution provided greater wealth for more people than ever before. Men could now afford extravagant gifts for the women they loved. Gem-studded jewelry became the favored choice.

Diamonds were increasingly in demand but there was a limited supply so they were still available to only a few. Then, in 1870, supply greatly increased when a major diamond deposit was discovered on the African continent. Diamond, the gem that most could only dream about, suddenly became available to a far wider public.

And so, with the rich new supply, the nineteenth century will see the diamond's full beauty revealed. The supply of rough diamonds from Africa not only influenced availability and jewelry design, but also resulted in greater experimentation with cutting and polishing. Soon diamonds showed a truly unique beauty; they now revealed a brilliance and fire unknown in any other gem. Set alone, the glorious diamond became the height of fashion.

During the nineteenth century, Queen Victoria was the most avid collector and visible promoter of the jewelry of the period. She not only maintained an immense collection, but spent many thousands of pounds with her Court jeweler, Garrard. In 1850, she excitedly accepted the magnificent 105.602 carat Koh-i-Noor (the largest in the world at that time), a gift from the East India Company.

❖ The Twentieth Century and the Tiffany Setting

Dramatic changes in jewelry design took place in the late nineteenth century. As the role of women changed from docile and demure to increasingly strong and independent, jewelry correspondingly became larger, bolder, and more assertive. Then, in reaction to the boldness, a romantic, free-thinking spirit emerged in the form of what came to be called Art Nouveau. This movement brought a fluid delicacy back to design that continued into the early twentieth century. And, as diamonds continued to be the central element in rings of love, it was the perfect environment to introduce the revolutionary new "Tiffany mount" at the close of the nineteenth century. This exciting setting began a tradition for the diamond solitaire (a ring with a single large stone at the center) that carried into the twentieth century and continues to be the most popular choice for the engagement ring.

Tiffany, the famous New York jeweler, invented a dramatic "open" mount. In this innovative setting, the stone was held up prominently by six tiny prongs (like little fingers). This setting allowed the fullest amount of light to enter the stone, so that it could exhibit maximum brilliance and sparkle. Unlike old style settings, which concealed most of the stone (and many of its flaws), the new Tiffany style revealed the diamond fully, and its overall quality—its cut, color, and clarity—was now clearly visible and could be fully appreciated.

Modern cutting and polishing techniques have released the full beauty of a stone so that light radiates from each of the facets. Modern materials such as platinum and new alloys have also provided greater freedom in design and setting, opening up fresh new vistas for twentieth-century craftsmen. Design now concentrates more on finding the right balance between personal style and highlighting the stone.

The skills of present-day designers continue to delight lovers with exquisite new ways of presenting the stone of their choice and incorporating the symbolism and traditions of centuries. When today's bride receives her engagement and wedding rings, she will become connected to men and women in love in both past and future generations. She will become part of a tradition of love that has spanned centuries.

*The famous
Tiffany 6-prong
setting.*
Photo: Diamond
Information Center

PART TWO

DIAMOND ENGAGEMENT
AND
WEDDING RINGS

CHAPTER 3

Selecting the Diamond

The diamond engagement ring has emerged as the universal symbol for the union of two people in love. Not only is it the formal beginning—the visible "announcement" of your engagement—but the centuries-old symbolism surrounding the diamond reflects the commitments made to each other and to a love that will last forever.

While some women prefer other gems to diamond, or opt for the special significance of a family heirloom, a diamond is the overwhelming choice of today's bride. Some brides-to-be have no doubt been taken by surprise with the unexpected presentation of an engagement ring, but it is probably safest to go about the task of selecting the ring *together*. While the element of surprise is very romantic, keep in mind that the engagement ring is meant to be worn for a lifetime. So it is particularly important that the bride-to-be really loves it; that it reflects her personal taste and style.

The following chapters will give you everything you need to know to purchase a diamond with greater confidence—whether you're shopping for an engagement ring, wedding or anniversary band, or simply a beautiful piece of diamond jewelry. The greater your awareness of the elements that determine diamond quality, the better your chances of knowing what you want, getting exactly what you're after, and deriving lasting pleasure from it.

Some modern diamond engagement rings.

Photo: Courtesy Mappin & Webb, London and the Diamond Information Center

❖ What is Diamond?

Chemically speaking, a diamond is the simplest of all gemstones. It is plain crystallized carbon—the same substance, chemically, as the soot left on the inside of a glass globe after the burning of a candle, the substance used in lead pencils.

The diamond differs from these in its crystal form, which gives it the desirable properties that have made it so highly prized—its hardness, which gives its unsurpassed wearability; its brilliance; and its fire. (But note that while diamond is the hardest natural substance known, it can be chipped or broken if hit hard from certain angles; and if the girdle has been cut too thin it can be chipped with even a modest blow.)

The transparent white (colorless) diamond is the most popular variety, but diamond also occurs in colors. When the color is prominent it is called a *fancy* diamond or *master fancy*. Diamond is frequently found in nice yellow and brown shades. Colors such as pink, light blue, light green, and lavender occur much more rarely. In diamonds, the colors seen are usually pastel. Deep colors such as red and dark blue are extremely rare. Historically, most colored diamonds have sold for more than their pure white counterparts, except for very pale yellow or brown varieties. V*ery* pale yellow or brown may not be fancy diamonds but *off color* stones that are very common and sell for much less than white or fancy diamonds.

Fancy colored diamonds that have obtained their color artificially, through exposure to certain types of radiation and heating techniques, are readily available. The bill of sale (and any accompanying certification, appraisal, etc.) should specify whether the color is natural or induced. If induced, the price should be much less, although the gem will often be just as beautiful as a natural.

❖ The Four Factors That Determine Diamond Value

Diamond quality and value are determined by four factors. These factors are called the "Four C's." If we were to rank them based on their importance in determining the *value* of a diamond, we would list them as follows:

1. Color (body color)
2. Clarity (degree of flawlessness)
3. Cut and proportion (often referred to as the *make*)
4. Carat weight

In terms of determining *beauty*, however, we would rank them in a different order:

1. Cut and proportion
2. Color
3. Clarity
4. Carat weight

Because each factor is a lesson in itself, we have devoted a chapter to each. We will begin with a discussion of diamond cutting and proportioning since we think it's the most important factor in terms of the stone's beauty, and because it's the least talked about . . . and understood. Also, it will familiarize you with the various terms used to describe the parts of the diamond.

CHAPTER 4

The Importance of Cutting and Proportioning

A *round brilliant-cut diamond*.
Photo: Lazare Kaplan International Inc.

The cutting of a diamond and its proportioning—called "make" in the jewelry trade—are of extraordinary importance because they have the greatest influence on the fire (variety and intensity of rainbow colors seen) and brilliance (liveliness, or sparkle) of the stone. It is the cutting and proportioning that releases the full beauty of the diamond, that releases the dazzling personality that sets it apart from all other gems. And yet, few people have any appreciation of its importance, and fewer still understand how to evaluate it. We hope that the information here will make an important difference in your understanding and appreciation of it.

❖ *The Cut of the Stone*

When talking about the cut of a stone, you should be familiar with a few general terms that apply to all faceted stones. These parts can vary in proportion to the rest of the stone and thus affect the stone's brilliance, beauty, and desirability.

Crown. The crown is also called the *top* of the stone. This is simply the upper portion of the stone, the part above the girdle.

24

Girdle. The girdle is the edge or border of the stone.

Pavilion. The pavilion is the bottom portion of the stone, measuring from the girdle to the bottom point.

Culet. The culet is the lowest part or point of the stone. It may be missing in some stones, which can indicate damage, or, particularly with colored stones, it may not be part of the original cut.

Table. The table is the flat top of the stone and is the stone's largest facet, often called the *face*.

Table spread. This term is used to describe the width of the table facet, often expressed as a percentage of the total width of the stone.

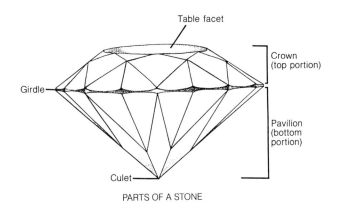

PARTS OF A STONE

There are many popular shapes for gemstones. Each shape affects the overall look of the stone, but if the stone is cut well its brilliance and value endure no matter which shape you choose. The shape you choose is simply a matter of taste. We will begin with the round, brilliant-cut stone, since this is the most popular.

A modern round, brilliant-cut diamond has 58 facets. When it is well-proportioned, this shape displays the stone's liveliness to the greatest extent because it enables the most light to be reflected back up through the top. This means round, brilliant-cut diamonds will have greater brilliance, overall, than other shapes. However, shape is a personal choice, and other shapes can also be very beautiful. The following diagram illustrates, in simple terms, the effect of cut and proportion on fire and brilliance in a round, brilliant-cut stone.

THE IMPORTANCE OF CUT TO BRILLIANCE

LIGHT REFLECTION IN AN IDEALLY PROPORTIONED DIAMOND
Ideal proportions insure the maximum brilliance. When light enters a properly cut diamond, it is reflected from facet to facet, and then back up through the top, exhibiting maximum fire and sparkle.

LIGHT REFLECTION IN A DIAMOND CUT TOO DEEP
In a diamond that is too deep, much of the light is reflected to opposite facets at the wrong angle and is lost through the sides. The diamond appears dark in the center.

LIGHT REFLECTION IN A DIAMOND CUT TOO SHALLOW
A diamond cut too shallow (to make it look larger) loses brilliancy. The eye sees a ring of dull reflection instead of the great brilliancy of a well cut diamond.

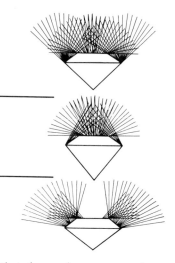

As a rule of thumb, if the top portion (crown) appears to be roughly one-third of the pavilion depth (distance from girdle to culet), the proportioning is probably acceptable.

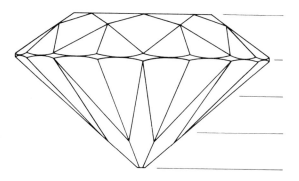

A well-proportioned stone.

❖ *Types of Diamond Proportioning*

Several types of diamond proportioning for round stones are currently used. Stones that adhere to these very precise formulas are referred to as having an "ideal" make. They vary slightly in relation to width and depth percentages traditionally quoted as "ideal," yet each creates a highly acceptable stone.

Round diamonds that have smaller tables exhibit more fire;

IDEAL CUT DIAMONDS

TABLE

IDEAL TABLE: the perimeter lines bow in; the effect is maximum brilliance and sparkle.

PAVILION DEPTH

IDEAL PAVILION: proper pavilion depth reflects the most light possible and can be identified by the small circle in the center.

CROWN ANGLE

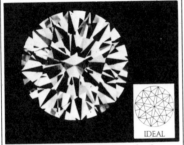

IDEAL CROWN ANGLE: allows for the maximum dispersion of light and can be identified by the "spear effect" i.e. the pavilion facets look wider in the side of the stone than in the table.

SIDE VIEW

IDEAL SIDE VIEW: when light enters an ideal cut diamond, it is reflected from facet to facet and comes back through the top of the diamond.

NON-IDEAL CUT DIAMONDS

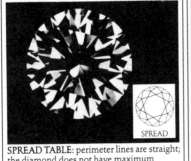

SPREAD TABLE: perimeter lines are straight; the diamond does not have maximum brilliance and sparkle.

DEEP PAVILION: light is lost through the sides because the diamond is too deep; result is a dark spot in the center.

Photo: Lazare Kaplan International Inc.

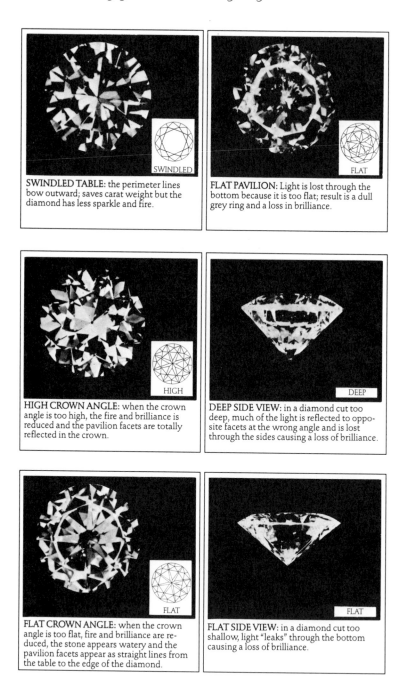

SWINDLED TABLE: the perimeter lines bow outward; saves carat weight but the diamond has less sparkle and fire.

FLAT PAVILION: Light is lost through the bottom because it is too flat; result is a dull grey ring and a loss in brilliance.

HIGH CROWN ANGLE: when the crown angle is too high, the fire and brilliance is reduced and the pavilion facets are totally reflected in the crown.

DEEP SIDE VIEW: in a diamond cut too deep, much of the light is reflected to opposite facets at the wrong angle and is lost through the sides causing a loss of brilliance.

FLAT CROWN ANGLE: when the crown angle is too flat, fire and brilliance are reduced, the stone appears watery and the pavilion facets appear as straight lines from the table to the edge of the diamond.

FLAT SIDE VIEW: in a diamond cut too shallow, light "leaks" through the bottom causing a loss of brilliance.

those with larger tables exhibit more brilliance. The latter seems to be more in fashion today.

The degree of fire (rainbow colors seen) and of brilliance (which results from the number of rays of light that are reflected from the back of the stone up through the top) depend primarily on the table *spread* (width), and the crown and pavilion angles.

But, as common sense may tell you, both can't excel in the same stone. A large table can create greater brilliance but will cause some reduction in fire; a small table area can increase fire but may reduce brilliance. The ideal would be a compromise that allows the greatest brilliance and fire simultaneously. No one has come to agreement, however, on what the percentages should be, since some people prefer fire to brilliance, and vice versa. This is why there are several accepted types of proportioning found in diamond, and "best" is a matter of personal preference. In terms of proportioning, the most important factors are called the "table percentage" and "depth percentage." These percentages are always included on diamond grading reports (certificates), such as those issued by the Gemological Institute of America (see Chapter 8).

In 1919 Marcel Tolkowsky calculated that the best theoretical compromise was a cut in which the width of the table facet was 53% of the total width of the stone (measuring across the stone at the girdle), with a pavilion angle of 40°45'. He felt this offered the most vivid fire with the least loss of brilliance. The Tolkowsky cut provides the basis for the modern American ideal cut.

Today there are several variations on Tolkowsky's formula, all considered "ideal." Generally, an ideal cut will have a table percentage between 53% and 57% and a depth percentage from approximately 58% to 60%. Ideal-cut stones can cost 15–25% more than other diamonds because of their increased beauty.

If you cannot afford an ideal make, but still want to ensure that your diamond will have acceptable brilliance and liveliness, look for stones with table percentages between 53% and 64%; avoid stones with a table percentage that exceeds 70% or, at least, expect to pay much less per carat for them. Look for stones with a depth percentage between approximately 58% and 62%; avoid stones with depth percentages over 64% or under 57% or, at least, expect to pay much less per carat.

Three recognized ideal proportions for round, brilliant-cut diamonds are:

1. Tolkowsky (also known as Standard American Ideal or American Cut)
2. Eppler (also known as European Cut)

3. Scan D.N. (Scandinavian Diamond Nomenclature, a popular European cut developed in 1970, used as a basis for grading in Scandinavia)

The basic differences between Tolkowsky's American cut and the other two can be seen in the table-spread variation and the height of the crown. All three are highly acceptable.

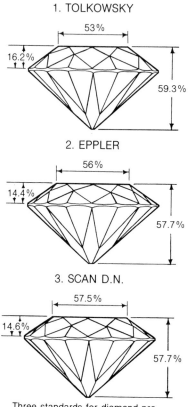

1. TOLKOWSKY

2. EPPLER

3. SCAN D.N.

Three standards for diamond proportioning — note the differences in table widths and crown heights.

We must point out, however, that there are individual stones that do not adhere to these proportions but still show strong fire and brilliance. Once again, your eye will be responsible for making the final determination. In general, when you look at a diamond that has brilliance and fire, the cut and proportioning probably are acceptable. When a stone appears lifeless, when it seems to have a dead center, or a dark center, it probably results from poor cutting and proportioning. The more time you take to look and compare diamonds of different qualities and prices, the better trained your eye will become to detect brilliance and fire, or lifelessness and dullness.

❖ *Faulty Cutting*

As you shop for and compare diamonds, be aware that many errors can occur in the cutting of a diamond that affect the appearance and value of the stone. Here are a few faults to watch for. We are using a round brilliant-cut as an example.

Look carefully for a sloping table or a table that is not almost perfectly perpendicular to the point of the culet.

The culet may frequently be the source of a problem. It can be chipped or broken, open or large (almost all modern cut stones

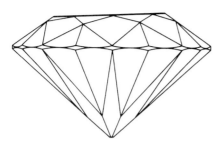

A brilliant-cut stone with a sloping table

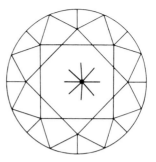

Off-center culet

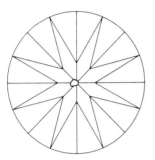

Open culet (viewed from the bottom)

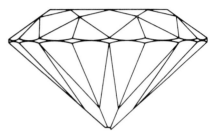

Broken or chipped culet

have culets that come nearly to a point), or it can be missing altogether.

If repairs to chipped areas result in misaligned facets, the stone's symmetry will be off.

Sometimes, too, as a result of repair, an extra facet will be formed, often in the crown facets, but also on or just below the girdle. These extra facets may slightly affect the stone's brilliance.

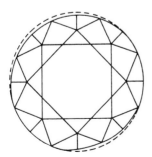

Poor symmetry

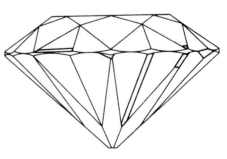

Stone with extra facets

❖ *Girdle Faults*

The girdle is often the source of faults. *Bearded* or *fringed* girdles are common. A fringed girdle exhibits small radial cracks penetrating the stone from the girdle. A bearded girdle is similar but not as pronounced a fault and can be easily repaired by repolishing, without much loss in diamond weight.

The relative thickness of the girdle affects the value of the stone. If the girdle is too thick, it loses not only in aesthetic appeal but in dimension. Too much of the stone's weight will be in the girdle, so, for its weight, it will be smaller in diameter than another stone of comparable weight.

If the girdle is too thin, it will chip or nick more easily. Such nicks can often be seen under the prongs of a setting. Some can be easily removed by repolishing, with minimal loss in weight or value. If the chips are numerous, the entire girdle can be repolished.

The girdle can also be wavy, rough, or entirely out-of-round.

A *natural* is another type of cutting fault. It is a small section of the diamond skin left on the polished diamond by the cutter. Usually, a natural results when a diamond cutter tries to get as large a diamond as possible from the rough stone. He leaves a small portion of the natural surface of the rough crystal on the girdle. If this natural is no thicker than the thickness of the girdle and is not so long as to distort the circumference of the stone, most dealers consider it a minor defect. If a natural is somewhat large and occurs slightly below the girdle, the cutter will probably polish it off, which will produce an extra facet below the girdle.

The gradations of girdle thickness

Wavy girdle   Out-of-round girdle

A *natural* at the girdle.

❖ *Deviations in Other Popular Cuts*

Within the popular fancy shapes, certain deviations have been established as standard. Some fall within the "acceptable" range, while others do not. Moderate deviations will not affect the beauty or value of a stone; however, deviations that exceed acceptable tolerances can seriously reduce a stone's beauty and value.

One of the most obvious deviations in proportion in fancy shapes is the *bow-tie*, or *butterfly* effect, a darkened area across the center or widest part of the stone, depending on the cut. The bow-tie is most commonly seen in the pear shape or marquise shape but may exist in any fancy shape. The degree of disproportion is directly related to the degree to which the bow-tie is pronounced. The more pronounced the bow-tie, the greater the degree of incorrect proportion.

As with the brilliant-cut diamond, fancy shapes can also be cut too broad or too narrow; and the pavilion can be too deep or too shallow.

Marquise with a pronounced bow tie, or butterfly.

Too broad

Too narrow

Culet too high

Culet too low

Open or misshapen culet

Pear-shaped stone,
cut correctly

❖ To What Extent Do Cut and Proportion Affect Value in Diamonds?

Stones of excellent cut and proportion cost significantly more per carat than those that are not cut well. The following will give a very basic idea of the monetary effect of some of the most frequently encountered defects in cut and proportion.

*Table is not a reasonably accurate octagon—2 to 15% off
*Girdle is too thick—5 to 20% off
*Symmetry of crown facets off—5 to 15% on round, less on fancy cuts since defect is not so easily seen
*Asymmetrical culet—2 to 5% off

*Misaligned culet—5 to 25% off
*Stone too shallow—15 to 50% off
*Stone too thick—10 to 30% off
*Slightly thin crown—5 to 20% off
*Slightly thick crown—5 to 15% off

As you can see, there is a fairly wide range here, depending on the severity of the error, and only an experienced professional can determine the extent to which the value of a given stone may be lessened. But a quick computation can show that a stone suffering from several errors (which is fairly common) could certainly have its price per carat significantly reduced.

❖ *A Word About Single Cuts*

Sometimes the stones used in diamond bands or rings containing small diamonds are *single-cut* rather than *full-cut*. This means they have only 17 facets instead of a full 58 facets. Since it has so few facets, the single-cut stone lacks the brilliance and liveliness of a full-cut stone. Rings containing single-cut diamonds should be much less expensive than rings containing full-cut stones.

CHAPTER 5

Body Color

W e think color is one of the most important factors to consider when selecting a diamond because it is one of the first things most people notice—whether or not the diamond is "white." It is also one of the most significant factors affecting value.

❖ How to Look at a Diamond to Evaluate Color

Before we can discuss color, you should know how to look at a diamond to evaluate color. Keep in mind that it is impossible to accurately determine the color grade in a mounted stone, but even an amateur can learn to see color differences in an un-mounted stone if the stone is viewed properly.

Because of the diamond's high brilliance and dispersion of light, the color grade cannot be accurately determined by looking at the stone from the top (face-up) position. It is best to observe color by examining the stone through the pavilion with the table down. Use a flat white surface such as a white business card, or a grading trough, which can be purchased from a jewelry supplier or through the Gemological Institute of America. Next, view the stone with the pavilion side down and the culet pointing toward you.

The following drawings show the best way to view loose diamonds.

*Position 1. Place table-side down and view the stone
through the pavilion facets.*

*Position 2. Table-side down, view the stone through
the plane of the girdle.*

*Position 3. Place the pavilion down with the culet
pointing toward you. View the stone through the
girdle plane.*

*Position 4. Place table-side down in a grading
trough and view the stone through the girdle
plane.*

*Position 5. Place pavilion-down in a grading
trough, with the culet pointing toward you. View
the stone through the pavilion facets.*

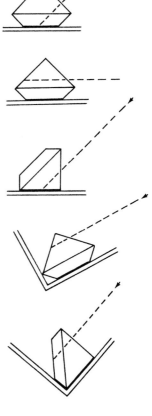

❖ *What Is Body Color?*

When we discuss body color we mean how much yellow or brown tint is observable in the stone. We are not referring to the rare shades of blue, green, canary yellow, red, etc., that are designated in the trade as *fancies*.

Today, the color designation frequently used to grade an absolutely water-clear, colorless diamond is the letter D. This letter designation is part of a color-grading system introduced by the Gemological Institute of America (GIA) and is used extensively in the diamond trade. The GIA classification progresses from D, the finest classification on this scale (colorless), through the alphabet to Z, getting progressively yellower. The grades D, E, F are exceptionally fine and are the only grades that should be referred to as colorless. (Technically, E and F are not colorless since they possess a trace of yellow, but the color is so slight that referring to them as colorless is acceptable.)

A diamond classified D has the finest possible color. It is essentially colorless and considered the most desirable. Diamonds with D color are becoming very rare, and a significant premium is paid for them. A diamond classified as having E color also possesses a very fine color, and we must point out that it is extremely close to D on the GIA scale, almost indistinguishable from D except to the very experienced. Nonetheless, E color costs significantly less per carat than D, despite the difficulty in seeing the difference.

F is also close to E, but shows a greater gradation in color than that observed between D and E.

❖ *What Color Grade Is Most Desirable?*

For the average consumer, the colors D, E, and F can all be grouped as exceptionally fine and may be referred to as "colorless," "exceptional white" or "rare white," as they are often described by diamond dealers. G and H may be referred to as "fine white" or "rare white." These grades are all considered very good. I and J colors are slightly tinted white. K and L show a tint of yellow or brown, but settings can often mask the slight tint. Grades M–Z will show progressively more and more tint of color, being yellowish or brownish. Grades D–J seem to have better resale potential than grades K–Z. This does not mean, however, that diamonds having color grades less fine than J aren't beautiful or desirable. They can make lovely, highly desirable jewelry.

❖ *To What Extent Does the Color Grade Affect Value?*

To an untrained eye, discerning the difference in color from D down to H in a mounted stone—without direct comparison—is almost impossible. Nevertheless, the difference in color greatly affects the value of the diamond. A 1-carat, *flawless*, excellently-proportioned *D-color* diamond might retail for $32,000, while the same stone with H color might sell for only $12,000. The same stone with K-color might sell for only $6,000. And, of course, if the stone were not flawless, it could sell for much less (see next chapter). This sounds complicated, but the range of

COMMONLY USED COLOR-GRADING SYSTEMS

The GIA and AGS are the most commonly used systems in the U.S.A. GIA is becoming the most favored. In addition, note that these systems indicate a greater number of classifications, providing greater precision in the grading. They are more stringent than any other system. The interval sizes are an indication of the degree of rarity only.

CIBJO stands for the International Confederation of Jewelry, Silverware, Diamonds, Pearls, and Stones. Participating member nations who use this scale include: Austria, Belgium, Canada, Denmark, Finland, France, Great Britain, Italy, Japan, Netherlands, Norway, Spain, Sweden, Switzerland, United States, and West Germany.

HRD uses a system applied by the Belgian "Hoge Raad voor Diamant" (Diamond High Council). The use of the term *Blue White* is discouraged today since it is usually misleading.

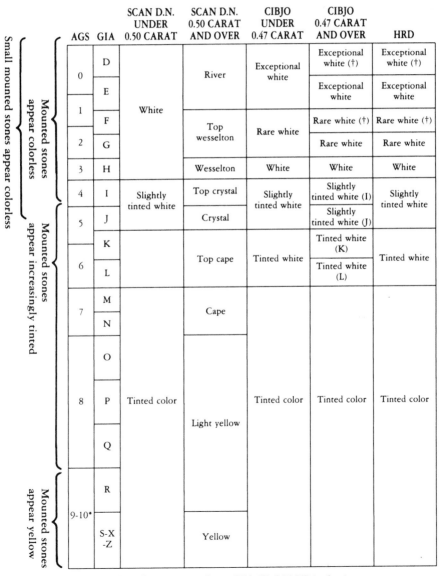

AGS	GIA	SCAN D.N. UNDER 0.50 CARAT	SCAN D.N. 0.50 CARAT AND OVER	CIBJO UNDER 0.47 CARAT	CIBJO 0.47 CARAT AND OVER	HRD
0	D	White	River	Exceptional white	Exceptional white (†)	Exceptional white (†)
0	E	White	River	Exceptional white	Exceptional white	Exceptional white
1	F	White	Top wesselton	Rare white	Rare white (†)	Rare white (†)
2	G	White	Top wesselton	Rare white	Rare white	Rare white
3	H	White	Wesselton	White	White	White
4	I	Slightly tinted white	Top crystal	Slightly tinted white	Slightly tinted white (I)	Slightly tinted white
5	J	Slightly tinted white	Crystal	Slightly tinted white	Slightly tinted white (J)	Slightly tinted white
6	K	Tinted color	Top cape	Tinted white	Tinted white (K)	Tinted white
6	L	Tinted color	Top cape	Tinted white	Tinted white (L)	Tinted white
7	M	Tinted color	Cape	Tinted color	Tinted color	Tinted color
7	N	Tinted color	Cape	Tinted color	Tinted color	Tinted color
	O	Tinted color	Cape	Tinted color	Tinted color	Tinted color
8	P	Tinted color	Light yellow	Tinted color	Tinted color	Tinted color
	Q	Tinted color	Light yellow	Tinted color	Tinted color	Tinted color
9-10*	R	Tinted color	Yellow	Tinted color	Tinted color	Tinted color
9-10*	S-X -Z	Tinted color	Yellow	Tinted color	Tinted color	Tinted color

Left-side vertical labels:
- Small mounted stones appear colorless
- Mounted stones appear colorless
- Mounted stones appear increasingly tinted
- Mounted stones appear yellow

*AGS grade "9" corresponds to GIA "R,S,T,U" inclusive.
AGS grade "10" corresponds to GIA "V,W" inclusive.

color will become clear to you the moment you begin looking at stones. It is our intention to inform you of the variations so that you will be watchful when you go to purchase a stone.

❖ *What Is Fluorescence?*

If the diamond you are considering is accompanied by a diamond grading report, it will indicate whether the diamond has some degree of *fluorescence*. This is a property that some stones possess which causes them to appear a different color in some lights than in other lights. A diamond that fluoresces might *look whiter than it really is* in certain light.

If a diamond fluoresces, it will produce a bluish, yellowish, or whitish glow when viewed in sunlight or daylight-type fluorescent light (those long tubes you see in the ceiling of many stores and office buildings). A professional always tests for fluorescence with a special lamp (an ultraviolet lamp) before color-grading a diamond to be sure the true body color is graded. Blue fluorescence is more common than yellow or white. It is not something you will see with the naked eye, but if a stone fluoresces blue, it can mask any yellowish tint that might be present so that it looks whiter than it really is. Some white diamonds that produce a blue fluorescence may actually look "blue-white" in the right light. A white diamond can also fluoresce yellow, and look *yellower* than it really is. But remember, the bluish or yellowish glow that is produced *only* occurs in daylight or fluorescent light. In other words, a slightly yellowish diamond that fluoresces blue could look whiter than it really is when viewed in the sun, but when viewed in candlelight, or in normal incandescent light (such as that in a household lamp), the blue will be totally gone and the diamond might have a yellow tint you never noticed before.

Generally, the absence or presence of fluorescence doesn't affect value. However, if the stone has a *strong yellow* fluorescence it may sell for less since it will make the stone appear yellower than it really is when worn in daylight or fluorescent light. The presence of *blue* fluorescence can be an added benefit—a little bonus—since it may make the stone appear whiter in some lights (but it won't add to the cost or value of the stone). However, if the stone has a *very strong blue* fluorescence there may be an "oily" or "murky" appearance to the diamond. If this is the case—if the stone appears murky or oily in daylight or fluorescent light—it should sell for less.

What Is A Premier?

At this point we should discuss a type of diamond that is not encountered often, but frequently enough to warrant a brief discussion. This type of diamond is called a *premier*. This does *not* mean the diamond is better than others.

A premier diamond has a *yellowish* body color that is masked by a *strong-blue* fluorescence. As with other diamonds that fluoresce blue, the premier will appear whiter than it really is when examined in daylight or under fluorescent lights. The premier will actually have a blue or bluish tint, sometimes tinged with a slight greenish cast. However, a premier *will always have a murky or oily appearance when viewed in daylight or fluorescent light*, resulting from the coupling of the yellow with the bluish coloration brought out in such light. The murkiness detracts from its beauty and causes a reduction in its value.

The price of a premier varies depending on the degree of yellow present and the degree of murkiness, as well as the other three variables—cut, clarity, and carat weight.

Do not confuse a premier diamond with one that exhibits some normal degree of fluorescence. Many diamonds exhibit some degree of fluorescence. Many have a very fine white body color to begin with. But most important, they differ from the premier because they will *not* appear oily or murky in daylight or fluorescent light.

❖ Some Plain Talk about Fancies

Let's spend a moment discussing *fancies*—colored diamonds. While white diamonds are preferred by most as the choice for engagement rings, those who love color are increasingly turning to colored diamonds. Diamonds have been found to occur naturally in almost every color and shade—blue, red, green, yellow, lavender, pink, gunmetal blue, coffee brown, and black. The color can be intense or very pale.

Some colored diamonds are very expensive because they are so rare. Others, such as certain shades of yellow or champagne, are often more affordable than some white diamonds. The most common fancy colors are various shades of yellow (very intense, bright yellow is sometimes called canary), orange, and brown. Among the most rare and most valuable are the reds and blues; and the least valuable (yet still expensive) are the blacks.

One must be aware, however, that it is possible with the use of sophisticated radiation technology to alter poor-quality brown-ish and yellowish diamonds so that they become beautiful fancy colored stones. These should sell for much less than their nat-urally occurring counterparts. Unfortunately, this is not always the case. Sometimes a jeweler may buy a fancy colored stone that has been represented as a natural when in fact it is a cheaper, treated stone, and then pass it on unintentionally to the unsus-pecting consumer as natural. But there are tests that the profes-sional gemologist can perform to differentiate the natural from the treated colored diamond—spectroscopic examination, elec-tro-conductivity, and ultraviolet response.

❖ Special Tips on the Subject of Color

Keep It Clean If You Want Your Stone's Color Exhibited to Its Best

Particularly when considering purchasing an old diamond ring, note whether the ring is impacted with dirt accumulated by years of wear. If it is, there is a possibility that the diamond will have a better color grade than it may appear to have at first glance. The dirt may contain varying amounts of fatty deposit (dishwasher grease, cosmetics, etc.), which has a tendency to yellow with age. Since this dirt is in contact with the back side of the diamond, it will have an adverse effect on the color, making it seem yellower than it actually is.

The same applies to your own diamond, so keep it clean in order to see and enjoy its full beauty.

White or Yellow Gold Setting?

The color of the setting can affect one's perception of the color of your stone—sometimes adversely and sometimes beneficially. A very white diamond should be held in a white metal such as white gold, platinum, or palladium. If you prefer a yellow gold setting, the ring can be made with a yellow gold "shank" to go around the finger, and white metal "head" to hold the diamond itself. An all yellow setting may make a very white diamond appear less white because the yellow color of the setting itself is cast into the diamond.

On the other hand, if the diamond you choose tends to be yellower than you'd like, mounting in yellow gold with yellow gold prongs may make the stone appear whiter in contrast to the strong yellow of the gold.

The yellow gold environment may mask the degree of yellow in a yellow diamond, or it may give a colorless diamond an undesirable yellow tint. The setting can also affect future color grading should you ever need an updated insurance appraisal. This is important for you to know, and a knowledgeable appraiser should certainly take the setting into consideration when color grading.

CHAPTER 6

The Effect of Flaws

*F*law classification (also referred to as clarity) is one of the most important criteria for determining the value of a diamond. The major grading system used in the United States is the GIA system. There are several other systems, but most American jewelers use GIA because it indicates a greater number of classifications and thereby provides a greater precision in determining the flaw grade. The GIA system is therefore considered the most stringent.

❖ Five Commonly Used Flaw Grading Systems

The following five systems are commonly used for grading flaws.

1. CIBJO (International Confederation of Jewelry, Silverware, Diamonds, Pearls, and Stones). Participating member nations who use this scale include Austria, Belgium, Canada, Denmark, Finland, France, Great Britain, Italy, Japan, Netherlands, Norway, Spain, Sweden, Switzerland, United States, and West Germany
2. Scan D.N. (Scandinavian Diamond Nomenclature)
3. GIA (Gemological Institute of America)
4. AGS (American Gem Society)
5. HRD (Hoge Raad voor Diamant—Diamond High Council of Belgium)

Basically, these systems grade the stone for its imperfections, both internal and external. Imperfections are called *inclusions* when internal, *blemishes* when external. Flaws can be white, black, colorless, or even red or green in rare instances. The "flaw" grade is more commonly referred to as the "clarity" grade today. The terms clarity and flaw, however, may be used interchangeably.

The following chart shows the relationships among these five systems.

COMMONLY USED FLAW (CLARITY) SYSTEMS

CIBJO UNDER 0.47 CARAT	CIBJO 0.47 CARAT AND OVER	HRD	SCAN D.N.	GIA	AGS
Loupe clean	Loupe clean	Loupe clean	FL	FL	0
			IF (Internally Flawless)	IF	1
VVS	VVS$_1$	VVS$_1$	VVS$_1$	VVS$_1$	
	VVS$_2$	VVS$_2$	VVS$_2$	VVS$_2$	2
VS	VS$_1$	VS$_1$	VS$_1$	VS$_1$	3
	VS$_2$	VS$_2$	VS$_2$	VS$_2$	4
SI	SI$_1$	SI	SI$_1$	SI$_1$	5
	SI$_2$		SI$_2$	SI$_2$	6
Piqué I	Piqué I	P1	1st Piqué	I$_1$ (Imperfect)	7
					8
Piqué II	Piqué II	P2	2nd Piqué	I$_2$	9
Piqué III	Piqué III	P3	3rd Piqué	I$_3$	10

VV = Very, Very
V = Very
S = Slight or Small
I = Inclusion or Included or Imperfect (Imperfection)

FL is the grade given to a stone that has no visible flaws, internal or external, when examined under 10X magnification. Only a highly qualified person will be able to determine this grade. Also, note that it is very difficult for the inexperienced to see flaws that may be readily observable to the experienced jeweler, dealer, or gemologist. (Often the novice is unable to see any flaws, even in SI grades, even with use of the loupe.) A flawless, colorless, correctly proportioned stone, particularly in a 1-carat size or larger, is extremely rare and is priced proportionately much higher than any other grade. Some jewelers insist there is no such thing in existence today.

IF is the grade given to a stone with no internal flaws and with only minor external blemishes—nicks, or pits or girdle roughness, not on the table—that could be removed with polishing. These stones, in colorless, well-proportioned makes, are also rare and priced proportionately much higher than other grades.

VVS_1 and VVS_2 are grades given to stones with internal flaws that are *very, very* difficult for a qualified observer to see. These are also difficult grades to obtain, and are priced at a premium.

VS_1 and VS_2 are grades given to stones with *very* small inclusions, difficult for a qualified observer to see. These stones are more readily available in good color and cut, and their flaws will not be visible except under magnification. These are excellent stones to purchase.

SI_1 and SI_2 grades are given to stones with flaws that a qualified observer will see fairly easily under 10X magnification. They are more prevalent and so command a lower price, and their flaws may sometimes be visible without magnification when examined from the back side or laterally. These grades are still highly desirable and, since they cannot normally be seen with the naked eye when mounted, may enable one to select a stone with a higher color, or in a larger size, when working with a limited budget.

The imperfect grades are given to stones in which the flaws may be seen by a qualified observer without magnification; they are readily available and are much less expensive. They are graded I_1, I_2 and I_3. (These grades are called 1st pique [pee-kay], 2nd pique, and 3rd pique in some classifications.) Stones graded "I" may still be desirable if they have good color and are well cut, and so should not be eliminated by a prospective purchaser who desires lovely diamond jewelry. As a general rule, however, imperfect grades are difficult to resell and do not appreciate in value as rapidly as better grades.

❖ *Types of Diamond Imperfections*

There are basically two types of flaws: internal flaws (inclusions) and external flaws (blemishes). Among these two categories are any number of flaws. We will discuss some of those flaws here, so that you have a working vocabulary of diamond imperfections.

❖ *Internal Flaws or Inclusions*

Pinpoint. This is a small, usually whitish (although it can be dark) dot that is difficult to see. There can be a number of pinpoints (a cluster) or a "cloud" of pinpoints (often hazy in appearance and difficult to see).

Dark spot. This may be a small crystal inclusion or a thin, flat inclusion that reflects light like a mirror. It may also appear as a silvery, metallic reflector.

Colorless crystal. This is often a small crystal of diamond, although it may be another mineral. Sometimes it appears very small, sometimes large enough to substantially lower the flaw grade to SI_2 or even I_1. A small group of colorless crystals lowers the grade from a possible VS_2 to I_3.

Cleavage. A small cleavage is a crack that has a flat plane, which, if struck, could cause the diamond to split.

Feather. This is another name for a crack. A feather is not dangerous if it is small and does not break out through a facet. Thermoshock or ultrasonic cleaners can make it larger.

Bearding or *girdle fringes.* These are usually the result of hastiness on the part of the cutter while rounding out the diamond. The girdle portion becomes overheated and develops cracks that resemble small whiskers going into the diamond from the girdle edge. Sometimes the bearding amounts to minimal "peach fuzz" and can be removed with slight repolishing. Sometimes the bearding must be removed by faceting the girdle. If the bearding is very minimal, a diamond can still be graded IF.

Growth or grain lines. These can be seen only when examining the diamond while slowly rotating it. They appear and disappear usually instantaneously. They will appear in a group of two, three, or four pale brown lines. If they cannot be seen from the crown side of the diamond and are small, they will not affect the grade adversely.

Knaat or twin lines. These are sometimes classified as external flaws because they appear as very small ridges, often with some type of geometrical outline; or as a small, slightly raised dot with a tail resembling a comet. They're difficult to see.

Laser treatment. This is used today to make flaws less visible, and thus improve the stone aesthetically. For example, a black spot can be "vaporized" and will practically disappear. However, the laser holes can be seen with a 10X loupe, looking like fine straight white threads penetrating the stone.

External Flaws or Blemishes

A *natural*. This usually occurs on the girdle and looks like a rough, unpolished area. It may look like a scratch line or small triangle (called a trigon). If a natural is no wider than the normal width of the girdle or does not disrupt the circumference of the stone, some jewelers will not consider it a flaw.

Often naturals are polished and resemble an extra facet, especially if they occur below the girdle edge.

A natural is a remnant of the original skin of the diamond, and is often left on the girdle showing that the cutter tried to cut the largest possible diameter from the rough.

Nick. This is a small chip, usually on the girdle, and can be caused by wear, especially if the girdle is on the thin side. Sometimes a nick or chip can be seen on the edge of the facets where they meet. If small, the bruised corner can be polished, creating an extra facet. This usually occurs on the crown.

Girdle roughness. This blemish appears as criss-crossed lines, brighter and duller finishing, and minute chipping. This can be remedied by faceting or repolishing.

Pits or cavities. Pits or holes on the table facet, especially if they are deep, will quickly lower the grade of the stone. Removing pits involves recutting the whole top of the stone, and can also shrink the stone's diameter.

Scratch. A scratch is usually a minor defect that can be removed with simple repolishing. Remember, however, that in order to repolish the stone, you must remove it from its setting, and then reset after it has been polished.

Polishing lines. Many diamonds exhibit polishing lines. If they appear on the pavilion side and are not too obvious, they do not lower the value. In some small diamonds these scratch lines can be obvious, and are usually the result of a badly maintained polishing wheel.

Abraded or rough culet. The culet has been chipped or poorly finished. This is usually a minor flaw.

❖ *How Does the Position of a Flaw Affect Diamond Grading and Value?*

As a general rule, the position of any given inclusion will downgrade and devalue a diamond progressively more and more as indicated below.

- *If seen only from the pavilion side,* or clearly only from the pavilion side, it has the least adverse effect, since it is the least visible from the top.
- *If positioned near the girdle,* while perhaps more visible than described above, it is still difficult to see, and hardly noticeable from the top. This flaw can be easily covered with the prong of a setting.
- *Under any crown facet* (other than a star facet), except when near the girdle, a flaw is more easily visible.
- *Under a star facet,* a flaw will be much more easily noticed.
- *Under the table* is the least desirable position since it places the flaw where it is most noticeable, and may have the greatest effect on brilliance or fire (depending on size, color, etc.).

Sometimes a small black or white flaw may be in such a position that it is reflected within the stone. This can occur as a reflection to the opposite side of the stone, or, it may reflect itself as many as eight times around the bottom or near the culet of the stone. A diamond with that flaw might otherwise be classified as a VS_1 or VS_2, but because of the eight-fold reflection resulting from its unfortunate position, the flaw grade will be lowered.

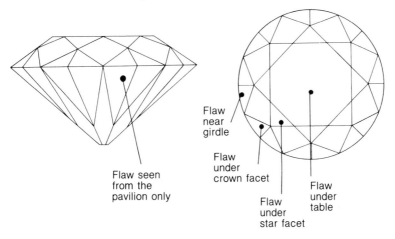

Flaw seen from the pavilion only

Flaw near girdle

Flaw under crown facet

Flaw under star facet

Flaw under table

❖ *An Important Closing Word About Flaws*

Remember, a diamond does not have to be flawless to be a very fine stone and of high value. Personally, we prefer a stone that might be slightly imperfect (SI) but with fine color and brilliance over a flawless stone with less sparkle and a less fine color. Color and brilliance are considered the most important factors in terms of a stone's desirability. And remember: Even a diamond graded I_3 is still 97% clean!

CHAPTER 7

Carat Weight

❖ What Is a Carat?

Diamonds are sold by the carat (ct)—not to be confused with karat (kt), which refers to gold quality in the United States.

The carat is a unit of weight, not size. (Since 1913 most countries have agreed that a carat weighs 200 milligrams, or ⅕ gram.) We wish to stress this point, since most people think that a 1-carat stone is a particular size. Most people, therefore, would expect a 1-carat diamond and a 1-carat emerald, for example, to appear the same size or have the same apparent dimensions. This is not the case.

If we compare a 1-carat diamond with a 1-carat emerald and a 1-carat ruby, we can easily illustrate this point. First, emerald weighs less than diamond and ruby weighs more than diamond. This means that a 1-carat emerald will look larger than a 1-carat diamond, and a 1-carat ruby will look smaller than a 1-carat diamond. Emerald, with a basic material that is lighter, will yield greater mass per carat; ruby, with its heavier basic material, will yield less mass per carat.

Let's examine this another way. Let's look at a 1-inch cube of pine wood, a 1-inch cube of aluminum, and a 1-inch cube of iron. The wood is like the emerald. It weighs less than the aluminum, which is like the diamond. The iron, which is like the ruby, weighs the most. Yet each has the same volume. This is called density, mass, or specific gravity.

In diamond, the carat weight has come to represent particular sizes. These sizes, as we've discussed, are based on the diamond's being cut to ideal proportion. Consequently, if properly cut, diamonds of the following weight should be approximately the size illustrated below. Remember, however, that these *sizes* will not apply to other gems.

❖ *How Does Carat Weight Affect Value in Diamonds?*

Diamond prices are usually quoted *per carat*. Diamonds of the finest quality are sold for the highest price *per carat*, and diamonds of progressively less fine quality are sold for a progressively lower price *per carat*. For example, the finest quality diamond in a certain size might sell for $30,000 *per carat*. Therefore, if such a stone weighed 1.12 carats, the stone would cost $33,600. On the other hand, a stone of the exact same weight, in a less fine quality, might sell for only $10,000 *per carat*, so it would cost only $11,200.

Also, as a rule, the price increases per carat as we go from smaller to larger stones, since the larger stones are more limited in supply. For example, stones of the same quality weighing ½ carat will sell for more per carat than stones weighing ⅓ carat; stones weighing ¾ carat will sell for more per carat than stones of the same quality weighing ½ carat. And stones of the same quality weighing 1 carat will sell for much more than stones weighing 90 to 96 points. (There are 100 points to a carat.) This is important information for anyone working with a limited budget. For example, if you want a 1-carat stone of a particular quality, but you can't afford it, you may find you *can* afford it in a 90-point stone—and a 90-point stone will give the impression of a full one-carat stone when set. You might be able to get your heart's desire after all.

As you will see, the price of a diamond does not increase proportionately—there are disproportionate jumps. And the larger the stone (all else being equal in terms of overall quality), the more disproportionate the increase in cost per carat may be. A 2-carat stone will not cost twice as much as a 1-carat stone. It could easily be four times as much. A 5-carat stone would not be five times the cost of a 1-carat stone—it could easily cost as much as ten times per carat the price of a 1-carat stone.

SIZES AND WEIGHTS OF VARIOUS DIAMOND CUTS

Weight (ct)	Emerald	Marquise	Pear	Brilliant
5				
4				
3				
2½				
2				
1½				
1¼				
1				
¾				
½				

DIAMETERS AND CORRESPONDING WEIGHTS OF ROUND, BRILLIANT-CUT DIAMONDS

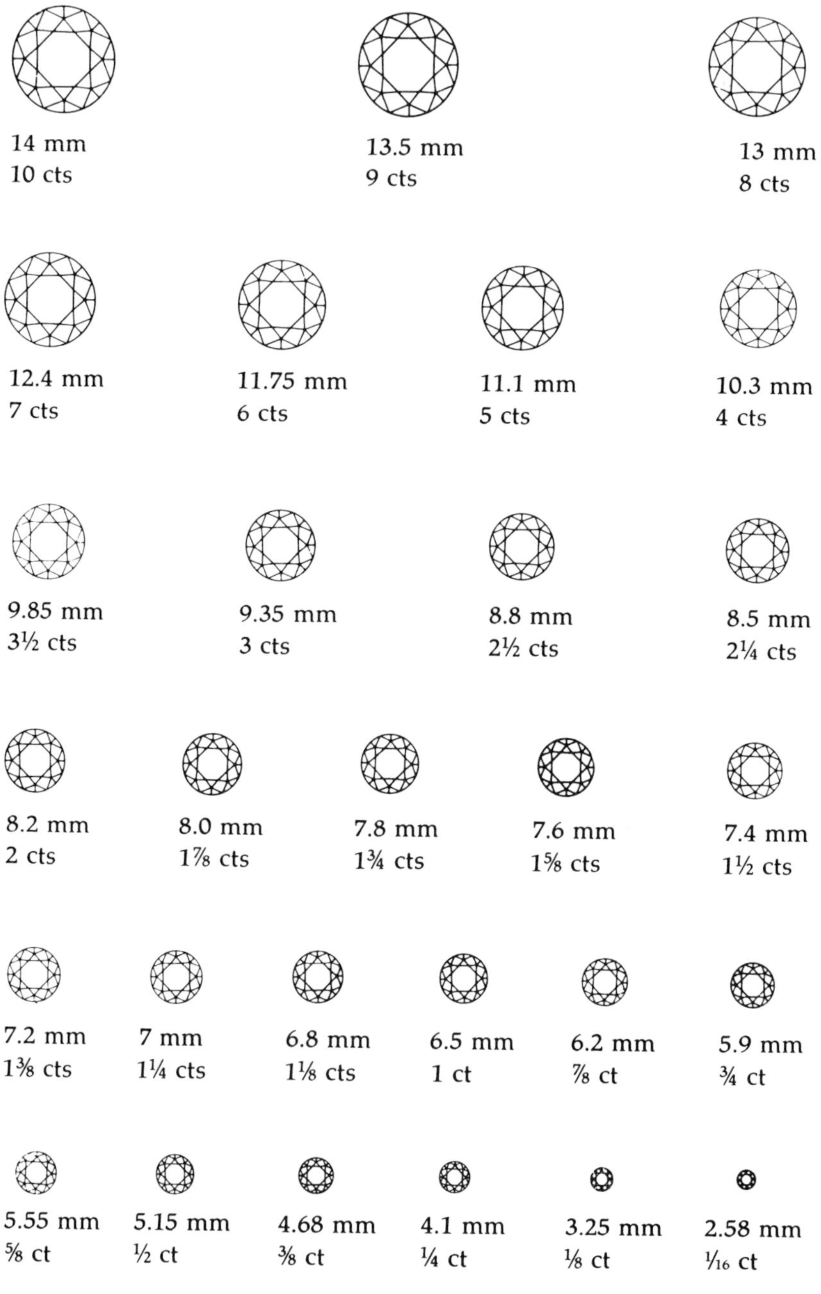

14 mm
10 cts

13.5 mm
9 cts

13 mm
8 cts

12.4 mm
7 cts

11.75 mm
6 cts

11.1 mm
5 cts

10.3 mm
4 cts

9.85 mm
3½ cts

9.35 mm
3 cts

8.8 mm
2½ cts

8.5 mm
2¼ cts

8.2 mm
2 cts

8.0 mm
1⅞ cts

7.8 mm
1¾ cts

7.6 mm
1⅝ cts

7.4 mm
1½ cts

7.2 mm
1⅜ cts

7 mm
1¼ cts

6.8 mm
1⅛ cts

6.5 mm
1 ct

6.2 mm
⅞ ct

5.9 mm
¾ ct

5.55 mm
⅝ ct

5.15 mm
½ ct

4.68 mm
⅜ ct

4.1 mm
¼ ct

3.25 mm
⅛ ct

2.58 mm
1/16 ct

What Are Points?

When discussing the carat weight of a diamond, jewelers often refer to the weight in terms of points. This is particularly true of stones under 1 carat. There are 100 points to a carat, so if a jeweler says that a stone weighs 75 points, he means it weighs $^{75}/_{100}$ of a carat, or ¾ carat. A 25-point stone is ¼ carat. A 10-point stone is $^1/_{10}$ carat.

What Is Spread?

The term *spread* is often used in response to the question "How large is this diamond?" But it can be misleading. Spread refers to the size the stone *appears* to be, based on its diameter. For example, if the diameter of the stone measured the same as you see in the Diamond Sizes Chart (see pages 53 and 54), which represents the diameter of a perfectly proportioned stone, the jeweler might say it *spreads* 1-carat. But this does not mean it weighs 1-carat. It means it looks the same size as a perfectly cut 1-carat stone. It may weigh less or more, frequently less.

Diamonds are usually weighed before they are set, as the jeweler must give you the exact carat weight since you are paying a certain price per carat. Note, also, that the price per carat for a fine stone weighing 96 points is much less than for one weighing 1 carat or more. So it is unwise to accept any "approximate" weight, even though the difference seems so slight.

When buying a diamond it is also important to realize that since carat refers to weight, the manner in which a stone is cut can affect its apparent size. A 1-carat stone that is cut shallow will appear larger in diameter than a stone that is cut thick (heavy). Conversely, a thick stone will appear smaller in diameter.

Furthermore, if the diamond has a thick girdle, the stone will appear smaller in diameter. If this girdle is faceted, it tends to hide the ugly, frosted look of a thick girdle, but the fact remains that the girdle is thick, and the stone suffers because it will appear smaller in diameter than one would expect at a given carat weight. These stones are therefore somewhat cheaper per carat.

CHAPTER 8

How to Read a Diamond Grading Report

Today, few fine diamonds are sold without a diamond grading report (or certificate, as they are also called).

The availability and widespread use of these reports can, when properly understood, enable even those without professional skills to make valid comparisons between several stones and more informed buying decisions. The key is in *knowing how to read the reports properly.*

Don't rely on color and clarity alone.

All too often couples compare diamonds based on only two factors—*color* and *clarity*—and think they are making sound comparisons. As a result, if two stones of approximately the same weight also have the same color grade and clarity grade, they think they are comparing "the same thing" and *erroneously* conclude that the cheaper stone is the best buy. In fact, the more expensive stone may really be a *better* stone—and possibly even a better *value*. More often than not, when there is a big price difference between two stones that appear to be the same quality, the stones are NOT the same quality—even if the color and clarity grades are the same.

Unless you know how to read the report and understand *all* the information on it, you can't make valid comparisons. A limited understanding of what is on the report may result in a costly mistake. Factors other than color and clarity affect price, sometimes dramatically.

Properly used, however, diamond grading reports provide information that can give you a *complete* picture with which you really can make sound comparisons. When you understand how to read them, and know what it *all* means, you'll be able to make sounder buying decisions, and know who is really offering the best *value*. This chapter will tell you everything you need to know to read a diamond report properly.

But before beginning, we must offer one important word of caution: *Don't make a purchase relying exclusively on any report without making sure the report matches the stone, and that the stone is still in the same condition described.* Always seek a professional gemologist, gemologist-appraiser, or gem-testing laboratory (see Appendix) to confirm that the stone accompanying the report is, in fact, the stone described on the report and that the stone is still in the same condition described. We know of instances where a report has been erroneously sent with the wrong stone. And, in some cases, a report fraudulently accompanies a stone.

❖ *Reading the Report*

Check the date issued. It is very important to check the report's date. It's always possible that the stone has been damaged since the report was issued. This sometimes occurs with diamonds sold at auction. Since diamonds can become chipped or fractured with wear, one must always check. For example, you might see a diamond accompanied by a report stating that it is D/Flawless. However, if the stone was badly chipped *after* the report was issued (possibly so badly chipped that a crack also penetrated the stone), the clarity grade could easily drop to VS_2. If this were the case, needless to say, its value would be dramatically reduced.

Who Issued the Report?

The next item to check is the name of the laboratory issuing the report. Is the report from a laboratory that is known and respected? If not, the information on the report may not be reliable. There are an increasing number of well-respected laboratories issuing reports on diamonds. The most well known internationally are issued by the Gem Testing Laboratory of the Gemological Institute of America (GTL). Other highly respected laboratories issuing diamond reports are American Gemological Laboratories (AGL), International Gemological Institute (IGI), European Gemological Laboratory (EGL), HRD (the Belgian Diamond High Council), Gemological Laboratory Gubelin, and

GIA GEM TRADE LABORATORY, INC.

A Wholly Owned Subsidiary of the Gemological Institute of America, Inc.

580 Fifth Avenue New York, New York 10036 (212) 221-5858	550 South Hill Street Los Angeles, California 90013 (213) 629-5435	1630 Stewart Street Santa Monica, Califorina 90404 (213) 828-3148

DIAMOND GRADING REPORT   0123456   3/07/89

THE ABOVE REPORT NUMBER HAS BEEN INSCRIBED ON THE GIRDLE OF THIS DIAMOND

THE FOLLOWING WERE, AT THE TIME OF THE EXAMINATION, THE CHARACTERISTICS OF THE DIAMOND DESCRIBED HEREIN BASED UPON 10X BINOCULAR MAGNIFICATION, DIAMONDLITE AND MASTER COLOR DIAMONDS, ULTRA-VIOLET, MILLIMETER GAUGE, DIAMOND BALANCE, PROPORTIONSCOPE.

RED SYMBOLS DENOTE INTERNAL CHARACTERISTICS. GREEN SYMBOLS DENOTE EXTERNAL CHARACTERISTICS. SYMBOLS INDICATE NATURE AND POSITION OF CHARACTERISTICS, NOT NECESSARILY THEIR SIZE. MINOR DETAILS OF FINISH NOT SHOWN. DIAGRAM MAY BE APPROXIMATE.

KEY TO SYMBOLS
- ° CRYSTAL
- ~ FEATHER
- · PINPOINT

EXTRA FACET SHOWN IN BLACK

SHAPE AND CUT . . ROUND BRILLIANT
- Measurements   6.50 – 6.58 X 3.90 MM.
- Weight . . . . . .   1.01 CARATS

PROPORTIONS . . .
- Depth   59.6%
- Table   62%
- Girdle   THIN TO MEDIUM, FACETED
- Culet   SMALL
- FINISH
- Polish   VERY GOOD
- Symmetry   GOOD

CLARITY GRADE . . VS1

COLOR GRADE . . . H
- Fluorescence . . . . . NONE

COMMENTS:

⚭ GEM TRADE LABORATORY, INC.

GIA Gem Trade Laboratory, Inc.

GIA CLARITY GRADING SCALE

	VVS₁	VVS₂	VS₁	VS₂	SI₁	SI₂	I₁	I₂
Flawless			X					
Internally Flawless								

Imperfect

GIA COLOR GRADING SCALE

D	E	F	G	H	I	J	K	L	M	N	O	P	Q	R	S	T	U	V	W	X	Y	Z	Fancy Light	Fancy	Fancy Intense
				X																					

Colorless | Near Colorless | Faint Yellow | Very Light Yellow | Light Yellow | Yellow

This report is not a guarantee, valuation or appraisal. The recipient of the report may wish to consult a jeweler or gemologist about information contained herein.

NOTICE: IMPORTANT LIMITATIONS ON REVERSE

A sample GIA Diamond Grading Report which includes important details pertaining to all quality factors. It includes a diagram of internal and external characteristics (flaws) and their placement.

American Gemological Laboratories

Olympic Tower
645 Fifth Ave, Suite 1105
New York, N.Y. 10022
(212) 935-0060
(212) 935-0071

Diamond Certificate

CERTIFICATE NO.   SAMPLE

DATE: 15 May 1989

SHAPE and CUT: Round Brilliant

CARAT WEIGHT: 1.22 Cts.

MEASUREMENTS: 6.95 – 7.06 x 4.04 mm.

PROPORTIONS:
Depth %   Good (4)
Table Diameter %   59.5%
Girdle Thickness   60%
Medium: Faceted

FINISH GRADE: Very Good – Good (3-4)

CLARITY GRADE: VVS_1 *
(10X Magnification)

COLOR GRADE: E*

UV Fluorescence   Moderate Blue

COMMENTS: *Minor details of finish
not plotted.
*Transitional color grade.

The information contained in this report represents the opinion of American Gemological Laboratories regarding the characteristics of the diamond(s) submitted for examination.

This analysis is based on measurements and also on observations made through a binocular darkfield microscope and in a controlled lighting environment utilizing master comparison stones. Mounted diamonds are graded only to the extent that mounting permits examination.

Internal characteristics shown with red symbols, external with green. Symbols indicate nature and position of identifying characteristics, not necessarily their size. Setting prongs on mounted stones are shown with black symbols. Minor details of finish not plotted.

This report prepared by: **American Gemological Laboratories, Inc.**

Martin J. Anderson

Martin J. Anderson, G.G.

Diamond Proportions

Crown
Pavilion Depth
Girdle Thickness
Cutlet
Girdle Diameter = 100%
Table %
Depth %

Clarity Scale (GIA)	F	IF	VVS₁	VVS₂	VS₁	VS₂	SI₁	SI₂	I₁	I₂	I₃

Color Scale (GIA)	D	E	F	G	H	I	J	K	L	M	N	O	P	Q	R	S through Z	Z+
	Colorless			Near Colorless				Faint Yellow			Very Light Yellow				Light Yellow		Fancy Yellow

Original

Schweizerische Stiftung fur Edelstein-Forschung (SSEF—another fine Swiss laboratory). These laboratories are listed in the Appendix, and can be contacted directly for further information. Whichever report you are reading, all provide essentially the same basic information.

American Gemological Laboratories   Diamond Report

Olympic Tower
645 Fifth Ave., Suite 1105
New York, N.Y. 10022
(212) 935-0060
(212) 935-0071

Clients are cautioned that the purpose of this document is to describe the quality parameters of the diamond(s) submitted for examination, therefore, the information may not necessarily provide adequate insurance documentation against damage, substitution or loss. Do not accept copies, alterations or corrections on this report for final transactions.

Report No: SAMPLE
Date: 15 May 1989

Quantity: One (1)
Shape/Cut: Round Brilliant

Weight: 0.76 Cts.

Diamond Proportions: Cutting

Girdle Diameter = 100%
Table %
Crown
Depth %
Pavilion Depth
Girdle Thickness
Culet

Color: – H –*

Clarity: VVS$_2$

Cutting: Good (5)

(LW) Ultra Violet: Moderate Blue*

Finish: Good (4)

Color Scale (GIA)

D E F	G H	I	J	K	L	M	N	O	P	Q	R	S through Z	Z+
Color-less	Near Colorless		Faint Yellow				Very Light Yellow					Light Yellow	Fancy Yellow

Clarity Scale (GIA)

F	IF	VVS$_1$	VVS$_2$	VS$_1$	VS$_2$	SI$_1$	SI$_2$	I$_1$	I$_2$	I$_3$

Cutting/Finish (AGL)

1	2	3	4	5	6	7	8	9	10
Excellent	Very Good			Good			Fair		Poor

Notice to Client: The information contained in this report represents the opinion of American Gemological Laboratories (A.G.L.) regarding the characteristics of the diamond(s) submitted for examination. Neither the American Gemological Laboratories nor any of its employees shall be responsible for any action that may be taken on the basis of this report.
The conclusions expressed are the American Gemological Laboratories' interpretation of the results obtained from gemological instruments and grading techniques designed for this purpose. Conclusions may vary due to the subjective nature of diamond analysis.

© 1977 American Gemological Laboratories, Inc.   *Original*

This report or the name of American Gemological Laboratories, Inc. may not be reproduced in whole or in part without the express prior written authorization from A.G.L.
This analysis is based on observations made through a binocular darkfield microscope and in a controlled lighting environment utilizing master comparison stones.
This report prepared by: **American Gemological Laboratories**

Martin J Andersson), G.G.

A sample Diamond Certificate and a sample Diamond Report from AGL. Notice the differences between the **certificate** *and the* **report***. The certificate provides greater detail. It also provides a diagram of internal and external characteristics (flaws).*

❖ *What Does It All Really Mean?*

As important as are color and clarity, each of the factors described below—often ignored—also affects a stone's appearance, desirability, *and value*. Understanding the total picture can save you costly mistakes in buying, and also help you understand more clearly how to make a fairer comparison between stones offered by different jewelers (where one might seem more attractive price-wise when color and clarity are the only factors being compared).

In addition to color and clarity, you must understand and check each of the following factors:

- Identity of stone
- Weight
- Dimensions
- Proportions
- Finish—symmetry and polish
- Girdle thickness
- Culet
- Fluorescence

Identity of the Stone

This is self-explanatory. Some diamond reports don't make a specific statement about identity because they are called *diamond reports* and are only issued for *genuine* diamonds. If the report is not called a "diamond grading report" then there must be a statement verifying the identity of the stone, attesting that it is genuine diamond.

Weight

Again, this is self-explanatory, but the *exact* carat weight must be given.

Dimensions Tell You More Than You Might Think

The dimensions given on a report are very precise. They are important in helping to establish that the diamond being examined is, in fact, the same diamond described in the report (the likelihood of having two diamonds with exactly the same carat weight and millimeter dimensions is rare). Also, if the diamond has been damaged and recut since the report was issued, the millimeter dimensions may provide a clue that something has been altered (and the carat weight as well). *Any discrepancy between the dimensions that you or your jeweler get by measuring the stone and those provided on the report should be a red flag to check the stone very carefully.*

Dimensions are measured in millimeters and must be taken to the *hundredth*. For example, 6.51 millimeters rather than 6.5 millimeters; 6.07 millimeters rather than 6.0, and so on. For any diamond, of any shape, dimensions should always be measured and recorded, especially for insurance/identification purposes.

Dimensions Can Affect the Price of Round Diamonds by at Least 10%—and Sometimes More.
For a round, brilliant cut diamond, the dimensions provide very important information that can affect price—information that indicates whether or not a stone is *out of round*. Depending on the degree of out-of-roundness (how much it deviates from being perfectly round), price can be affected by at least 10%–15%, or much more if it is very noticeably out-of-round. The greater the deviation, the lower the price should be.

To tell whether or not a diamond is out-of-round, look at the measurements given. Notice that there are *two* millimeter dimensions supplied for the diameter (width) of the stone. This is because diamonds are very rarely perfectly round. And because so few are perfectly round, some latitude is allowed for deviation—*up to 0.10 millimeter* (one-tenth of a millimeter). As long as the deviation is not greater than 0.10, it is considered "round"; any stone that deviates by more than that is "out-of-round."

Determining Whether or Not a Stone Is Out-of-Round Is Simply a Matter of Subtraction.
To find out whether or not the diamond is out-of-round is easy. Simply take the two width dimensions provided on the report and subtract the smaller number from the larger one. If the difference is 0.10 or *less*, it is considered "round"; if the difference is *greater* than 0.10, it is "out-of-round." For example, if we look at a report accompanying a 1-carat diamond and it gives the two dimensions as 6.51 millimeters and 6.53 millemeters, we simply subtract 6.51 from 6.53. The difference is 0.02. The stone is not out-of-round. However, if the dimensions were 6.51 and 6.62, the difference would be 0.11. This would be unacceptable. Since it is more than 0.10, this stone would be considered *out-of-round* and would sell for less-per-carat than one that is not. The more noticeably out-of-round, the lower the price.

Tip: When reading a report for a round diamond, always subtract the smallest width dimensions from the largest to check for out-of-roundness. If the difference is more than 0.10, adjust the price downward . . . the more out-of-round, the lower the price.

Dimensions for Fancy Shapes. While the dimensions for fancy shapes (shapes other than round) are not as important as they are for round diamonds, there are length-to-width ratios that are considered "normal" and deviations may result in prices as much as 15% lower or more. The following ratios are acceptable:

Pear	1.50:1 to 1.75:1
Marquise	1.75:1 to 2.25:1
Emerald	1.50:1 to 1.75:1
Oval	1.50:1 to 1.75:1

Let's look at a marquise for example. If a report for a marquise diamond showed the length to be 15.00 millimeters and the width to be 10.00 millimeters, the length-to-width ratio would be 15 to 10, or 1.50:1 and would be acceptable. If, however, the dimensions were 30.00 millimeters in length by 10.00 in width, the ratio would be 30 to 10, or 3:1. This would be unacceptable. The ratio is too great (the stone would be much too long for its width). A marquise with an unacceptable length-to-width ratio should sell for at least 10% less than other stones, and sometimes more. *Note:* A long marquise is not necessarily bad, and some people prefer a longer shape, but it is important to understand that they should sell for less than one with a "normal" length. Always keep in mind the length-to-width ratio of fancy cuts, and adjust the price for stones that are not in the acceptable range.

Proportions

Good Proportions Increase the Cost as well as the Beauty of a Diamond; Poor Proportions Reduce Both. Good proportioning is as critical to a diamond as it is to the woman (or man) who wears it! The proportioning, especially the height of the crown in relation to the depth of the pavilion, and the width of the table facet in relation to the width of the stone—is what determines how much brilliance and fire the stone will have.

Proportioning is the key to unlocking the full beauty of the diamond.

The information provided on diamond reports pertaining to proportions is critically important for *round, brilliant-cut diamonds*. Unfortunately, it is only of minimal use with fancy shapes. For fancies, you must learn to rely on your own eye to tell whether or not the proportioning is acceptable, to pick up flatness or dark spots such as a "bow-tie" that might result from poor proportioning. (See Chapter 4).

Proportioning Can Dramatically Affect Price. For round, brilliant-cut stones, the information on diamond reports regarding proportions is as important as the color or clarity grade. Cost is also significantly affected by it. The proportioning of a diamond is referred to in the jewelry industry as a stone's "make." An excellent "make" results in a more beautiful, more desirable diamond and sells for more; a poor "make" results in a less beautiful diamond and sells for less.

Diamonds that are cut close to "ideal" proportions, stones with "excellent" makes, can easily cost 15% to 25% more than the norm; diamonds with poor makes sell for less—very badly proportioned stones for as much as 50–60% less.

"Table Percentage" and "Depth Percentage" Are the Keys to Evaluating Proportioning

To determine whether or not a stone's proportioning is good, look at the section of the report that describes "depth percentage" and "table percentage." These numbers indicate how well a stone has been cut in terms of the proportioning, and must adhere to very precise standards in terms of what is acceptable and what is not. While your eye may be able to see differences in the sparkle and brilliance, *these percentages must fall within a certain range in order to be considered acceptable, excellent, or poor.* We will not discuss how one calculates these percentages, but it is important for you to know what the acceptable ranges are—what is considered good, what bad. Some reports (not those from GIA) also provide information about the "crown angle." The crown angle tells you the angle at which the crown portion has been cut. This angle will affect the depth and table percentage. Normally, if the crown angle is between 34 and 36 degrees, the table and depth will be excellent; between 32 and 34, good; 30–32 degrees, fair; and less than 30 degrees, poor.

Table Percentage

Look for stones with a table percentage between 53% and 64%.

- "Ideal" table percentage— from 53 to 57%
- "Excellent" table percentage—up to 60% (up to 62% in stones under ½ carat)
- "Acceptable" table percentage—up to 64%
- "Fair" (should sell for less)— over 64–70%
- "Poor" (should sell for much less)—over 70%

A stone with a table percentage between 53% and 57% (combined with an excellent depth percentage) will sell for MORE than other stones. Stones with a table percentage that exceeds 64% should sell for less per carat than other stones. Stones with a table percentage over 70% are significantly less brilliant than other stones and should sell for MUCH LESS per carat.

Tip: *Look for stones with table percentages betwen 53% and 64% (remember that stones with a table percentage between 53–57%, with an excellent depth percentage, will probably sell for MORE); avoid stones with a table percentage that exceeds 70%, or at least expect to pay much LESS for them.*

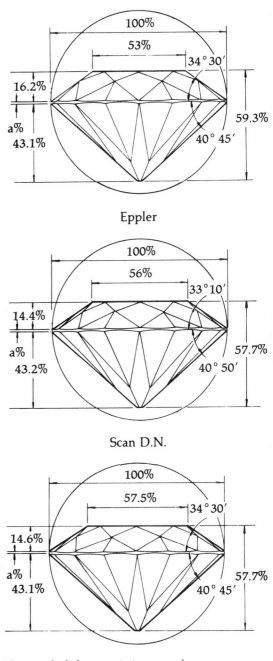

Three standards for proportioning—note the differences in table and depth percentages. All of these show excellent proportioning.

Depth Percentage

The IDEAL depth percentage ranges from approximately 58–60%. The following ranges indicate how good or poor the depth percentage is:

- "Ideal" depth percentage—approximately 58–60%
- "Excellent" depth percentage—61–62%
- "Acceptable" depth percentage—62–64%
- "Poor" depth percentage—over 64%

A depth percentage from approximately 58–62% would indicate excellent proportioning; 62–64% would indicate good proportioning. You should note, however, that girdle thickness will affect depth percentage—a high depth percentage could result from a thick or very thick girdle so, when checking the depth percentage, also study the "girdle" information on the report.

If the depth is UNDER 57% or over 64% the cost should be less because the depth percentage is either too high or too low so the stone will either be too deep or too shallow. If the depth percentage is too high, the stone will look smaller than its weight indicates. If the depth percentage is exceptionally high, brilliance can be significantly reduced and a darkish center may also be present. If the depth percentage is too low, brilliance will also be significantly affected. We've seen diamonds that are so shallow, stones with such low depth percentages, that they had no brilliance and liveliness. Once they become dirty, they look no better than a piece of glass.

Tip: *Look for stones with a depth percentage between 58–64%.* Pay close attention to stones with depth percentages that are too high (over 64%) or too low (under 57%). We avoid these stones. Whatever you decide, they should sell for much less per carat.

Finish—What Does Finish Mean?

Finish actually deals with the stone's polish and symmetry.

Polish. The polish serves as an indicator of the care taken by the cutter. Evaluating the stone's polish and symmetry is a factor that cannot be ignored in evaluating the overall quality of a diamond, and its cost and value.

The polish should be "good"—or the price should be less. Be sure that the report describes the polish as "good" . . . or look for a lower price per carat. Anything less than good means the cutter didn't take the time to polish out the parallel lines that are caused in the cutting process. You may be able to see these lines if you examine the stone carefully from the top, in the area of the lower-girdle facets or pavilion facets, if the polish is not good. The price per carat should be less on stones with "fair" or "poor" polish; it may be more for stones that have "very good" or "excellent" polish.

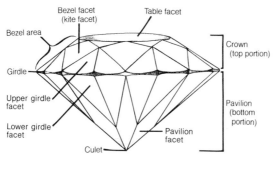

The Parts of a Stone
and the Facet Names

Symmetry. Symmetry describes several factors—(1) how the facet edges align with one another; (2) whether or not the facets from one side of the diamond match corresponding facets on the opposite side; and (3) whether or not facets in the top portion of the diamond are properly aligned with corresponding ones in the bottom portion. When the symmetry is described as "fair to good"—or worse—be sure to check what is out of line.

First, *check the facet edges to see whether or not they align with one another*—do they meet where they are supposed to meet? If not, how far off is the alignment? Has an extra facet been formed?

Next, *check to see whether or not the facets from one side of the diamond correspond to those on the opposite side.* For example, is the bezel (kite) facet on one side of the table the same as the bezel facet opposite it?

Finally, *does the top portion of the diamond line up properly with the bottom?*

This is the most important element of symmetry to check— the alignment of the top to the bottom. If it is not good, it will make a visual difference in the beauty of the stone and its price. To check, simply view the stone from the side to see

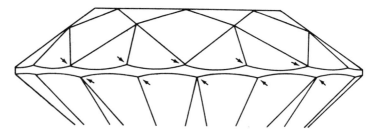

Misalignment of crown and pavilion

whether or not the upper-girdle facets align with the lower-girdle facets. If they do not, you know the cutting is sloppy and, more important, the overall beauty of the diamond is diminished. The beauty and the price will both be affected by the symmetry that has gone into the cutting. And if the alignment of the top and bottom is off, the price will probably be affected more than it would by other symmetry faults.

How Does the Girdle Affect Value?

The girdle is another important factor described on diamond grading reports. With regard to the girdle, it is the thickness, specifically, that is evaluated. This thickness is important for two reasons: (1) it affects value; (2) it affects the stone's durability.

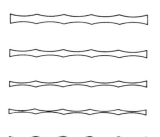

The gradations of girdle thickness

The "Ideal" Girdle Thickness Is "Medium" to "Slightly Thick." Girdle thickness can range from extremely thin, to very thin, thin, medium, slightly thick, very thick to extremely thick. Diamonds with girdles that are extremely thin or extremely thick normally sell for less than other diamonds. In the case of a girdle that is extremely thin, there is an increased risk of *chipping*. Remember that diamonds are brittle, so a very thin edge poses a greater risk.

In the case of a diamond that has an extremely thick girdle, the cost will also be somewhat less because the stone will look smaller than another diamond of the same weight with a more normal girdle thickness. This is because extra weight is being consumed by the thickness of the girdle itself.

There is only one area in which a very thick girdle is acceptable. In the case of shapes that have one or more points, such as the pear-shape, heart, or marquise, it is acceptable to have thick to very thick girdles *in the area of the points*. Here the extra thickness in the girdle helps protect the points themselves from chipping.

Generally, a diamond with an extremely thin girdle should sell for less than one with an extremely thick girdle because of the stone's increased vulnerability to chipping. However, if the girdle is much too thick (as in some older diamonds), the price can also be significantly less because the stone can look significantly smaller than other stones of comparable weight.

The Culet

The culet is actually another facet—a tiny, flat polished surface. The culet should be small or very small so that it isn't noticeable from the top. Some diamonds today are pointed. This means that there really is no culet, that the stone has been cut straight down to a point instead (although most culets appear to be a "point," when examined under magnification one can see that it really is a small flat facet). A stone with a large culet will sell for less than another diamond because the larger the culet, the more visible it will be from the top. Stones described as having a large or "open" culet—as in old-European or old-mine cut diamonds—are less desirable because the culet is clearly visible from the top and results in reduced sparkle or brilliance at the very center of the stone. These stones normally need to be recut, and their valuation should take the need for recutting into consideration. Normally the cost is determined by estimating the amount of weight loss one would expect if the stone were recut, and reducing the stone's value by that amount. Normally this can be anywhere from 5% to 25%. Also, a chipped or broken culet will seriously detract from the stone's beauty and significantly reduce its value.

Color and Clarity Grades

The color and clarity grades are the factors most people are familiar with, and we have already discussed them in detail in Chapters 5 and 6. They are important factors in terms of determining the value of a diamond, but they do not tell the whole story as we hope you can now see. We won't take the time to go into color and clarity grading again here, but we do want to remind you of several important related points.

A Word About FLUORESCENCE and Its Effect on Color and Value. Generally, the absence or presence of fluorescence doesn't affect value. However, if the stone has a *very strong yellow* fluorescence, it should sell for less since it will appear yellower than it really is when worn in daylight or fluorescent lighting. The presence of *blue* fluorescence will not detract, and in some cases should be considered a "freebie" since it may make the stone appear whiter than it really is in daylight or fluorescent lighting. However, if the report shows a *very strong blue* fluorescence, there may be an "oily" or "murky" appearance to the diamond. If this is the case—if the stone appears murky or oily to you as you look at it (especially in daylight or fluorescent light)—the stone should sell for less.

Placement of Flaws May Affect Price. The clarity grade is also fairly well understood by most, but keep in mind that the *placement* of the flaws—where they occur within the stone—may affect the cost. A stone with a noticeable inclusion (for example, one in the center of the table where it might be seen, or might affect fire or brilliance) will sell for less than one that has several inclusions that are less visible (for example, near the girdle, in the pavilion). See Chapter 6.

❖ A Final Word about Reports

Diamond grading reports provide a very useful tool to aid in comparing diamonds and evaluating quality and value. But the key to their usefulness is proper understanding of how to read them, and how to look at the stone. Those who take the time to learn and understand what they are reading and, therefore, what they are really buying, will have a major advantage over those who do not.

CHAPTER 9

Comparing Diamond Prices

All too often people look for easy answers to complex problems. Many would like to have a simple list of diamond grades and corresponding prices, by size. Unfortunately, market conditions are constantly changing, and, more important, significant differences in price often result from subtle differences in quality not readily discernible to any but the professional (see Chapter 8 on reading diamond grading reports). Therefore, it is not possible to provide a simple answer to this complex problem.

But that does not mean we cannot provide you with some useful information. We can offer some general guidelines that will help you understand the *relative* effects of each of the four primary factors that are used to determine the value of diamonds. They are not intended as hard price lists of what you should be paying in a jewelry store. Keep in mind that these prices are for unmounted stones. Fine settings can add substantially to the price.

Extreme differences between the prices given on the following pages and a price you might be quoted for a diamond should be examined carefully—if the price is *much* lower, be sure to check the quality and whether or not it is as represented (see the list of appraisers and laboratories in the Appendix); if the price is *much* higher, check to be sure the seller is offering good value by comparison shopping in your community.

Having said this, note that the prices given here are for round, brilliant-cut diamonds with "good" proportioning (stones with "excellent" proportioning will sell for more; stones with poor proportioning can sell for much less). Diamonds having "fancy" shapes (shapes other than round) normally sell for anywhere from 5% to 15% less. However, if a particular shape is in very high demand, the price can be higher than it is for round stones. Well-cut marquise-shaped diamonds were selling for more than round diamonds in the late 1980s, but changes in fashion affect their popularity and price.

Finally, before relying too heavily on the prices listed in this chapter, be sure to read Chapter 8 on how to read and understand diamond grading reports. This will give you additional input on adjusting diamond prices according to the more subtle factors that affect quality and value. Then be sure to have the facts verified by a qualified gemologist-appraiser (see Appendix).

RETAIL PRICE GUIDES

Note the effect of color, clarity, and carat weight on the price per-carat of a well-made round brilliant-cut diamond

> PRICE PER CARAT
> **PRICE PER STONE** U.S. DOLLARS - 1990

⅓ - Carat Round Brilliant (.30⁺)
COLOR GRADE

Flaw (Clarity) Grade		D	E	G	I	K	M
	IF	6,800	6,450	5,600	4,050	3,225	2,400
		2,275	**2,150**	**1,865**	**1,350**	**1,075**	**800**
	VVS₁	6,450	6,000	5,250	3,600	2,850	2,250
		2,150	**2,000**	**1,750**	**1,200**	**950**	**750**
	VS₁	5,550	5,175	4,350	3,600	2,700	1,950
		1,850	**1,725**	**1,450**	**1,200**	**900**	**650**
	SI₁	3,900	3,750	3,150	2,850	2,400	1,800
		1,300	**1,250**	**1,050**	**950**	**800**	**600**
	SI₂	3,700	3,000	2,850	2,700	2,100	1,650
		1,200	**1,000**	**950**	**900**	**700**	**550**
	I₁	3,075	2,850	2,700	2,250	1,950	1,500
		1,025	**950**	**900**	**750**	**650**	**500**

RETAIL PRICE GUIDES

Note the effect of color, clarity, and carat weight on the price per-carat of a well-made round brilliant-cut diamond

PRICE PER CARAT
PRICE PER STONE U.S. DOLLARS - 1990

½ - *Carat Round Brilliant (.50⁺)*

COLOR GRADE

Flaw (Clarity) Grade		D	E	G	I	K	M
	IF	14,250 **7,125**	11,400 **5,700**	9,600 **4,800**	6,800 **3,400**	4,400 **2,200**	3,000 **1,500**
	VVS₁	11,400 **5,700**	10,400 **5,200**	8,400 **4,200**	6,000 **3,000**	4,200 **2,100**	3,200 **1,600**
	VS₁	9,200 **4,600**	8,200 **4,100**	6,400 **3,200**	5,200 **2,600**	3,800 **1,900**	2,600 **1,300**
	SI₁	6,400 **3,200**	6,000 **3,000**	5,200 **2,600**	4,400 **2,200**	3,400 **1,700**	2,400 **1,200**
	SI₂	5,000 **2,500**	4,800 **2,400**	4,400 **2,200**	4,000 **2,000**	3,200 **1,600**	2,200 **1,100**
	I₁	4,000 **2,000**	3,800 **1,900**	3,400 **1,700**	3,000 **1,500**	2,600 **1,300**	2,100 **1,050**

PRICE PER CARAT
PRICE PER STONE U.S. DOLLARS - 1990

¾ - *Carat Round Brilliant (.70⁺)*

COLOR GRADE

Flaw (Clarity) Grade		D	E	G	I	K	M
	IF	16,000 **12,000**	12,000 **9,000**	10,250 **7,700**	7,350 **5,500**	5,200 **3,900**	3,600 **2,700**
	VVS₁	12,000 **9,000**	11,200 **8,400**	9,150 **6,850**	6,800 **5,125**	5,000 **3,750**	3,400 **2,550**
	VS₁	10,000 **7,500**	8,900 **6,700**	6,800 **5,100**	5,800 **4,350**	4,400 **3,300**	3,000 **2,250**
	SI₁	7,600 **5,700**	6,300 **4,725**	6,000 **4,500**	4,800 **3,600**	3,800 **2,850**	2,800 **2,100**
	SI₂	6,400 **4,800**	6,000 **4,500**	5,200 **3,900**	4,200 **3,150**	3,400 **2,550**	2,700 **2,000**
	I₁	4,600 **3,450**	4,400 **3,300**	4,000 **3,000**	3,400 **2,550**	3,000 **2,250**	2,400 **1,800**

RETAIL PRICE GUIDES

Note the effect of color, clarity, and carat weight on the price per-carat of a well-made round brilliant-cut diamond

PRICE PER CARAT	
PRICE PER STONE	U.S. DOLLARS - 1990

A *"Light"* Carat Round Brilliant *(.90+)*

COLOR GRADE

Flaw (Clarity) Grade		D	E	G	I	K	M
	IF	17,000	13,100	11,000	8,350	5,500	4,000
		15,300	**11,800**	**9,900**	**7,500**	**5,000**	**3,600**
	VVS$_1$	13,200	12,000	9,500	7,000	5,300	3,750
		11,900	**10,800**	**8,550**	**6,300**	**4,800**	**3,400**
	VS$_1$	11,000	9,500	7,600	6,100	5,000	3,600
		9,900	**8,550**	**6,850**	**5,500**	**4,500**	**3,240**
	SI$_1$	7,800	7,400	6,450	5,500	4,375	3,400
		7,100	**6,675**	**5,800**	**5,000**	**3,950**	**3,050**
	SI$_2$	7,000	6,600	6,000	5,000	4,000	3,200
		6,300	**5,900**	**5,400**	**4,500**	**3,600**	**2,900**
	I$_1$	5,000	4,750	4,375	4,000	3,600	3,000
		4,500	**4,300**	**3,950**	**3,600**	**3,240**	**2,700**

PRICE PER CARAT	U.S. DOLLARS - 1990

1 - *Carat Round Brilliant (1.00+)*

COLOR GRADE

Flaw (Clarity) Grade	D	E	G	I	K	M
IF	32,400	20,700	14,250	9,500	7,400	6,100
VVS$_1$	20,700	17,000	12,000	8,550	6,850	5,700
VS$_1$	13,875	11,475	9,000	7,200	6,100	5,150
SI$_1$	9,300	8,700	7,200	6,275	5,300	4,600
SI$_2$	7,800	7,400	7,000	6,000	5,200	4,300
I$_1$	5,700	5,600	5,250	5,000	4,400	3,800

RETAIL PRICE GUIDES

Note the effect of color, clarity, and carat weight on the price
per-carat of a well-made round brilliant-cut diamond

PRICE PER CARAT
PRICE PER STONE U.S. DOLLARS - 1990

2 - Carat Round Brilliant (2.00⁺)
COLOR GRADE

Flaw (Clarity) Grade		D	E	G	I	K	M
IF		41,600	33,600	23,200	14,875	10,200	7,400
		83,200	**67,200**	**46,400**	**29,750**	**20,400**	**14,800**
VVS₁		33,600	30,000	21,250	13,500	9,450	7,000
		67,200	**60,000**	**42,500**	**27,000**	**18,900**	**14,000**
VS₁		22,875	20,050	14,875	12,100	8,650	6,100
		45,750	**40,100**	**29,750**	**24,200**	**17,300**	**12,200**
SI₁		14,000	13,125	11,400	9,250	7,000	5,250
		28,000	**26,250**	**22,750**	**18,500**	**14,000**	**10,500**
SI₂		12,000	11,000	9,000	7,800	6,600	5,200
		24,000	**22,000**	**18,000**	**15,600**	**13,200**	**10,400**
I₁		7,550	7,100	6,650	5,950	5,150	4,400
		15,100	**14,200**	**13,300**	**11,900**	**10,300**	**8,800**

CHAPTER 10

How to Protect Yourself Against Fraud and Misrepresentation

As you have seen, many factors affect quality and value in diamonds and colored gems. When looking at a stone already set in a ring, especially a diamond, it is very difficult, if not impossible, for the average buyer to *see* differences—differences that significantly affect cost. This is the primary reason why you should ask the right questions when shopping around and comparing rings from different jewelers. It is equally important to deal only with knowledgeable, reputable jewelers (see Chapter 23), to make sure the jeweler is willing to back up the description in writing on the bill of sale, and to *verify the description with a qualified gemologist-appraiser.*

❖ How can you tell if a stone is really a diamond?

As we have said many times, unless you are an expert—or seek expert advice—you cannot be sure about the identification of a stone. Nevertheless, there are a few simple tests you can perform that will quickly reveal most fraudulent diamonds.

Some things to look for to detect diamond imitations

Is newsprint readable or observable through the stone? In round, brilliant-cut diamonds, if the stone is unmounted, or mounted in such a way as to allow you to place it table-down over newsprint, check whether you can *see* or *read any portion of the lettering.* If so, it is not a diamond.

Is the stone glued into the setting? Diamonds are *seldom* glued in. Rhinestones often are.

If a ring, is the back open or closed? If the stone is a properly set diamond, the back of the ring box or setting will always be open at least slightly, allowing a portion of the pavilion to be readily observable. (Some very small rose-cut diamonds or chips, as seen in some antique jewelry, may be mounted with a closed back.) If a ring has a closed back, it is probably not diamond.

Recently a young woman called and asked if we would examine an antique diamond ring she'd inherited from her great-grandmother. She mentioned that as she was cleaning it, one of its two diamonds had fallen out of the setting, and inside the setting she saw what she described as pieces of "mirror." She added, "Isn't that strange?" Of course our suspicions were immediately aroused, and upon examination of the ring, they were completely confirmed.

When we saw the piece, we could immediately understand why she felt this ring was a fine heirloom. The ring was beautiful. Its design was classic. It held two "diamonds" appearing to be approximately 1 carat each. The ring mounting was lovely, finely worked filigree platinum. But the design of the mounting, which had been common in her great-grandmother's day, made viewing the stones from the side of the ring almost impossible. One could see the top of the stone, and the beautiful platinum work, but little more. Furthermore, the back was almost completely enclosed, except for a small round hole at the back of the setting (which would have led one to assume the stones were the real thing, since it wasn't completely closed, as was the case with most imitations at that time). The "set" diamond appeared to be a well-proportioned "old mine" cut (the cut of that day) with very good color. The loose stone, however, with some of the "shiny stuff" still clinging to it, lacked brilliance and fire.

This was one of the finest examples of fraud we had seen in a long time. The "stones" were well cut and proportioned; the mounting was beautifully worked in a precious metal; the stones were held by very small prongs, which was typical of good design at that time. But inside the mounting, backing the stones, was silver foil. The stones were *glass*, backed with metallic foil to give brilliance and liveliness!

The use of silver foil is an effective method used to "create" a diamond. It acts as a mirror to reflect light so that the stone appears so brilliant and lively that it can pass as a diamond. The foiling seen today consists of making the back facets into true mirrors, giving the backs of these mirrors a protective coating of gilt paint. These are then set in jewelry so that their backs are hidden.

It's a sad story, but not an altogether uncommon one. We don't know how many more rings as cleverly done exist today, but approximately 5% of the *antique jewelry* we see is set with fake gems. Fine glass imitations (often referred to as paste) have been with us since the Venetians of Renaissance time perfected the art of glassmaking. Of course fraud has been around since time immemorial. Don't allow yourself to be deluded into believing that something you possess is "genuine" simply because it is "antique" or has "been in the family" for a long time.

Count the facets visible on the top. In cheaper glass imitations there are usually only nine visible top facets, as opposed to 33 visible top facets in a diamond or "good" simulation. However, some small diamonds, such as those seen in side stones in some rings and some wedding bands, do show only nine facets on top (referred to in the trade as single cut rather than brilliant cut). Of course, such diamonds are set in open-back mountings, whereas rhinestones would usually be set in closed-back mountings.

Examine the girdle of the stone. Most diamonds have a frosted appearance (unpolished and with a ground-glass-like appearance). There are some diamond imitations that also have a frosted appearance but, of all of these, a diamond has the whitest "frostiness"—like clean, dry ground glass. (Note, however, that some diamonds do have polished or faceted girdles, and so this frostiness will not be observed.) You can develop an eye for this by asking a reliable jeweler to point out the differences between a polished girdle, an unpolished girdle, and a faceted girdle.

Check the symmetry of the cut. Since diamond is so valuable and symmetry so important to its overall appearance and desirability, the symmetry of the faceting on a diamond will be very carefully executed, whereas in diamond simulations the symmetry of the facets may be sloppy. For example, the eight kite-shaped facets (sometimes called bezel facets) will often be missing one or more points on the side, or on the top or bottom, showing a small straight edge rather than a point. This sloppy faceting can be an important indication that the stone in question is not a diamond, since it indicates that proper care was not taken (but some poorer-grade diamonds or old-cut diamonds may also show this sloppiness).

Are the crown and the pavilion of the stone properly aligned? While occasionally a diamond may show partial misalignment, imitations are frequently and often badly misaligned.

Are the facet edges or faces scratched, chipped, or worn? Diamond imitations include some stones that are very soft and/or brittle, such as zircon, GGG (a man-made simulation), Fabulite (a man-made diamond simulation also known as Wellington Diamond), and glass. Because of their lack of hardness and, in the case of zircon, possible brittleness, these imitations will show wear easily, and one can often detect scratches or chips on the facet edges or faces. The edges are somewhat more vulnerable and scratches or chips may be more easily seen there, so check the edges first. Then check the flat faces for scratches. Check the areas that would be most exposed, as well as around the prongs (where a setter might accidentally have scratched the stone while setting it).

Zircon, which is not particularly soft, is very brittle, and it will almost always show chipping at the edges of the facets if the stone has been worn in jewelry for any length of time (a year or more). Glass and Fabulite will also show scratches after minimal exposure to handling and wear. (Fabulite also differs from diamond in its fire—it will show even more fire than diamond, but with a strong bluishness to it.)

Also, with a very good eye or the aid of a magnifier, one can notice an absence of sharpness to the lines or edges where the facets come together. In diamond these facet edges are very sharp because of the stone's spectacular hardness. In most simulation, since the stone is so much softer, the final polishing technique rounds off these edges.

Some diamond look-alikes, however, are more durable and resistant to noticeable wear. These include colorless synthetic spinel, colorless synthetic sapphire, colorless quartz, YAG (man-made), and CZ (cubic zirconia, also man-made). While these may scratch or chip over time with regular wear and daily abuse, scratches or chips will probably not be easily observed. These stones, however, can be distinguished from diamond simply by examining as already described.

Examine the stone, loose or mounted, for fluorescence under ultraviolet light. We do not feel this is something readily accomplished by an amateur, nor comprehensible to the average person because of the numerous variables and scientific complexities.

If, after the above tests, you still have doubt, take the stone to a qualified gemologist with lab facilities and ask him to identify the stone. If it is a diamond, have the gemologist note the nature of the stone's fluorescence since it can prove a valuable tool for identification if ever needed.

An Important Word About CZ

CZ is the best diamond simulation made to date, and even some jewelers have mistaken CZ for diamonds.

Shortly after the appearance of CZ, several well-known Washington, D.C., jewelers found themselves stuck with CZ instead of the fine 1-carat diamonds they thought they had. The crooks were very clever. A well-dressed couple would arrive at the diamond counter and ask to see various 1-carat round, brilliant-cut loose diamonds. Because of their fine appearance and educated manner, the jeweler's guard was relaxed. The couple would then leave, not making a purchase decision just then, but promising to return. When the jeweler went to replace his merchandise, "something" didn't seem quite right. Upon close examination, the jeweler discovered that the "nice couple" had pocketed the genuine diamond and substituted CZ.

CZ is almost as brilliant as diamond, has even greater fire (which masks its lesser brilliance), and is relatively hard, giving it good durability and wearability. CZ is also being produced today in fancy colors—red, green, and yellow—and it can provide a nice diamond "alternative" as a means to offset or dress up colored semiprecious stones in jewelry if diamonds are unaffordable.

But make sure you know *what* you are buying. For example, if you are shown a lovely amethyst or sapphire ring dressed up with "diamonds," ask whether the colorless stones are diamonds. And if you are having your own piece of jewelry custom made, you might want to consider using CZ. You can ask your jeweler to order them for you. Also, they make stunning stud earrings and other jewelry that can be worn every day . . . and you need not worry if they are stolen—your real gems will be safe in your vault!

How Can You Tell If You Have a CZ? Some of the tests already discussed may help you detect a CZ. The following, however, may eliminate any remaining doubt.

If it is a loose stone, have it weighed. CZ is much heavier than a diamond of similar size. If you are familiar with diamond sizes (see page 53 and 54) or have a spread gauge (which can be purchased for under $5), you can estimate the diamond carat weight by its spread. The loose stone can be weighed on a scale, which most jewelers have handy, and you can determine how much it should weigh if a diamond. If the weight is much greater than the diamond weight should be, based on its spread, then it is not a diamond. A CZ is approximately 75% heavier than a diamond of the same spread. For example, a 1-carat (diamond spread) CZ weighs 1¾ carats; 25/100 carat (diamond spread) CZ weighs approximately 40/100 carat.

Look at the girdle. If it is frosted, unlike diamond, it will have a subdued whiteness resembling slightly wet or oiled frosted glass. Unfortunately, one must have some experience looking at girdles in order to differentiate between the appearance of a frosted CZ and a frosted diamond girdle.

Test the stone with a carbide scriber. CZ can be scratched with a finepoint carbide scriber; also available at most jewelry supply houses for under $10. If the scriber is forcibly pushed perpendicularly to any of the facets (the table being the easiest) and then drawn across this flat surface, you will scratch the facet. You cannot scratch a diamond except with another diamond. But be sensible . . . and considerate. Don't heedlessly scratch merchandise that doesn't belong to you—particularly if the jeweler or seller doesn't represent the stone as diamond.

Examine the stone, loose or mounted, for fluorescence. Many jewelers have an "ultraviolet lamp" and will be happy to show you the fluorescence of the stone, if it has any. *Some diamonds do not fluoresce: all CZ does!* The fluorescence of CZ—the colors and intensities it will exhibit—are different from diamond.

If after the tests you have some questions, take the stone to a qualified gemologist with laboratory facilities and ask for an identification.

❖ *Types of Misrepresentation*

Beware of Diamond Bargains—Misrepresenting Diamonds to Be Better Quality than They Are

Beware of bargains. Most are not. Legitimate retailers don't give something away for nothing, or for less than it costs them. When a bargain seems too good to be true, it usually is (unless the seller doesn't know its true value). A large jewelry store in Philadelphia was recently found guilty of misrepresenting the quality of diamonds it was selling. They were consistently representing their diamonds to be *several* color grades and/or flaw grades *better* than they actually were. As a result, their prices seemed much more attractive than those of other jewelers. Customers thought they were getting a much better buy from this firm than from others in the Philadelphia area, when, in fact, this may not have been the case. Since customers didn't know the true quality of the stones they were buying, they couldn't make a fair comparison with what other jewelers were offering. Other jewelers in the area were, in fact, offering stones comparable to what was actually being sold by this "bargain" firm for *less*.

Another firm in another major city has been guilty of a similar practice. Based on several rings brought into our laboratory for appraisal, we learned that this firm not only misrepresented diamond quality, but was willing to put the important details *in writing* on the bill of sale!

They figured out that most people *assume* when they put it in writing that they *must* be properly representing the item—and most never bother to have the facts verified. While our clients were savvy enough to get an independent evaluation and, as a result, were able to get their money refunded, we wonder how many customers of this firm don't have what they've been told they have.

Another variation on this clever ploy is frequently encountered in New York's famous 47th Street jewelry district. Many retailers in this area are quick to tell you they are "anxious to do business" and are willing to give customers "a very special buy." Frequently one hears phrases such as, "because I bought it right"—whatever that means—or "I pass the savings on to you," or, "I'm not greedy—I don't care who I sell to at wholesale, after all, a sale is a sale." And so on. When they give you the price, it is without question the best price—much cheaper than anything you've seen anywhere else. When asked whether or not they're willing to put the facts in writing, they may refuse (for one of several seemingly plausible reasons). However, they're willing to have you take the ring out to have it appraised, *before* you make the purchase. Again, most people think that since the seller has no objection to getting it appraised first, they must not have anything to hide . . . so why bother to go to all the trouble to check it out? So they assume the jeweler is telling the truth and never bother to get it appraised first.

Those who do wish to have the diamond examined first often face another problem. They don't know any appraiser, or certainly not any in the neighborhood. Many visitors to 47th Street are from out of town and don't know anyone local. Unscrupulous sellers often count on this because it gives them the opportunity to recommend several "reliable" appraisers. Unfortunately, reliable in this case means the *seller* can rely on the *appraiser* to tell the prospective buyer what the seller wants him to. One must always be careful of recommendations from the seller. Never accept a jeweler's recommendation of appraisers without also checking the appraiser's credentials yourself (see Chapter 24). While legitimate jewelers usually know better than anyone else who the best gemologist appraisers are in their communities, and their recommendations should be respected, you must still be sure to check the credentials to protect yourself from scams. Unfortunately, especially in the jewelry districts of major cities, far too many appraisers are not qualified, and some are in collusion with unscrupulous jewelers.

One of our clients had just such an experience with a 47th Street firm. She was offered a 5-plus carat diamond ring at a price that was less than one-fifth the price most retailers had been quoting her. When she asked the seller if he would back up his description of the quality of the diamond in writing, he said it was against store policy, but he would be happy for her to take the ring to an appraiser before she purchased it. Since she was from out of town (which he had already learned from chatting with her), he recommended several local appraisers. She insisted, however, that she would rely on only one appraiser, Mr. Bonanno, and would only consider purchasing the ring if he saw it first. Surprisingly, the seller agreed and sent the ring to us.

Not surprisingly, the quality was not as represented. It was easy to see that the flaw grade had been misrepresented (by four grades), but the color still looked very fine, and the price being asked was still "too good" for the stone. We suspected that the color may have been altered. In fact, we wondered if the stone might have been "painted." Painted diamonds have been coated with a substance that *temporarily* whitens the color. This coating doesn't come off with normal cleaning and may take months or years to wear off. We decided to clean the stone chemically and found that it was, indeed, painted. The coating dissolved in the chemical and the stone's true body color was revealed. The actual body color of the diamond was *seven color grades lower than represented!*

In this particular case, given the true value of the diamond, the price being asked for the ring was certainly not the "steal" it appeared to be. It wasn't a bad price, but other retailers may have been offering comparable stones at comparable prices, or less. More important, this seller was dishonest. The buyer might never have discovered the stone was painted, and would have wondered why the stone seemed so much yellower than she'd remembered it after a few years. Furthermore, dishonest practices such as these put other jewelers in a bad light, unnecessarily. In such cases, the dishonest jeweler *appears* to be offering the best value while the honest jeweler, who may actually be offering the best *value*, appears to be charging "too much."

Take time to do your homework first, to learn what to look for and what questions to ask. Then shop carefully and compare stones being offered by several fine jewelers in your community. This will give you a chance to get a clearer sense of what something should legitimately sell for. Only then can you decide whether or not something sounds "too good to be true" or which jeweler seems to have the right ring for you, at a *fair* price.

And remember: No one gives away a valuable gem. There are very few "steals," and even fewer people qualified to truly know a "steal" when they see one.

There are five areas in which diamond fraud or misrepresentation usually occur:

- Weight misrepresentation
- Color alteration and misgrading
- Flaw concealment and misgrading
- Certification alteration and counterfeit production
- Come-on and flamboyant advertising

Weight

Giving "total weight" where more than one stone is involved, rather than the exact weight of the main stone, is misrepresentation. Sometimes a customer buying a diamond ring with side stones, when asking about the "size" of the diamond, is given a diamond weight that actually represents the total weight of all the stones but is presented in such a way that the customer believes it to be the weight of the main, central stone. This is in strict violation of Federal Trade Commission (FTC) rulings. In giving the weight, particularly on any display card, descriptive tag, or other type of advertising for a particular piece of jewelry, the weight of the main stone(s) should be clearly indicated as well as the total weight of all the stones.

Thus, if you purchase a "3-carat diamond" ring with three stones—one large center stone and two small side stones (as found in many engagement rings)—the center stone's weight should be clearly stated; for example, "The weight of the center stone is 2.80 carats, with 2 side stones that weigh .10 carats each, for a total weight of 3 carats."

There is a tremendous price difference between a single stone weighing 3 carats and numerous stones having a total weight of 3 carats. A single 3-carat stone could sell for $100,000, while 3 carats consisting of numerous stones (even with some weighing as much as a carat or more) of good quality could sell anywhere from $5,000 to $10,000, depending on how many and what quality.

Use of the Word SPREAD in Response to Questions About Weight or Size. A consumer inquiring about the weight of a diamond usually asks the wrong question, as discussed earlier, due to confusion between size and weight. Usually the jeweler will be asked how large the stone is, rather than how much it weighs. In any case, the answer should provide the exact carat weight. Where the response includes the word spread ("This stone has an x-carat spread" or "This stone spreads x carats"), beware. A stone that spreads 1 carat is not the same thing as a stone that weighs 1 carat. It simply means it looks like a 1-carat stone in its width (or width and length if it is a fancy-cut diamond).

In diamond-trade language a spread stone is one with thin proportions—it's somewhat "pancaked." The cut and proportion may be poor, and the stone will therefore lack life and should sell for less per carat than a well-cut stone. If you see a diamond that looks like it is about 1 carat, and the price seems particularly attractive, make sure you ask what the *exact actual weight is*. Look at the stone carefully, focusing your attention on its brilliance and fire, and ask yourself if it's really pretty and lively, and whether you really like it.

A fine 1-carat stone will cost much more per carat than a stone that is only .90 carat, for example, but seems as large because of its spread.

To illustrate our point even more clearly in terms of dollar value, a first-quality diamond weighing from 1 full carat to 1.06 carats has a cost per carat approximately 45% more than a .94 carat that spreads 1 carat. (Some "slightly spread" stones are still very pretty and lively, but their price should be 15 to 25% less than other stones of the same size.)

An **illusion** *setting*

Illusion Mounting. This refers to mounting a stone in a setting that creates the illusion that the stone is larger than it actually is. This in and of itself may not be misleading, or in any way fraudulent. In fact, it may be preferable to the customer. But don't be misled as to the size of a stone mounted in this manner. Make sure you *know* what you are getting.

Color

Enhancing Color Artificially

Touching the culet, or side, of a slightly yellow stone with a coating of purple ink, such as found in an indelible pencil, neutralizes the yellow, producing a whiter-looking stone. This can be easily detected by washing the stone in alcohol or water. If you have any questions about the color, tactfully request that the stone be washed (in front of you) for "better examination." A reputable jeweler should have no objection to this request.

Improving the color by utilizing a sputtering technique (also called "painting" the diamond). This involves sputtering a very thin coating of a special substance over the stone or part of the stone (usually the back, where it will be harder to detect when mounted). The girdle area can also be "painted" with the substance and create the same effect. This substance also neutralizes the yellow and thereby improves the color. This technique is not frequently used, but stones treated in this manner do appear often enough to be worth mentioning. *The color grade can be improved as much as 5 to 7 grades by this method.*

The substance does *not* wash off. It can be removed in two ways: by rubbing the stone briskly and firmly with a cleanser or by boiling the stone carefully in sulfuric acid.

If the stone is already mounted and is coated on the back, using cleanser is not feasible. The sulfuric acid method is the only way. But please note, *it is extremely dangerous, and must be done by an experienced person. We cannot overstate the hazards of conducting this test.*

Coating the diamond with chemicals and baking it in a small lab-type furnace. This technique also tends to neutralize some of the yellow, thereby producing a better color grade. This coating will be removed eventually by repeated hot ultrasonic cleanings, which will gradually erode the coating. A more rapid removal can be accomplished by the more dangerous method of boiling in sulfuric acid.

Radiation treatment. Exposing off-colored diamonds, such as yellowish- or brownish-tinted stones, and also badly flawed stones, to certain types of radiation can result in the production of fancy colored stones—canary yellow, greens, blues, or pinks.

This treatment greatly enhances their saleability because these fancy colors are very desirable. In and of itself, radiation is not fraud; in fact, it may enable one otherwise unable to afford a fancy to be able to afford one. But again, just be sure it is properly represented and you know what you are buying, and that you are getting it at the right price—which is much lower than that of the natural fancy.

Treated stones must be represented as "treated stones" and should be priced accordingly. Unfortunately, too often, in passing through many hands, the fact that they have been "treated" or "radiated" or "bombarded" is overlooked or forgotten—intentionally or accidentally.

Whether the color is natural or treated can be determined by spectroscopic examination, which can be provided by a gem testing laboratory (see appendix). Not many gemologists, however, are competent with spectroscopic procedures, and it may be time-consuming. If you wish to verify a fancy stone as natural, ask the gemologist if he or she is experienced in conducting such testing. If not, the gemologist may be able to recommend someone who is.

Erroneous Color Grading. This may be deliberate, or it may be the result of the jeweler's limited knowledge. One is safer considering the purchase of a stone that has had important data, such as color, described in a diamond grading report (or certificate) issued by one of several different laboratories now offering this service. Many jewelry firms now offer diamonds accompanied by grading reports. Diamond grading reports issued by GIA are used most widely in the United States. Diamonds accompanied by reports usually sell for slightly more per carat, but provide an element of security for the average consumer, as well as credible documentation if one wishes to sell this stone at some future time. If the stone you are considering is accompanied by such a report, be sure to read Chapter 8. Also, be sure to verify that the report is genuine.

Flaw Concealment

Where possible, flaws are concealed by their settings. The good stone setter will try to set a stone in such a manner that the prong (or prongs) will help to conceal any visible flaws. This is one reason flaws near or at the girdle will downgrade a stone less than those found in the center of a stone. Aside from the fact that they are simply less visible here, they may also become "invisible" when the stone is set.

Similarly, flaws can be concealed under the bezel in a bezel-set stone. A bezel setting is a rim of metal that encases the girdle, as in a pair of eyeglasses; the rim of metal holding the lens could be called a bezel setting. While this type of setting hasn't been seen much in diamond jewelry in the past, we are beginning to see more and more bezel settings in diamond jewelry because it can protect the girdle, and can accent an unusual shape very nicely. And, of course, this too can conceal in the same manner as prong settings. However, note that the bezel setting also prevents examination of the girdle. This makes examination for naturals, small chips, slight repairs, and the girdle thickness itself impossible unless the stone is removed from the setting.

Is concealment fraud or misrepresentation? There is nothing fraudulent as long as the stone is properly represented. The only danger is that not only may the customer not see it but the jeweler may not have noticed it.

We know of situations where a jeweler purchases mounted goods from a dealer at a fair price, thinking the price is unusually good because the jeweler can't spot the flaw. The jeweler then does one of two things—sells the ring at a normal markup, but possibly representing it as a finer quality and therefore a better value for the price than it really is . . . unknowingly. Or the jeweler may take advantage of an opportunity here to make a higher profit, and mark the ring up to what is thought would be a fair price, when in fact it is now overpriced . . . again, unknowingly.

Can concealment affect value? In most diamonds other than FL or IF, the presence of a minor flaw concealed under a prong will not affect the price significantly. However, a diamond represented as FL or IF may have a small blemish or inclusion hidden under a prong, which should have been classified as IF or VVS$_1$. The difference here may represent a very large price differential on larger stones with fine body color.

Certification of Diamonds

In the United States today, most fine diamonds of 1 carat or larger have been *certificated* by a laboratory such as GIA or AGL prior to being set and are accompanied by a diamond grading report or certificate issued by one of these well-known gem labs (see Chapter 8). This means that the stone will not only have been certified as genuine, but will have an accompanying *certificate* or *report* that will fully describe it, providing all the important information such as color grade, flaw grade, weight, cut, proportion, etc. If you are considering the purchase of a very fine diamond *weighing 1 carat or more*, which is not accompanied by such a report, we would strongly recommend that a written report be obtained from GIA or other respected laboratory prior to purchase. This should be done even if it means having a stone that is already set removed from the setting and reset. Given the significant difference in cost that can result from a grading error in these rarer grades, we believe this procedure is worth the inconvenience.

Unfortunately, the confidence of the public in stones accompanied by certificates has given rise to the practice of altering and counterfeiting them. While you can be relatively sure that "certificated" stones sold by reputable, established jewelry firms are what they claim to be, there are some suppliers and dealers who are seizing opportunities to prey on the unsuspecting.

Altering Certificates

This involves changing information on an otherwise valid certificate—changing the flaw or color grade stated. If you have any question regarding information on the certificate, a phone call to the lab giving them the certificate number and date will enable you to verify the information on your certificate.

Counterfeit Certificates

This practice is outright fraud and consists of several techniques.

- Producing a "GIA" (or other equally credible lab) certificate that is not in fact a GIA certificate. An astute appraiser may detect the difference in the seal on the certificate. Again, if you have any reason to be suspicious, a call to the lab in question will usually expose this fraud.
- Producing a certificate from a nonexistent lab. This is becoming an increasing problem today. Stones accompanied by fancy "certificates" from impressive sounding labs that don't exist are appearing more and more frequently. If it is not from one of the recognized labs, it should be carefully checked. Have jewelers in the area heard of this lab? Has the Better Business Bureau had any complaints? If the lab seems legitimate, call to verify the information on the certificate, and, if all seems in order, you can probably rest comfortably. Otherwise, you may need to have the facts verified by another gemologist or recognized lab.

The jeweler may not allow this verification—and some won't, simply because they've been victims themselves or it isn't worth the inconvenience to them. In this case, you might ask the jeweler to get the stone certificated by one of the recognized labs. Many jewelers today are happy to provide this service. If not, then you must decide how badly you want the stone, how much you feel you can trust the jeweler, and what degree of monetary risk you can afford.

Switching the Stone Described on a Certificate

In this situation the certificate is bona fide but the stone has been switched. To protect both the consumer and the certificating lab, some labs today are taking advantage of ingenious techniques to ensure against switching by permanently marking the stone in some way. For example, GIA can now actually inscribe the certificate number, which is visible only under magnification, directly onto the diamond itself, along the girdle. By so doing, one can very easily be sure a specific stone matches a specific certificate simply by matching the numbers. There is an additional fee for this service.

In the absence of such a mark, one clue to a switched stone might be provided by the carat weight and the dimensions given on the certificate. If the measurements match exactly, the probability is slim that the stone has been switched (provided the certificate hasn't been altered). Again, a phone call can verify such information. If the measurements don't match, you know there is a mistake somewhere that warrants immediate investigation. If the measurements do match, then all the specifications provided on the certificate—fluorescence, depth percentage, table spread, crown angles, symmetry, color, clarity—should be checked to see if the stone and the certificate match.

Unfortunately, if the stone has been mounted, it may be difficult to get precise measurements to compare. In this case, if there is any cause for suspicion, the consumer has little recourse unless the seller allows the consumer to have the certificate and stone verified by a qualified gemologist-appraiser (removing the stone from the setting). This arrangement requires an understanding in writing that the stone can be returned within a certain time limit if the customer learns it is not as represented.

Always make sure in this situation, for both your protection and the jeweler's, that the jeweler writes down on the bill of sale or memo all of the stone's dimensions as best as can be determined: diameter or length and widths, depth percentage, and weight. This is to ensure that you aren't accused of switching the stone after leaving the premises, in the event you must return the stone.

Baiting and Flamboyant Advertising

We've all seen come-on or misrepresentative advertising. Quite simply, it is advertising that lures the buyer into a store or into making a purchase. The Better Business Bureau, in their booklet "Facts You Should Know About Jewelry," describes these practices very well. (This booklet is available upon request from your local Better Business Bureau.) Some of the practices are:

Bait advertising. Articles are advertised at bargain prices, but the seller has no intention of selling them. When you arrive, the article advertised is "sold out," but they have something else, which, of course, costs more. Often, too, these goods are of inferior quality.

Buying "wholesale." In this case the seller claims to be selling products at wholesale prices, when in fact they are selling merely at a discount. Few firms sell truly at wholesale.

Deposit scheme. The seller asks the customer for a deposit, which will be returned if the buyer is dissatisfied. In reality, the seller will only provide credit toward the purchase of other goods.

Buying "on approval." The seller induces the customer to take merchandise "on approval" simply by signing a receipt. The receipt turns out to be a binding contract to pay for the merchandise.

Fictitious allowances. These occur with trade-ins. The seller jacks up the price of the item you are buying to cover the trade-in allowance.

Fictitious comparative prices. This is advertising with two prices: an "original" price and a "sale" price. The "original" price is fictitious, or much higher than the item is worth.

Fictitious list prices. The list price for the item is much higher than the sale price—but, of course, the list price is not true.

Fictitious preticketing. The seller attaches a price tag showing a high fictitious price on "reduced" merchandise.

These methods are used in the selling of gems and jewelry, just as they are for selling automobiles, clothing, food, or any other commodity. Beware of them. Learn to judge for yourself the value of the gems and the current selling price, so that you can trust your judgment.

Come-on Ads

In recent years many ads have been circulated offering diamonds, rubies, or emeralds for unbelievable prices such as $19.95 for a diamond ring. These ads are just one more new and increasingly sophisticated form of deception. The next time you see one, study it carefully and take note of the various tactics used to deceive the buyer.

The ads often appear in respected publications. This, in itself, lends credibility. Often the seller offers a money-back guarantee to further lure the buyer into believing this must be safe. Frequently the seller claims the stone is "genuine." Because of truth-in-advertising laws, the buyer believes that the goods must be genuine if the advertiser claims they are. Usually the seller offers a certificate that provides even further assurance.

In fact, the buyer will receive precisely what was advertised. The stones will be genuine and of the size advertised. Also, the money-back guarantee and certificate usually prove to be true and valid. However, you must read between the lines. With a closer look, the facts reveal that you will get less than you would expect.

Size. Often the ads will offer ¼ carat *total* weight for rubies, sapphires, or emeralds and "0.25 points" for diamonds. This means that each ring consisting of rubies, sapphires, or emeralds has stones that *total* ¼ carat; moreovoer, the ¼ carat may consist of several small stones or chips, not one ¼-carat stone.

The diamond size is extremely deceptive. A .25-point stone is not ¼ *carat*, as one might expect, but ¼ of one point (there are 100 points in a carat). With the diamond, you would be receiving a stone weighing 1/400 of 1 carat, not ¼ carat! In any case, the diamond offered is extremely small, probably the size of a fleck of dandruff.

Genuineness. The stones one receives from this type of advertisement are genuine. However, there is no description of color, flaw grade, or cut. One expects to receive a lovely stone—a beautiful, sparkling diamond, a transparent, lively emerald, ruby, or sapphire.

The buyer receives flawed, badly cut diamonds and cloudy, flawed, unattractive colored gems. In other words, the buyer receives exactly what was paid for. Moreover, the stones will have *no resale value* whatsoever.

The money-back guarantee and the certificate. Again, in point of fact, these promises are true. However, given the small price paid, would it be worth the trouble to return the goods for a refund? Also, what guarantee is there that the supplier will still be in business or located at the same address by the time you receive your jewelry and return it?

With regard to "certification," certificated by whom? Is this specified? And even if you doubt the certificate, would you bother sending $25 or more to have a gemologist appraise the jewelry or verify the certificate?

These are just a few of the deceptions buried in these schemes. As we have said, everything printed in these advertisements is true, but is the ring of sufficient value to warrant buying it at all? Examine each ad very carefully, apply what you now know, and you should be able to see through most of these tricks.

PART THREE

COLORED GEMSTONES
IN ENGAGEMENT AND
WEDDING RINGS

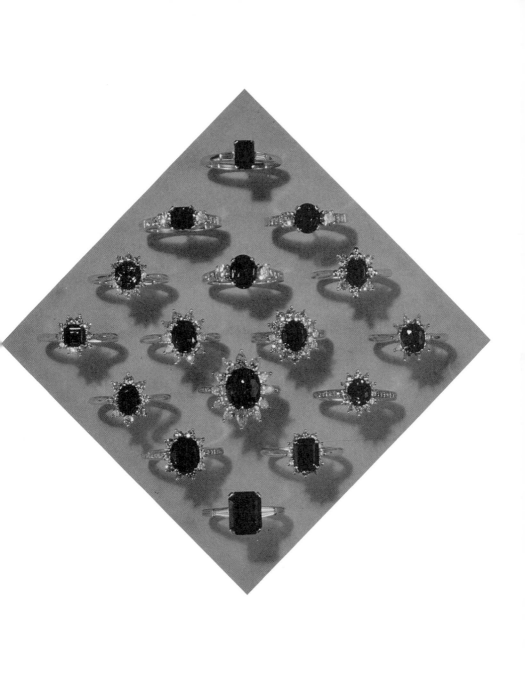

CHAPTER 11

The Allure of Colored Gemstones

*F*ascination with colored gemstones dates back to the very beginning of civilization. Long before the discovery of diamonds, the blue of sapphire produced visions of the heavens; the red of ruby was a reminder of the very essence of life. As early as Roman times, rings containing colored gems were prized as symbols of power and friendship. In fact, the most powerful (and most beloved) wore rings on every joint of every finger, which reflected the status of their position.

As betrothal rings, colored gemstones also hold an illustrious position. In addition to the beauty of particular colors, certain powers attributed to certain colored gems made them not only beautiful but meaningful choices. We see many examples of colored stones in engagement and wedding rings, from many centuries ago to the present, used both alone and combined with diamonds.

Right: A medieval ruby
betrothal ring Photo: Christie's

Left: A medieval sapphire ring

Following the discovery of diamonds in South Africa, which made diamonds more widely available and affordable, colored gemstones were briefly ignored during the earlier part of this century. While there have always been those who preferred colored gemstones despite the trends, colored stone engagement rings have only recently re-emerged as a choice for the modern bride. The selection of a sapphire and diamond engagement ring by His Royal Highness Prince Charles for Lady Diana, followed not long thereafter with his brother Prince Andrew's selection of a ruby and diamond engagement ring for Sara Ferguson, sparked a revival of interest in colored gemstones for the bride-to-be.

While rubies, sapphires, and emeralds have historically been among the most coveted gems, particularly for important occasions, there are many alternatives in colored gems for today's bride, depending on budget and personal preference. Many find birthstones make an attractive choice because of the very personal connection to the bride herself. Keep in mind that most birthstones come in several colors. You may be surprised to learn that the color you associate with your birthstone may be only one of several available. For example, most people think garnet is dark red and are surprised to learn it can be green, orange, yellow, white, purple—virtually every color in the rainbow except blue. Before discarding your birthstone as a choice, check out all the colors in which it may be available. Accented with diamonds, one can use a birthstone and combine the symbolism of diamond with the personal significance of the birthstone for a lovely, deeply meaningful, and often much more affordable ring.

In addition to birthstones, the choice of a particular colored stone may be connected to mystical powers, attributes or symbolism with which the stone has been historically identified. There is an almost limitless wealth of information about colored gems, enough to stir the imagination of even the greatest cynic.

CHAPTER 12

The Magic and Mystery
of Colored Gems

The world of colored gems is endlessly fascinating. Since ancient times, colored stones have been thought to possess certain magical powers or the ability to endow the wearer with certain attributes. Emeralds were thought to be good for the eyes; yellow stones were believed to cure jaundice; red stones to stop the flow of blood. At one time it was believed that a ruby worn by a man indicated command, nobility, lordship, and vengeance; worn by a woman, however, it signified pride, obstinacy, and haughtiness. A blue sapphire worn by a man indicated wisdom, and high and magnanimous thoughts; on a woman, jealousy in love, politeness, and vigilance. The emerald signified for man joyousness, transitory hope, and the decline of friendship; for woman, unfounded ambition, childish delight, and change.

Colored gems, because of the magical powers associated with them, achieved extensive use as talismans and amulets; as predictors of the future; as therapeutic aids; and as essential elements to many religious practices—pagan, Hebrew, and Christian.

The following stones were strongly associated with the twelve tribes and the twelve apostles.

The Twelve Tribes of Israel

Levi—garnet	*Simeon*—chryso-lite (peridot)	*Reuben*—sard (brown chalcedony)
Zebulon—diamond	*Issachar*—sapphire	*Judah*—emerald
Gad—amethyst	*Naphtali*—agate	*Dan*—topaz
Benjamin—jasper	*Joseph*—onyx	*Asher*—beryl

The Twelve Apostles

Peter—jasper
Andrew—sapphire
James—chalcedony
John—emerald
Philip—sardonyx
Bartholomew—sard
(brown chalcedony)

Matthew—chrysolite (peridot)
Thomas—beryl
James the Less—topaz
Jude—chrysoprase
Simon—hyacinth (zircon)
Judas—amethyst

The following is a list of the zodiacal gems passed on from very early history, and the powers or special characteristics attributed to each:

Aquarius
(Jan. 21–Feb. 21)
Garnet—believed to guarantee true friendship when worn by an Aquarian

Pisces
(Feb. 22–Mar. 21)
Amethyst—believed to protect a Pisces wearer from extremes of passion

Aries
(Mar. 22–Apr. 20)
Bloodstone—believed to endow an Aries wearer with wisdom

Taurus
(Apr. 21–May 21)
Sapphire—believed to protect from and cure mental disorders if worn by a Taurus

Gemini
(May 22–June 21)
Agate—long life, health, and wealth were guaranteed to a Gemini if an agate ring was worn

Cancer
(June 22–July 22)
Emerald—eternal joy was guaranteed to a Cancer-born if an emerald was taken with him on his way

Leo
(July 23–Aug. 22)
Onyx—would protect a Leo wearer from loneliness and unhappiness

Virgo
(Aug. 23–Sept. 22)
Carnelian—believed to guarantee success in anything a Virgo tried if worn on the hand of the Virgo

Libra
(Sept. 23–Oct. 23)
Chrysolite (peridot)—would free a Libra wearer from any evil spell

Scorpio (Oct. 24–Nov. 21)	**Beryl**—should be worn by every Scorpio to guarantee protection from "tears of sad repentance"
Sagittarius (Nov. 22–Dec. 21)	**Topaz**—protects the Sagittarian, but only if the Sagittarian always shows a topaz
Capricorn (Dec. 22–Jan. 21)	**Ruby**—a Capricorn who has ever worn a ruby will never know trouble

The preceding list of zodiac signs is from a Hindu legend, but there are others. An old Spanish list, probably representing an Arab tradition, ascribes the following stones to the various signs of the zodiac:

Aquarius—Amethyst	*Leo*—Topaz
Pisces—(indistinguishable)	*Virgo*—Magnet (lodestone)
Aries—Crystal (quartz)	*Libra*—Jasper
Taurus—Ruby and diamond	*Scorpio*—Garnet
Gemini—Sapphire	*Sagittarius*—Emerald
Cancer—Agate and beryl	*Capricorn*—Chalcedony

It was believed that certain planets influenced stones, and that stones could therefore transmit the powers attributed to those planets. A further extension of this belief can be seen in the practice of engraving certain planetary constellations on stones. For example, a stone engraved with the two bears, Ursa Major and Ursa Minor, would make the wearer wise, versatile, and powerful. And so it went. And from such thought came the belief in birthstones.

❖ *The Evolution of Birthstones*

The origin of the belief that a special stone was dedicated to each month, and that the stone of the month possessed a special virtue or "cure" that it could transmit to those born in that month, goes back to at least the first century. There is speculation that the twelve stones in the great breastplate of the Jewish High Priest may have had some bearing on this evolution. In the eighth and ninth centuries, the interpreters of Revelation began to ascribe to each of those stones attributes of the twelve apostles. The Hindus, on the other hand, had their own interpretation.

But whatever the reason, one fact is clear. As G. F. Kunz

points out, in *The Curious Lore of Precious Stones,* "there is no doubt that the owner of a ring or ornament set with a birthstone is impressed with the idea of possessing something more intimately associated with his or her personality than any other stone, however beautiful or costly. The idea that birthstones possess a certain indefinable, but none-the-less real significance has long been present, and still holds a spell over the minds of all who are gifted with a touch of imagination and romance."

❖ *Present-Day Birthstones*

The following is the list of birthstones adopted in 1952 by major jewelry industry associations.

Month	Birthstone	Alternate Stone
January	Garnet	
February	Amethyst	
March	Bloodstone	Aquamarine
April	Diamond	
May	Emerald	
June	Pearl	Moonstone or Alexandrite
July	Ruby	
August	Sardonyx (Carnelian)	Peridot
September	Sapphire	
October	Opal	Tourmaline
November	Topaz	Citrine
December	Turquoise	Lapis lazuli, zircon

Besides the lists of birthstones and zodiacal or talismanic stones, there are lists of stones for days of the week, hours of the day, for states of the union, for each of the seasons.

❖ *The Importance of Color and Its Mystical Symbolism in Gems*

Yellow	Worn by a man, denoted secrecy (appropriate for a silent lover); worn by a woman, it indicated generosity.
White (colorless)	Signifies friendship, integrity, and religion for men; purity, affability, and contemplation for women.

Red	On a man, indicated command, nobility, lordship, and vengeance; on a woman, pride, haughtiness, and obstinacy.
Blue	On a man, indicated wisdom and high and magnanimous thoughts; on a woman, jealousy in love, politeness, vigilance.
Green	For men, signified joyousness, transitory hope, decline of friendship; for women, unfounded ambition, childish delight, and change.
Black	For men, meant gravity, good sense, constancy, and strength; for young women, fickleness and foolishness, but for married women, constant love and perseverance.
Violet	For men, sober judgment, industry, and gravity; for women, high thoughts and spiritual love.

❖ *What Colored Stones are Available Today?*

Today, gems are worn primarily for their intrinsic beauty and are chosen primarily for aesthetic reasons. While we may own a birthstone that we wear on occasion, our choice is dictated more by personal color preferences, economics, and fashion. The world of colored gems today offers us an almost endless choice. New gems have been discovered and are being made available through the major jewelry companies. If you like red, there are rubies, garnets, red tourmalines, red spinels, and even red diamonds. If you prefer blue, there are sapphires, iolite, blue spinel, blue topaz, blue tourmaline, tanzanite, and even blue diamonds. For those who prefer green, there are emeralds, tsavorite (green garnet), green zircons, green tourmalines, green sapphires, peridots, and even green diamonds.

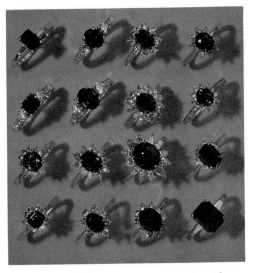

Some classic colored-gemstone engagement ring styles.
Photo: Benjamin Zucker, Precious Stones Company, New York

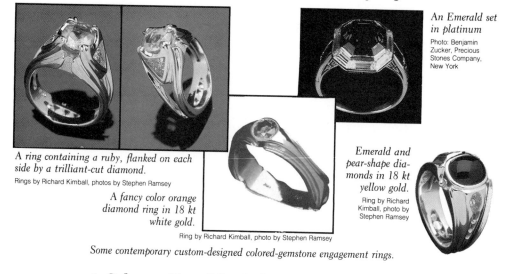

An Emerald set in platinum
Photo: Benjamin Zucker, Precious Stones Company, New York

A ring containing a ruby, flanked on each side by a trilliant-cut diamond.
Rings by Richard Kimball, photos by Stephen Ramsey

A fancy color orange diamond ring in 18 kt white gold.
Ring by Richard Kimball, photo by Stephen Ramsey

Emerald and pear-shape diamonds in 18 kt yellow gold.
Ring by Richard Kimball, photo by Stephen Ramsey

Some contemporary custom-designed colored-gemstone engagement rings.

❖ Select a Durable Colored Stone for Your Engagement Ring

In selecting a colored stone for your engagement ring, it is important to choose a stone that is durable and to avoid those which are especially fragile. After all, you want your engagement ring to last a lifetime. Some gems, such as emerald, a gem with a reputation for being fragile, might not make the best choice as an engagement ring for a very active woman if she is going to wear it every day. Unless you can afford a very fine emerald, one that is relatively free of inclusions that might make it more vulnerable to breakage, you may want to consider another more durable green gemstone such as tsavorite (green garnet, a rare and beautiful gem, more durable and more affordable than emerald). If emerald is the gem of "her dreams," and nothing else will do, be sure to choose a design that offers special protection for the stone.

❖ Guides to Popular Gems

The following charts show what stones are available in various colors and their wearability, and availability. Chapter 15 describes the stones (listed by family), and provides important information particular to each.

Now you will know what to ask the jeweler to show you—and don't forget to do a lot of shopping, looking and asking questions, until you really have developed a feel for that particular stone and the market for it.

Gem Alternatives by Color

Color Family	Popular Name of Stone	Gem Family
Red— *from red to shades of pink*	Ruby—red bluish red to orange red	Corundum
	Garnet—several red color varieties	Garnet
	Pyrope—brownish red to red	Garnet
	Almandine—violet to pure red	Garnet
	Spessartite—orange red to reddish brown to brownish red	Garnet
	Rhodolite—red to violet	Garnet
	Spinel—red to brownish red and pink	Spinel
	Pink sapphire—pinkish red	Corundum
	Zircon—brownish red to deep, dark red	Zircon
	Rubellite—red to violet red and pink	Tourmaline
	Morganite—pink to orange pink	Beryl
	Kunzite—violet pink to pink violet	Spodumene
Orange	Padparadsha sapphire—pinkish orange	Corundum
	Topaz—brownish orange and yellow orange	Topaz
	Spinel—brown to orange	Spinel
	Zircon—orange to golden brown	Zircon
	Hessonite—orange brown	Garnet
	Malaya—pink orange to brownish red	Garnet
	Tourmaline—orangy brown, yellow orange	Tourmaline
Yellow	Sapphire—yellow	Corundum
	Beryl—golden yellow	Beryl
	Chrysoberyl—yellow, yellow green, yellow brown	Chrysoberyl
	Citrine—yellow to yellow brown	Quartz

Yellow (cont'd)	*Grossularite*—yellow to yellowish green to yellowish brown	Garnet
	Zircon—yellow to yellow brown	Zircon
Green	*Emerald*—yellowish green to bluish green	Beryl
	Tsavorite—yellowish green to bluish green	Garnet
	Tourmaline—all shades of green	Tourmaline
	Peridot—yellow green to green	Peridot
	Zircon—green to yellow green to gray green	Zircon
	Alexandrite—daylight: bluish to blue green; artificial light: violet red	Chrysoberyl
	Sapphire—yellow green to blue green to gray green	Corundum
	Demantoid—yellow green to emerald green	Garnet
Blue	*Sapphire*—cornflower blue to greenish blue to inky blue	Corundum
	Tanzanite—violet blue	Zoisite
	Spinel—gray blue, greenish blue, true pastel blue	Spinel
	Aquamarine—pastel to deep blue to blue green	Beryl
	Indicolite—inky blue, greenish blue	Tourmaline
	Topaz—pastel to dark blue to blue green	Topaz
	Zircon—pastel blue	Zircon
	Water sapphire—violet blue	Iolite
Violet	*Amethyst*—lilac to violet to reddish purple to brownish purple	Quartz
	Sapphire—purple to violet	Corundum
	Rhodolite—red violet	Garnet
	Spinel—grayish violet to pure purple	Spinel
	Morganite—lavender	Beryl

CHAPTER 13

Determining Value in
Colored Gems

❖ The Importance of Color

Color is the most important determining factor affecting value in colored gems. It is also, too often, the principal determinant in erroneous identification. Unfortunately, most people don't realize how many gems look alike in color. Dealers too, can be misled or caught off-guard. Too often recognition and identification are based on color alone because so few jewelers and consumers alike are aware of the large number of similarly colored stones available today.

Today, colored stones are very much in vogue and consumers have a wider variety from which to choose than ever before. If you want an emerald-green stone but can't afford a true emerald, you might choose a green garnet (tsavorite), a green sapphire, or a green tourmaline.

Color is affected by many variables that make accurate evaluation difficult. Color is affected primarily by light—the type of light and its intensity. In addition, evaluating the color of a gem can be very subjective in terms of what is considered pleasing and desirable. Nonetheless, there have been major efforts in recent years to bring some degree of standardization to the colored-gem market. GIA now offers an instrument called the ColorMaster, which is a type of visual colorimeter (a color-grading machine). The American Gem Laboratory (AGL) also has a color-grading system called Color Scan. Both have their shortcomings at this time but are still of assistance in color grading. Nothing, however, can replace the value of a trained eye, coupled with years of experience in the colored-stone field.

As a general rule, the closer a stone comes to being the pure spectral hue of that color, the better the color. For example, if we are considering a green stone, the purer the green, the better the color. In other words, the closer it comes to being a pure spectral green, having no strong undertone of any other color such as blue or yellow, the better the color.

❖ *Key Elements in Describing Color*

The spectral colors go from pure red to pure violet, not including brown, white, black, and gray. These latter colors, in combination with the spectral colors, affect the tone of the color seen and make the classification of color so difficult. For example, if there is white present with red, you will have a lighter tone of red; if there is black, you will have a darker shade.

The following factors are commonly used to describe color:

- Hue—the precise spectral color
- Intensity—the brightness or vividness (dullness or drabness) of the color
- Tone—the depth of color (light or dark)
- Distribution—the even (or uneven) distribution of the color

Both intensity and tone of color can be significantly affected by the proportioning of the cut. In other words, a good lapidary (gem cutter) working with a fine stone will be able to bring out its inherent beauty to the fullest, making it very desirable. A poor cutter may take the same rough material and create a stone that is not really desirable, because a poor cut will significantly reduce the vividness and alter the depth of color, usually producing a stone that is much too dark to be attractive.

In general, stones that are either very pale or very dark sell for less per carat. There seems to be a common belief that the darker the stone, the better. This is true only to a point. A rich, deep color is desirable, but not a depth of color that approaches black. Consumers must shop around and continue to train their eye to differentiate between a stone with a nice depth of color and a stone that is too dark.

As a general rule, it is even more important to shop around when considering colored stones than it is when buying diamonds. One must develop an eye for all the variables of color—

hue, intensity, tone, and distribution. Some stones simply exhibit a more intense, vivid color than other stones (all else being equal), but only by extensive visual comparison can you develop your own eye.

Let's discuss the ruby, for example. The finest red rubies are Burmese. While they are not a pure red, these are the closest to pure red. The tone may vary, however, from very light to very dark. As with most stones, the very light stones and the very dark stones sell for less per carat. Burmese rubies are the most highly prized, and the most expensive, because of the desirability of their color and their scarcity.

Thai rubies can vary tremendously in hue and tone, going from a light to dark red with differing degrees of a blue undertone, giving them a purplish cast and making them look like the much cheaper reddish-purple gemstone, the garnet. While some shades of Thai ruby are very expensive, most of these stones are much less expensive than the Burmese.

African rubies have a tint or undertone of brown or orange, which makes them also much cheaper than the Burmese reds, but more valuable than the Thai ruby, depending on the color of the Thai ruby.

Ceylon (Sri Lanka) rubies are also encountered with relative frequency. However, these are usually classified as pink sapphires since the tone is consistently pale. (Sapphire and ruby are the same stone, physically and chemically. The red variety is called ruby, while the equally popular blue—and other colors—are called sapphire.)

Next, let's look at emeralds. Some of the finest emeralds today come from Colombia. The Colombian emerald is the color of fresh, young green grass—a pure spectral green with a faint tint of either yellow or blue. The "drop of oil" emerald from Colombia is considered absolutely the finest, and is a deep green (do not confuse with dark green, which has black in it) with a very slight blue undertone. This is the most valuable color and is unique to Colombian varieties.

The African emerald is also a nice shade of green, but it has a blue undertone with a slight darkening effect (probably due to traces of iron), which makes the stone less valuable than the Colombian. However, it usually has fewer flaws than the Colombian, and cuts a more vivid stone. Therefore, some of the African stones, depending on depth of color, compare very favorably to the Colombian aesthetically, while costing less per carat.

❖ The Importance of Environment

The color of a stone can be drastically affected by the kind of light and the environment (color of wallpaper, color of shirt, fluorescent light, etc.) in which the examination takes place. If examined under a fluorescent light, for example, a ruby may not show its fullest red, because most fluorescent lights are weak in red rays, which will cause the red in the ruby to be diminished and to appear more purple red in body color. The same ruby examined in daylight or under incandescent light (ordinary electric light bulb), which is not weak in red rays, will appear a truer, fuller red. The same ruby would look even redder if examined against a piece of yellow-orange paper. Loose rubies are often shown in little envelopes, called "parcel papers," that have a yellow-orange inner paper liner to enhance the red color to the fullest.

Another example of color being affected by the type of light in which it is observed can be seen in the gem Alexandrite. Alexandrite can be a bluish-green gem in daylight or under daylight-type fluorescent light, and a deep red or purple-red under incandescent light.

The most important thing to keep in mind before buying a colored gem is: *Look at the particular gem you are considering in more than one type of light!* Examine it outside in sunlight; look at it under a normal house-lamp (lamp or light with normal lightbulbs); view it in shade or under the long fluorescent tubes that light most office buildings today. Most stores will have both fluorescent lighting and incandescent "spot" lights. Windows can provide daylight light. Perhaps a "broom closet" is available to give you the effect of lamplight at home in the evening. Also, be sure to examine colored gems in the type of lighting environment you will most often be wearing them.

A Word About Color Distribution or Zoning

Even though zoning doesn't really describe color, it is very important in evaluating color. In some stones, color isn't always evenly distributed but may exist in zones—adding color to colorless areas surrounding the zone. This is frequently observed in amethyst, ruby, and sapphire. These zones may be noticed by looking through the side of the stone, moving it slowly, while tilting it and rotating it.

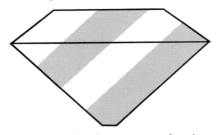

A stone showing *zones* of color.

Sometimes a stone in the rough is colorless, or nearly so, but has a spot or layer of color. If the cutter cuts the stone so that the culet is in the color spot, the whole stone will appear that color. If there is a layer and the cutter cuts the stone so that the layer lies in a plane nearly parallel to the table, the whole stone will look completely colored. Evenness of color and complete saturation of color are very important in determining the value of colored gems.

❖ *Clarity*

As with diamonds, clarity refers to the absence of internal flaws or inclusions. Flawlessness in colored stones is even rarer than in diamonds. However, while clarity is important, and the cleaner the stone the better, flawlessness in colored stones does not usually carry the premium that it does with diamonds. Light, pastel-colored stones will require better clarity because the flaws are more easily visible; in darker-toned stones the flaws may not be as important a variable because they are masked by the depth of color.

The type and placement of flaws are more important considerations in colored stones than the presence of flaws in and of themselves. For example, a large crack (called a feather) that is close to the surface of a stone can be dangerous because it weakens the stone's durability and breaks the light continuity. Also, it may show an iridescent effect that could detract from its beauty. (Iridescence usually means that a fracture or feather breaks through the surface somewhere on the stone.) Such a flaw would certainly reduce the stone's value. But if the fracture is small and positioned in an unobtrusive part of the stone, it will have a minimal effect on its durability, beauty, and value. Some flaws actually help a gemologist or jeweler to identify a stone. There are also certain types of flaws that are characteristic of specific gems and specific localities and, again, may detract only minimally from the value. In some cases the presence of a particular flaw may provide positive identification of the exact variety or origin and actually cause an increase in the per-carat value. We should note, however, that a very fine colored gem that really is flawless will probably bring a disproportionately higher price per carat because it is so rare.

Types of Flaws Found in Colored Gems

There are numerous types of flaws found in colored gems. Since certain ones are found in some gems but not in others, they provide the gemologist with an important means of positive identification in many cases. For anyone interested in learning more about flaws in colored gems, *Gem Identification Made Easy* (GemStone Press, South Woodstock, Vt., 1989) provides over 70 color photographs of flaws seen under magnification and explanations on how to use basic pocket-size instruments to detect these flaws and identify gemstones (see Appendix: Selected Readings). Types of flaws a gemologist will look for include the following:

Needle- or fiber-like inclusions. Some of these inclusions can be found in garnet, sapphire, ruby, aquamarine, and amethyst.

Two-phase inclusions. This is an inclusion that has a "frank-furter" outline with an enclosed bubble—which may or may not move as the "frank" is tilted from end to end. These can be observed in topaz, quartz, synthetic emeralds, and sometimes tourmalines.

Three-phase inclusions. These look like irregularly shaped pea pods, usually pointed at both ends, containing a bubble and a cube shape or rhomboid solid adjacent to the bubble. The three-phase inclusion may be liquid (pea pod), solid (cube or rhomboid), or gas (bubble). These are found in genuine Colombian emeralds, verifying the emeralds' origin and genuineness.

Twinning planes. These are found in rubies and sapphires and occasionally in some of the feldspar gems (such as moonstone).

They have the appearance of parallel cracks that resemble panes of glass lying in parallel planes. In rubies and sapphires these can often be found to crisscross at 60° and 120° to each other. These types of inclusions can prove the genuineness of a ruby or sapphire, but if too numerous they may both weaken the stone and diminish its brilliance.

Liquid-filled or healing feather. This type of inclusion is found in the corundum family, although it is more frequently observed in sapphires than in rubies. It is often shaped like a maze.

Veils. These are small bubble-like inclusions arranged in a layer-like formation that can be flat or curvaceous, broad or narrow, long or short. They may be easily observed in some synthetic emeralds.

Fingerprint. These are small crystal inclusions arranged in curved rows in such a way as to resemble a fingerprint or maze design. They can be seen in quartz and topaz. They closely resemble the liquid-filled healing feathers seen in rubies and sapphires.

Dark ball-like inclusions. These are found exclusively in Thai rubies. They are dark, opaque balls surrounded by an irregularly shaped, wispy, brown cloud-like formation. These are never seen in Burmese stones (which often contain needle-like inclusions not found in Thai stones).

Cleavage fault. This is a type of break in the stone rather than an actual inclusion. It is observed in topaz, diamond, feldspar, kunzite, hiddenite. It is a plane-type crack and can weaken the stone if it is exposed to extreme temperature change (thermoshock) or struck a severe blow, which could break the stone apart.

Bubbles. Nice round bubbles usually indicate a synthetic or glass, though they can be found in amber. In synthetic corundum (ruby, sapphire) they can be round, pear-shaped, or tadpole-shaped. In the latter two, the points of the pear and the tail of the tadpole always point in the same direction.

Curved striae. These are concentric curved lines seen in synthetic sapphire and synthetic ruby, made by older processes, but are difficult to observe in light-colored stones, such as pale synthetic pink or yellow sapphire.

Swirl marks. These are found in glass. They appear in serpentine or curved shapes and curlicues, and usually appear as a darker shade of color.

Halo or disk-like inclusions. Many of the Ceylon sapphires contain flat, disk-like inclusions, sometimes referred to as halos. Very often they will contain a small black mark at the center, and sometimes a crystal can be seen, rather than a black mark. These are small zircon crystals that cause the formation of the halos.

If the flaws weaken the stone's durability, affect color, are easily noticeable, or are too numerous, they will significantly reduce price and value. Otherwise, they may not affect price to any great extent at all. And in some cases, if they provide positive identification and proof of origin, they may actually have a positive effect on price, increasing the cost rather than reducing it (as with Burmese rubies and Colombian emeralds). And because flawless colored stones are rare, they may bring a disproportionately higher price per carat.

Again, as a consumer it is important to shop around and become familiar with the stone you wish to purchase and to train your eye to discern what is acceptable or objectionable.

❖ *The Importance of Cut*

The cutting and proportioning in colored stones are important for two main reasons:

1. They affect the depth of color seen in the stone.
2. They influence the liveliness projected by the stone.

While color is the most important criteria in determining value in colored stones, if a colored stone is of good quality material to begin with, a good cut will enhance its natural beauty to the fullest and allow it to exhibit its finest color and liveliness. If we take the same material and cut it poorly, its natural beauty will be lessened, causing it to look too dark, or too light, or even "dead."

Therefore, when we examine a colored stone that looks lively to our eye and has good color—not too dark and not too pale—we can assume that the cut is reasonably good. If the stone's color is poor, or if it lacks liveliness, we must immediately examine it for proper cut. If it has been cut properly, we can assume the basic material was poor. However, if the cut is poor, the material may be very good and can perhaps be recut into a beautiful gem. In this case we may want to confer with a knowledgeable cutter to see if it is worthwhile to recut, considering cutting costs and loss in weight. If you don't know any cutters, a reputable jeweler, gemologist-appraiser, or local lapidary club may be able to recommend one.

❖ *Cutting and Proportion in Colored Stones— A Few Considerations*

Is the shade pleasing, and does the stone have life and brilliance? If the answer is yes to both considerations, then the basic material is probably good, and you must make a decision based on your own personal preferences and budget.

Is the color too light or too dark? If so, and if the cut looks good, the basic uncut material was probably too light or too dark. Consider purchasing it if personally pleasing, but only if the price is right (significantly lower than stones of better color).

Is its brilliance even, or are there dead spots or flat areas? If the brilliance is not uniform, or the stone looks dead or flat, do not purchase it. The cut may look good, but probably is not right for the particular stone. For example, tourmaline in a normal emerald cut may look flat, while special faceting on the back facets can add tremendous brilliance. But the average consumer can't really determine to what extent the cut is responsible for the flatness and whether it's due to poor quality, rough material.

Is the stone cut so shallow that its wearability is reduced? If the stone is cut too shallow it may not be feasible to wear it in a ring, although it may be worn with reasonable safety in a pendant, or as earrings, since these types of jewelry are less exposed to blows or knocks and subsequent damage.

Will this stone be worn frequently and be prone to collecting dirt or grease? In shallowly cut pastel or light-colored stones, such as aquamarine, zircon, amethyst, and topaz, the apparent body color and brilliance are diminished considerably if grease or dirt collects on the back side. This is often the case with a ring worn daily and subjected to cooking, dishwashing, cosmetic application, bath oils, etc. These stones should be frequently cleaned.

❖ *Weight*

As with diamonds, weight in colored gems is measured in carats. Before 1913 the carat weight varied depending upon the country of origin—the Indian carat didn't weigh the same as the English carat; the French carat was different from the Indian or English. This is important if you have or are thinking of buying a very old piece that still has the original bill of sale indicating carat weight—the old carat weighed more than the new (since 1913) metric carat, which is 200 milligrams (⅕ gram). Therefore, an old "3-carat" stone will weigh more than 3 carats by the new standards. The use of metric is often deleted today, and we simply refer to the carat, meaning the 200-milligram carat.

All gems are weighed in carats, except pearls and coral. (Pearls and coral are sold by the grain, momme, and millimeter. A grain is ¼ carat; a momme is 18.75 carats.)

Normally, the greater the weight, the greater the value per carat, unless we reach unusually large sizes—in excess of 50 carats—after which size may become prohibitive for use in a ring and price per carat may drop because such large sizes are more difficult to sell (unless it is a rare stone in that size).

Also, remember again not to confuse *weight* with *size*. Some stones weigh more than others; the density (specific gravity) of the basic material is heavier. A 1-carat ruby will have a different size than a 1-carat emerald or a 1-carat diamond.

Some stones are readily available in large sizes (over 10 carats), such as tourmaline. For other stones, gem material in sizes over 5 carats may be very rare and considered large, and will command a proportionately higher price (precious topaz, emerald, alexandrite, demantoid and tsavorite garnets, ruby, and red beryl). With these stones a 10-carat stone can command any price—a king's ransom. A 30-carat blue diamond was sold in 1982 for $9 million.

Scarcity of certain sizes among the different colored stones affects the definition of "large" in the colored-gem market. A fine 5-carat alexandrite or ruby is a very large stone; an 18-carat tourmaline is a nice size stone.

As with diamonds, stones under 1 carat sell for less per carat than stones of 1 carat or more. But here it becomes more complicated. The definition of "large" or "rare" sizes differs tremendously, as does price, depending on the stone. For example, an 8-carat tourmaline is an average-size stone, fairly common, and will be priced accordingly. A 5-carat tsavorite is extremely rare, and will command a price proportionately much greater than a 1-carat stone. Precious topaz used to be readily available in 20-carat sizes and larger, but today even 10-carat stones of very fine color are practically nonexistent and their price has jumped tremendously.

❖ Colored Gemstone Certificates

Systems for grading colored gemstones are relatively new and standards are not yet established worldwide. As a result, certificates or grading reports for colored gemstones are not yet used extensively and have a more limited value than those for diamonds. Diamond grading reports are widely relied upon to describe and confirm the factors that affect diamond quality, using standards that are very precise and accepted internationally. Very few colored stones are accompanied by such reports. However, with today's new-type synthetics and look-alikes, they can be useful to verify identity (type of gem) and genuineness. For colored gems of unusual size and exceptional quality, we strongly recommend obtaining a "report" from a recognized laboratory (see Appendix).

The most widely recognized reports for colored gemstones include those issued in the United States by American Gemological Laboratories, Inc. (AGL), and GIA Gem Trade Laboratory, and, in Switzerland, by Laboratory Gubelin and Schweizerische Stiftung fur Edelstein-Forschung (SSEF).

At the least, colored gemstone reports should *identify* the gemstone and verify whether it is *natural* or *synthetic*. One can also request a *grading* report which, in addition to identity and genuineness, will also describe the color, clarity, brilliance and other important factors that affect quality and value. This information is always useful for insurance purposes and can also be helpful if you are comparing several stones.

Where there is sufficient gemological information available after close examination of the stone, some reports will also disclose whether or not the stone's color is *natural* or *enhanced* and, if enhanced, by what method. (Reports issued by Laboratory Gubelin, one of the most respected laboratories in the world, as a matter of policy will not disclose treatments. They believe that since most gemstones have been routinely treated in some manner

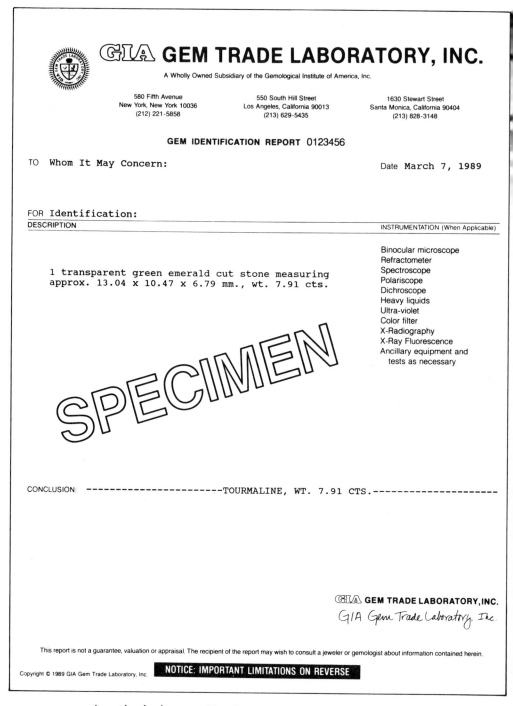

GIA GEM TRADE LABORATORY, INC.

A Wholly Owned Subsidiary of the Gemological Institute of America, Inc.

580 Fifth Avenue	550 South Hill Street	1630 Stewart Street
New York, New York 10036	Los Angeles, California 90013	Santa Monica, California 90404
(212) 221-5858	(213) 629-5435	(213) 828-3148

GEM IDENTIFICATION REPORT 0123456

TO   Whom It May Concern:

Date **March 7, 1989**

FOR Identification:

DESCRIPTION	INSTRUMENTATION (When Applicable)
1 transparent green emerald cut stone measuring approx. 13.04 x 10.47 x 6.79 mm., wt. 7.91 cts.	Binocular microscope Refractometer Spectroscope Polariscope Dichroscope Heavy liquids Ultra-violet Color filter X-Radiography X-Ray Fluorescence Ancillary equipment and tests as necessary

SPECIMEN

CONCLUSION: ----------------------TOURMALINE, WT. 7.91 CTS.----------------------

GIA GEM TRADE LABORATORY, INC.

GIA Gem Trade Laboratory, Inc.

This report is not a guarantee, valuation or appraisal. The recipient of the report may wish to consult a jeweler or gemologist about information contained herein.

Copyright © 1989 GIA Gem Trade Laboratory, Inc.

NOTICE: IMPORTANT LIMITATIONS ON REVERSE

A sample colored gemstone **Identification Report** *from GIA.*

American Gemological Laboratories

Colored Stone Certificate

Olympic Tower
645 Fifth Avenue
New York, N.Y. 10022
(212) 935-0060
(212) 935-0071

CERTIFICATE NO: CS SAMPLE

DATE: 15 May 1989.

IDENTIFICATION: Natural Sapphire, Kashmir*

CLARITY GRADE: MI.*

SHAPE AND CUT: Cushion Antique Mixed Cut

CARAT WEIGHT: 2.24 Cts.

MEASUREMENTS: 8.61 x 6.08 x 4.65 mm.

PROPORTIONS: Good (4)

Depth %: 76.5%

Brilliancy %: Range: 50-90%

Average: 80%

Finish: Very Good - Good (3-4)

COLOR GRADE: 4/85*

Color Rating/Tone: 4/80-85

Light Source: Vita lite

Color Scan

B 70 V 15 G/Gy 15

COMMENTS: *Total quality integration rating: Excellent. **Based on available gemological information, the origin of this material would be classified as Kashmir. *No significant gemological evidence of heat induced appearance modification present. **Faint to moderate color zoning², texture, and moderate dichroic effect present.

NOTE: All color determinations are subject to the color temperature of the light source and the color sensitivity of the observer. The quality and commercial desirability of any color is determined by examining the interrelationships of all factors indicated under Color Grade. Conclusions may vary due to the subjective nature of colored stone analysis.

Tone (AGL) (0 = Colorless, 100 = Black)

0	5	10	15	20	25	30	35	40	45	50	55	60	65	70	75	80	85	90	95	100
	V Light		Light			Light-Med		Medium				Medium-Dark			Dark-V Dark		

Proportions/Finish (AGL)

	1	2	3	4	5	6	7	8	9	10
	Excellent		Very Good		Good		Fair		Poor	

Color Rating (AGL)

1	2	3	4	5	6	7	8	9	10
Excellent		Very Good		Good		Fair		Poor	

Clarity Scale (AGL)

F1	L1	L2	MI1	MI2	HI1	HI2
Free of Incl.	Lightly Included		Moderately Included		Highly Included	

Proportions/Cutting

Girdle Diameter = 100%

Table %

Depth %

Crown

Pavilion

Depth

Girdle Thickness

Cutlet

A sample Colored Gemstone Certificate *from AGL. Notice it provides information pertaining to the* quality *and* origin *of the gemstone as well as its identity.*

for centuries, it is unimportant and that comparative quality, beauty and rarity are the important considerations.) Also, depending upon the information available after examination, some laboratories will indicate the country of origin, if requested. Laboratory Gubelin and AGL will indicate country of origin when possible; GIA will not indicate country of origin.

When considering a colored gemstone that is accompanied by a report, keep in mind the different types of reports available. What does the report really tell you? Is it confirming identity and genuineness only? If so, remember that quality differences can dramatically affect cost. A genuine 1-carat ruby, sapphire or emerald can sell for $10 or $10,000, depending upon quality differences. *Being genuine doesn't mean a stone is valuable.* Only by looking at many stones, asking the right questions, and making comparisons can you develop an understanding of the differences that affect quality, beauty, and value.

CHAPTER 14

Fraud and Misrepresentation in Colored Gems

As stated previously, the occurrence of misrepresentation and fraud in jewelry transactions is low. Most jewelers are reputable professionals in whom you can place your trust. However, in the colored-gem market more misrepresentation occurs than in the diamond market, primarily because of the scientifically more complex nature of colored stones. So it is even more important for you to be aware of the deceptive practices one might encounter when buying a colored gem, both to protect yourself from the more obvious scams, and to better understand the importance of dealing with a reliable jeweler.

Take care to be sure that your gemstone is what it is represented to be. When buying an expensive colored gem, we cannot overemphasize the importance of seeking verification from a qualified gemologist—preferably one with extensive experience in the colored gem market.

❖ Misrepresenting Synthetic as Natural

Today there is much misrepresentation of the synthetic as natural. Synthetic gems have been manufactured for many years. Good synthetic sapphires, rubies, and spinels have been made since the early 1900s. Very good synthetic emeralds began to be produced commercially in the 1940s. These synthetics, while they looked like the real thing to the average consumer and were very attractive because of their affordable price, could be readily distinguished from the real thing by a competent jeweler.

Today, this may not be the case, particularly with ruby and

emerald. While the older techniques for producing these synthetics are still used, new sophisticated methods have enabled the production of synthetic rubies and emeralds that are not readily discernible, because they do not possess the familiar characteristics common to the older type synthetics with which the dealer and jeweler are so familiar. Many have been represented and sold as genuine. A highly qualified gemologist can, however, differentiate between these new, fine synthetics and natural stones. The following incident dramatically illustrates the situation today.

We knew a jeweler with an excellent reputation for being honest, reliable, and expert in his field. He has been in the business for many years and has extensive gemological training. Nonetheless, he recently sold a new-type synthetic ruby as a natural ruby for just under $10,000.

His customer, who had purchased the stone at a reasonable price, proceeded to resell it to a third party for a quick profit. The third party took it to a very competent gemologist whom he knew to be up to date on the scientific procedures necessary to differentiate even the new synthetics from natural rubies. And the truth was learned!

The second and third parties in this case lost nothing (one of the benefits of buying from a reputable jeweler). However, the jeweler suffered both a heavy financial loss and heavy damage to his reputation.

You may ask how he made such a mistake. It was easy. He was knowledgeable, like many other jewelers, and thought he knew how to distinguish a natural from a synthetic. But he had not kept current on the new technological advances and the new synthetics entering the marketplace. So he made the purchase of this lovely stone over the counter from a private party who had procured it in the Orient. These new synthetic rubies are produced in the United States and then "find their way" to the Orient—the source of the naturals where they are more easily sold as the real thing. And he had no recourse at all, because he had no way of locating the seller, who had simply walked in off the street.

As this story illustrates, today it is essential for the consumer to have a highly qualified gemologist verify authenticity—particularly with fine rubies, emeralds, and sapphires. Thousands of dollars may be at stake, for too many jewelers innocently represent these new synthetics as genuine because they themselves bought them as genuine. Don't delude yourself into believing that if a piece is purchased from a well-respected firm it must therefore be what it's claimed to be. It may be inconvenient, and it may require an additional charge, but we believe it is better to be safe now than sorry later.

With today's sophisticated equipment, and a greater knowledge of crystals, it is possible for man to create almost any gemstone. For example, synthetic alexandrite has been successfully produced since 1973, and is another example of a gem that is difficult to distinguish from its natural counterpart. These gemstones, though not as expensive as the genuine, are also not inexpensive themselves.

As a general rule, remember that almost any expensive gem—opals, alexandrite, ruby, emerald, sapphire, and even turquoise—could be a synthetic, that many synthetics are themselves expensive, and that most have become more difficult to distinguish from their natural counterparts, so there is innocent "confusion" and subsequent errors in how they are represented by the jeweler. Take special care with fine colored gems to make sure the gem you're considering is as represented. If you are interested in learning more about how to separate genuine diamonds and colored gems from imitations and "look-alikes," *Gem Identification Made Easy* (GemStone Press, South Woodstock, Vt., 1989) explains what to look for gemstone by gemstone and provides simple, step-by-step instructions on the proper use of instruments to accomplish this task.

❖ Simulated Stones

These should not be confused with synthetics. A simulated stone is usually a very inexpensive man-made stone. It is usually glass, but can also be plastic. These stones simulate the stone's color only and are very easily differentiated from the genuine. There are glass simulations of all the colored stones, and glass and plastic simulated pearls, turquoise, and amber are among the most common.

❖ Look-Alike Substitution

This practice involves misrepresenting a more common, less expensive stone for another rarer, more expensive gem of similar color. Today, with so many gems available in every color, both deliberate and accidental misrepresentation can occur.

❖ *Color Alteration*

Heating and Radiation Treatments

Heat treatment and radiation are commonly used to change or enhance the color of certain gems. Subjecting certain stones to sophisticated heating procedures is a practice that is hundreds of years old and is accepted within the jewelry industry as long as the change is permanent. Most sapphires and rubies are heated. The treatment may lighten, darken, or completely change the color. A skilled gemologist or gem testing lab can often determine whether or not a gem's color has been altered by heating; in some cases it is not possible to know for sure with current technology. In a few cases it is possible to ascertain that the color is natural. If the color is very fine, and known to be natural, the cost can be much higher than the norm.

Radiation techniques are now in common use. Sometimes radiation is used in combination with heating. It seems to have a permanent effect on some stones, but not on others. There is still some question regarding radiation levels and the long-term effects on health.

Heating procedures are commonly used on the following stones:

Zircon—to produce blue or colorless stones

Amethyst—to produce "yellow" stones sold as citrine and topaz; and "green" sold as praseolite

Topaz—to produce shades of blue or pink

Sapphire—to lighten the blue color; to darken a light color; or to change lavender shades to pink

Aquamarine—to deepen the blue color

Tanzanite—to produce a more desirable shade of blue

Tourmaline—to lighten the darker shades (usually of the green variety)

Morganite—to change the color from orange to pinkish lavender

The color obtained by these heating processes is usually permanent.

Radiation techniques are commonly used on the following stones:

> Aquamarine—to deepen its color (often in conjunction with heat)
> Diamond—to change the color from an off-white to a fancy color—green, yellow, etc.
> Sapphire—to produce the beautiful golden-colored sapphire seen today
> Topaz—to change from colorless or nearly colorless to blue

As far as we know now, the color changes resulting from radiation treatment for the stones listed above are usually permanent. There is one exception. Some "yellow" sapphires that have obtained their color from radiation treatment will lose it if heated by the flame of a common cigarette lighter. If you are considering a "yellow," it may be worthwhile to try this simple flame test. Also, "blue" sapphires which have obtained their color by radiation techniques *will quickly lose* their color (in a matter of weeks). Irradiated "blue sapphire" is not accepted by the jewelry trade.

The color of fancy colored diamonds can usually be verified as being natural or radiated. However, with most other radiated stones, identification procedures for determining whether color is natural have not been developed as of this date.

Dyeing

Dyeing has been practiced since earliest times, particularly with the less expensive gemstone callled chalcedony (a variety of quartz). The gems frequently dyed are jade, opal, coral, lapis, and to a lesser degree poor-quality star rubies, star sapphires, and emeralds.

Oiling

This technique is commonly used on emeralds. The emerald is soaked in oil (which may or may not be tinted green). Its purpose is to fill fine cracks, which are fairly common in emerald. These cracks look whitish and therefore weaken the green body color of the emerald. The oil fills the cracks, making them "disappear," and thereby improves the color by eliminating the white.

This is an accepted procedure and will normally last for many years. However, if the stone is put in a hot ultrasonic cleaner (which is dangerous to any emerald and never recommended), or soaked in an organic solvent such as gasoline, xylene, or substances containing these, such as paint remover, the oil may be slowly dissolved out of the cracks and the whitish blemishes will then reappear and the stone's color will be weakened. If this should happen, the stone can be re-oiled.

Foil-backed Stones

This technique is not frequently encountered, but should be mentioned. It is used on stones set in fully or partly "closed-back" mountings. This technique involves lining the inside of the setting with a colored foil that projects its color into the stone, deepening the stone's color. Always be apprehensive when considering a piece of jewelry that has a closed back. This technique has been observed in both antique and modern jewelry.

We recently examined a heavy, yellow-gold ring set with five fine, flawless emeralds of a gem-green body color. The stones were set into the gold and therefore their backs were not observable. Suspicion arose since the emeralds were all flawless and the color was so uniformly fine. Upon examination, we discovered that the green body color was projected into the stones by a fine emerald-green foil back. The stones were probably not even emerald, but almost-colorless aquamarine. Since both aquamarine and emerald belong to the same mineral family (beryl), an inexperienced jeweler or gemologist using normal, basic procedures to identify the stones could have erroneously labeled them as fine emeralds.

❖ *Composite Stones—Doublets and Triplets*

Composite stones are exactly what the term implies—a stone *composed* of more than one part. There are two types of composite stones we will mention: doublets and triplets.

Doublets are composite stones consisting of two parts, sometimes held together by a colored cement.

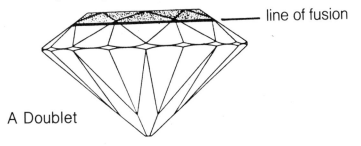

line of fusion

A Doublet

Triplets are composite stones consisting of three parts, usually glued together to a colored middle part.

Doublets

Doublets are especially important to know about since they were so widely used in antique jewelry before the production of synthetics. However, they are also reappearing in modern jewelry.

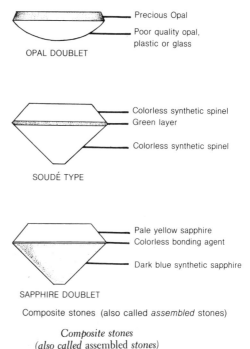

OPAL DOUBLET — Precious Opal / Poor quality opal, plastic or glass

SOUDÉ TYPE — Colorless synthetic spinel / Green layer / Colorless synthetic spinel

SAPPHIRE DOUBLET — Pale yellow sapphire / Colorless bonding agent / Dark blue synthetic sapphire

Composite stones (also called *assembled* stones)

Composite stones
(also called assembled *stones)*

The most commonly encountered doublet, often referred to as a false doublet, consisted of a red garnet top fused to an appropriately colored glass bottom. With the right combination, any gem could be simulated by this method. For example, blue sapphire was created by fashioning a doublet that consisted of a red garnet top and a blue glass bottom. An emerald could be created by fusing the red garnet top to a green glass bottom. And so it went.

Garnets were used for the top halves of these false doublets because they possessed nice luster and excellent durability and were readily available in great quantity, which made them very inexpensive.

There are also doublets made from two parts of a gem, usually a colorless stone cemented together in the middle with an appropriately colored glue. For example, a colorless synthetic spinel top and bottom can be held together in the middle (at the girdle) by red, green, or blue glue to simulate ruby, emerald, or sapphire.

There are also blue sapphire doublets (called true doublets) in circulation that are composed of two parts of genuine sapphire— but genuine pale *yellow* sapphire. The top and bottom are pale yellow sapphire cemented with blue glue, resulting in a very fine "blue sapphire." These are especially convincing.

Another type of sapphire doublet is composed of a genuine pale yellow sapphire top fused to a synthetic blue sapphire bottom.

This might fool many a gemologist because four tests would provide positive ID as a genuine sapphire.

The same techniques are used to make ruby doublets, although the ruby doublets don't look as convincing. And the same basic techniques can also be used for emerald doublets (with beryl instead of sapphire). There are also opal doublets. These usually consist of a thin top layer of genuine opal cemented to a base that can be either a poorer grade of opal or some other substance altogether.

The most commonly encountered opal doublets are those made to look like the precious black opal. This doublet is usually composed of a translucent or transparent top that is cemented by black cement to a bottom portion of cheaper opal or other material that acts as a support. Please note that the top of these "black opal" doublets is usually never genuine black opal, though they certainly look like it.

Opal doublets are also made by cementing a thin piece of fine opal to a larger one of less fine opal to create a larger overall appearance. The doublets can be identified by observing the join of the two pieces at the girdle and noting the dark line of the cement between the two pieces.

Triplets

Triplets are frequently encountered in the opal market and have substantially replaced the doublet. A triplet is exactly like the opal doublet except that it has a cabochon-shaped colorless quartz cap (the third part) that covers the entire doublet, giving the delicate doublet greater protection from breakage and providing greater luminescence (brightness) to the stone.

With careful examination, a competent jeweler or gemologist should be able to easily differentiate a doublet or triplet from a natural. We should note, however, that detection of an opal doublet may be very difficult if it is set in a mounting with a rim (bezel set) covering the seam where the two pieces are cemented together. It might be necessary to remove the stone from its setting for positive identification. (Removal must be performed only by a very competent manufacturing jeweler, due to opal's fragile nature—and he may do it only at your own risk, not wanting to assume responsibility for any breakage.) In the case of a black opal with a value of several thousand dollars, it is well worth the additional cost and inconvenience to be sure it is not a doublet worth only a few hundred dollars. Always be apprehensive of a flat-topped opal that is bezel-set.

❖ *Misleading Names*

Many colored stones are called by names that lead one to believe they are something they are not. This practice is frequently encountered, especially outside the United States. When any stone is described with a qualifier, as in "Rio Topaz" or "Ceylon Sapphire," be sure to ask whether the stone is a genuine, natural stone, and whether or not the color is natural. Ask why there is a qualifier.

Let's examine these two examples. In the case of Rio topaz, the stone is not a topaz at all, but a heat-treated amethyst, and the name, therefore, is clearly misleading. However, in the case of the Ceylon sapphire, "Ceylon" refers to the location (Ceylon, now Sri Lanka) from which that gem was mined, and Ceylons usually have a particular tone of blue and are very lively. Furthermore, because of their particular color, Ceylon sapphires sell for more per carat than certain other varieties, such as Australian or Thai. Therefore, in this case, "Ceylon" is very important to the stone's complete description.

Let's look at one more example, the Ceylon-colored sapphire. In this case, the qualifier is the word "colored." In most cases the presence of this word implies some type of color alteration or treatment. A Ceylon-colored sapphire is not a Ceylon sapphire but a sapphire that has been treated to obtain the Ceylon color.

There is nothing actually wrong with selling "Rio topaz" or "Ceylon-colored sapphire," or other similarly named stones, as long as they are properly represented and priced. Then the decision becomes yours—either you like it or you don't; it meets your emotional need for a topaz or Ceylon sapphire or it doesn't; and the price is right or it isn't. The following lists provide some examples of names to be aware of—"descriptive" names that are important to the stone's complete description; and "misleading" names, misnomers, which are meant to do exactly that, mislead.

Misleading Names

Descriptive Names	Misnomers (and What They Really Are)

DIAMOND

Canary diamond (refers to fancy yellow color)	*Alaska black diamond* (hematite)
	Alaska diamond (hematite)
Fancy Diamond (refers to colored diamond)	*Arkansas diamond* (quartz)
	Bohemian diamond (quartz)
	Brazilian diamond (quartz) (Diamond is also found in Brazil but is not referred to as "Brazilian diamond," but simply as "diamond.")
	Bristol diamond (quartz)
	Buxton diamond (quartz)
	Cape May diamond (quartz)
	Ceylon diamond (zircon)
	Hawaiian diamond (quartz)
	Herkimer diamond (quartz)
	Kenya diamond (rutile)
	Matura diamond (zircon)
	Mogok diamond (topaz)
	Pennsylvania diamond (pyrite)
	Radium diamond (smoky quartz)
	Rainbow diamond (rutile)
	Rangoon diamond (zircon)
	Rhine diamond (quartz; original rhinestone)

EMERALD

Colombian emerald (refers to the finest variety of emerald, mined in Colombia)	*African emerald* (green fluorite)
	Brazilian emerald (tourmaline) (Genuine emerald is also found in Brazil; slightly different from Colombian emeralds
Brazilian emerald (refers to emeralds mined in Brazil)	
Zambian emerald (emerald mined in Zambia)	
	Chatham emerald (synthetic)
	Esmeralda emerald (green tourmaline)

EMERALD
(continued)

Evening emerald (peridot)
Gilson emerald (synthetic)
Lechleitner emerald (partially synthetic)
Lithia emerald (green spodumene—hiddenite)
Mascot emerald (doublet)
Oriental emerald (green sapphire)
Soudé emerald (doublet)
Zerfass emerald (synthetic)

JADE

Ax stone (nephrite jade)
California jade (both jadeite and nephrite jade)
Greenstone (nephrite jade, New Zealand)
Imperial jade (fine, gem-quality jadeite jade)
Jade (both nephrite jade and jadeite jade)
Kidney stone (nephrite jade)
Maori (nephrite jade from New Zealand)
Spinach jade (nephrite jade)

African jade (green massive garnet)
Amazon jade (microcline feldspar; amazonite)
Australian jade (chrysoprase quartz)
California jade (a variety of idocrase)
Colorado jade (amazonite feldspar)
Fukien jade (soapstone)
Honan jade (soapstone)
Indian jade (aventurine quartz)
Jadine jade (Australian chrysoprase)
Korea jade (serpentine [bowenite])
Manchurian jade (soapstone)
Mexican jade (dyed green calcite)
New jade (serpentine [bowenite])
Oregon jade (dark green jasper [quartz])
Pennsylvania jade (serpentine, variety williamsite)
Potomac jade (massive green diopside, Md., U.S.A.)

Soochow jade (serpentine or soapstone)

Styrian jade (pseudophite)

Swiss jade (dyed green jasper [quartz])

Virginia jade (amazonite, variety of feldspar)

PEARLS

Oriental pearl (genuine, natural pearl)

Cultured pearl (pearl made by man's implanting a bead into the oyster, which then covers the bead with the pearl substance, nacre. Can't be differentiated from natural pearl except by X ray or very strong microscopic examination).

Biwa pearl (a cultured pearl, lacking the "bead" implantation, grown in lakes rather than salt water. These can be produced more easily and more quickly than the saltwater pearl).

Atlas pearls (imitation—satinspar type gypsum beads)

Laguna pearls (imitation)

La Jausca pearls (imitation)

Nassau pearls (pink conch pearl, common and usually inexpensive)

Patona pearls (pink conch pearl)

Patricia pearls (pink conch pearl)

Pompadour pearls (pink conch pearl)

Red Sea pearls (coral beads)

Tecla pearls (pink conch pearl)

RUBY

African ruby (ruby from Africa)

Burma ruby (ruby from Burma —most desirable red color; most expensive)

Ceylon ruby (ruby from Sri Lanka [Ceylon])

Thai ruby (ruby from Thailand)

Adelaide ruby (garnet, Australia)

Almandine ruby (garnet)

Ancona ruby (quartz)

Australian ruby (garnet)

Balas ruby (spinel)

Bohemian ruby (garnet)

Brazilian ruby (tourmaline)

Brazilian ruby (topaz; rare)

Californian ruby (garnet)

Cape ruby (garnet)

Ruby spinel (spinel)

Siberian ruby (tourmaline)

SAPPHIRE

Australian sapphire (sapphire from Australia)

Burmese sapphire (sapphire from Burma; finest and most expensive)

Ceylon sapphire (fine sapphire from Ceylon; very fine— lighter blue than Burmese)

Kashmir sapphire (fine sapphire from Kashmir)

Montana sapphire (sapphire from Montana)

Oriental sapphire (an older term that means "genuine")

Thai sapphire (sapphire from Thailand)

Brazilian sapphire (blue tourmaline. Brazil also has sapphire but they are called simply "sapphire.")

Lux sapphire (iolite)

Water sapphire (iolite)

TOPAZ

Precious (Imperial) topaz (usually fine apricot brown)

Madeira topaz (citrine quartz)*

Occidental topaz (citrine quartz)

Palmeira topaz (citrine quartz)

Rio del Sol topaz (citrine quartz)

Rio topaz (citrine quartz)

Saffranite topaz (citrine quartz)

Scottish topaz (citrine quartz)

Smokey topaz (smokey quartz)

Spanish topaz (citrine quartz)

*Much of the citrine quartz as seen on the market today is produced by heating the purple variety (amethyst). This heating alters the color from purple to shades of yellow, yellow brown, or golden yellow.

CHAPTER *15*

Popular Colored Gemstones

*H*ere we would like to provide an alphabetical listing of popular colored gemstones, including birthstones. Some of the most popular colored stones mentioned in the preceding chart on colored gemstone alternatives are also described.

❖ *Alexandrite*

Alexandrite is not a birthstone but makes a wonderful choice for the changeable woman who loves red and green. Alexandrite is a fascinating transparent gem that appears grass green in *daylight* and raspberry red under *incandescent light*. It is a variety of chrysoberyl reputedly discovered in Russia in 1831 on the day Alexander II reached his majority—hence the name. In Russia, where the national colors also happen to be green and red, it is considered a stone of very good omen. It is also considered Friday's stone or the stone of "Friday's child." Alexandrite is a relatively recent gem. Nonetheless, it has definitely come into its own and is presently commanding both high interest and high prices. While not too uncommon in small sizes, it has become relatively scarce in sizes of 2 carats or more. A fine 3-carat stone can cost $25,000 today. If you see an alexandrite that measures more than ½ inch in width, be suspicious—it may well be a synthetic or imitation. Alexandrite is normally cut in a faceted style, but some cat's-eye type alexandrites, found in Brazil, would be cut as a cabochon to display the eye effect. These are usually small; the largest we've seen was approximately 3 carats.

Prior to 1973, there were really no good synthetic alexandrites.

While some varieties of synthetic corundum and synthetic spinel were frequently sold as alexandrite, they really didn't look like the real thing but were hard to differentiate since so few had ever seen the real thing. However, they are easy for a gemologist to spot. In 1973 a very good synthetic alexandrite was produced, which is not easy to distinguish from the real thing. While a good gemologist today can tell the synthetic from the genuine, when these synthetics first appeared on the market many were mistaken for the real thing. So be especially careful to verify the authenticity of your alexandrite, since it might have been mistakenly identified years ago and passed along as the real thing to you today. This could save you a lot of money!

❖ *Amethyst*

Amethyst, a transparent purple variety of quartz, is one of the most popular of the colored stones. Recognized in contemporary times as the birthstone of February, it was once believed to bring peace of mind to the wearer. It was also believed to prevent the wearer from getting drunk, and if the circle of the sun or moon was engraved thereon, it was thought to prevent death from poison.

Available in shades from light to dark purple, it is relatively hard, fairly brilliant, and overall a good, versatile, wearable stone, available in good supply even in very large sizes (although large sizes with deep color are now becoming scarce). Amethyst is probably one of the most beautiful stones available at a moderate price, although one must be careful because "fine" amethyst is being produced synthetically today. Amethyst may fade from heat and strong sunshine. Guard your amethyst from these conditions and it will retain its color indefinitely.

❖ *Aquamarine*

To dream of aquamarine signifies the making of new friends; to wear aquamarine earrings brings love and affection. Aquamarine, a universal symbol of youth, hope, and health, blesses those born in March. (Prior to the fifteenth century it was thought to be the birthstone for those born in October.)

Aquamarine is a member of the important beryl family, which includes emerald, but aquamarine is less brittle and more durable than emerald. Aquamarine ranges in color from light blue to bluish green to deep blue, which is the most valuable and desirable color. Do not purchase a shallow-cut stone, since the color will become paler as dirt accumulates on the back. It is a very wearable gem, clear and brilliant, and, unlike emerald, is available with excellent clarity even in very large sizes, although these are becoming scarce. Aquamarines are still widely available in sizes up to 15 carats, but 10-carat sizes with fine color and clarity are becoming rare and are more expensive. Long considered a beautiful and moderately priced gem, it is now entering the "expensive" classification for stones in larger sizes with a good deep blue color.

One must be careful not to mistake blue topaz for aquamarine. While topaz is an equally beautiful gem, it is usually much less expensive since it is usually treated to obtain its desirable color. For those who can't afford an aquamarine, however, blue topaz is an excellent alternative—as long as it is properly represented . . . and priced.

Also, note that many aquamarine-colored synthetic spinels are erroneously sold as aquamarine.

❖ Beryl (Golden Beryl and Morganite)

As early as A.D. 1220 the virtues of beryl were well known to man. Beryl provided help against foes in battle or litigation, made the wearer unconquerable but at the same time friendly and likable, and also sharpened his intellect and cured him of laziness. Today beryl is still considered important, but primarily for aesthetic reasons. The variety of colors in which it is found, its wonderful clarity (except for emerald), its brilliance, and its durability (again with the exception of emerald) have given the various varieties of beryl tremendous appeal.

Most people are familiar with the blue variety, aquamarine, and the green variety, emerald. Few as yet know the pink or orange variety, morganite, and the beautiful yellow to yellow green variety, referred to as golden beryl. These gems have only recently found their place in the jewelry world but are already being shown in fabulous pieces made by the greatest designers. While not inexpensive, they still offer excellent value and beauty.

Beryl has also been found in many other colors—lilac, salmon, orange, red, sea green, as well as colorless. While most of these varieties are not as yet available to any but the most ardent rock hound, the orange varieties are fairly common and can still be found for under $125 per carat.

❖ *Bloodstone (Heliotrope)*

Believed by the ancient Greeks to have fallen from heaven, this stone has held a prominent place throughout history, and even into modern times, as a great curative. It was (and still is in some parts of the world) believed capable of stopping every type of bleeding, clearing bloodshot eyes, acting as an antidote for snakebite, and relieving urinary troubles. Today there are people who wear bloodstone amulets to prevent sunstroke and headache, and provide protection against the evil eye.

The birthstone for March, bloodstone is a more or less opaque, dark green variety of quartz with specks of red jasper (a variety of quartz) spattering red throughout the dark green field. It is particularly popular for men's rings (perhaps they need more protection from illness?). It is most desirable when the green isn't so dark as to approach black and the red flecks are roundish and pronounced. It has fair durability and is fairly readily available and inexpensive.

❖ *Carnelian*

If you're the timid sort, carnelian is the stone for you. "The wearing of carnelians is recommended to those who have a weak voice or are timid in speech, for the warm-colored stone will give them the courage they lack so that they will speak both boldly and well," reports G. F. Kunz.

This stone is especially revered by Moslems, because Muhammad himself wore a silver ring set with a carnelian engraved for use as a seal.

Napoleon I, while on a campaign in Egypt, picked up with his own hands (apparently from the battlefield) an unusual octagonal carnelian, on which was engraved the legend "The Slave Abraham Relying Upon The Merciful [God]." He wore it with him always and bequeathed it to his nephew.

Carnelian, one of the accepted birthstones for August, is a reddish orange variety of quartz. A moderately hard, translucent to opaque stone, its warm uniform color and fair durability have made it a favorite. It is often found in antique jewelry and lends itself to engraving or carving (especially in cameos). It is still a relatively inexpensive stone with great warmth and beauty and offers an excellent choice for jewelry to be worn as an accessory with today's fashion colors.

❖ *Emerald*

Emerald is the green variety of the mineral beryl and one of the most highly prized of all gems. Aside from being the birthstone for May, it was historically believed to bestow on its wearer faithfulness and unchanging love, and was thought to enable the wearer to forecast events.

The finest-quality emerald has the color of fresh young green grass—an almost pure spectral green, possibly with a very faint tint of blue, as in the "drop of oil" emerald from Colombia, which is considered to be the world's finest. Flawless emeralds are rare, so the flaws have come to serve almost as "fingerprints," while flawless emeralds are immediately suspect. Although a hard stone, emerald will chip easily since it tends to be somewhat brittle, so special care should be given in wearing and handling.

Because of emerald's popularity and value, imitations are abundant. Glass (manufactured complete with "flaws"), doublets, or triplets—such as "aquamarine emeralds" and "Tecla emeralds," which are clever imitations made by inserting layers of green glass (or, more frequently, a green cementing agent) between pieces of aquamarine or quartz "crystal"—are often encountered. Also, fine synthetic emeralds have been produced for many years with nearly the same physical and optical properties (color, hardness, brilliance) as genuine emerald. These synthetics are not inexpensive themselves, except by comparison to a genuine emerald of equivalent quality.

Techniques to enhance color and reduce the visibility of flaws are also frequently used. A common practice, one that goes back to early Greek times, is to boil the emerald in oil (sometimes tinted green). Oiling emerald is a practice that is accepted by the jewelry industry since it is actually good for the stone in light of its fragile nature. Oiling hides some of the whitish flaws, which are actually cracks, filling them so they become less visible. The oil becomes an integral part of the emerald unless it is subjected to some type of degreasing procedure. For this reason, *ultrasonic cleaners should not be used to clean emerald.*

A good friend of mine took her heirloom emerald ring to her jeweler for a "really good cleaning." Luckily for the jeweler, she never left the store and was standing right there when the ring was put into the cleaner and removed. She couldn't believe her eyes. She was shocked by the loss of color and the "sudden appearance of more flaws." The ultrasonic cleaner had removed the oil that had penetrated the cracks, and an emerald several shades lighter and more visibly flawed emerged. Had she not been there, she would never have believed the jeweler hadn't pulled a switch.

Oiling is considered an acceptable practice, but be sure the price reflects the actual quality of the stone.

As with all highly desired gems, the greater the value and demand, the greater the occurrence of fraudulent practices. Examples of almost every type of technique to simulate emerald can be found—color alteration (using green foil on closed backs), synthetics, substitutes (of less valuable green stones), doublets or other composites, etc. Therefore, be especially cautious of bargains, deal with reputable jewelers when planning to purchase, and always have the purchase double-checked by a qualified gemologist-appraiser.

❖ *Garnet*

If you are loyal, devoted, and energetic, perhaps the garnet is your stone. Or if not, perhaps you should obtain some! Red garnets were "known" to promote sincerity, stop hemorrhaging or other loss of blood, cure inflammatory diseases, and relieve anger and discord. And if you engrave a well-formed lion image on it, it will protect and preserve honors and health, cure the wearer of all disease, bring honors, and guard from all perils in traveling. All in all, quite a worthwhile stone.

The garnet family is one of the most exciting families in the gem world. A hard, durable, often very brilliant stone, available in many colors (greens, reds, yellows, oranges), it offers great versatility. Depending on the variety, quality, and size, lovely garnets are available for under $20 per carat or more than $3,000 per carat. Garnet is also mistaken for other (usually more expensive) gems. Green garnet, tsavorite, is one of the most beautiful, and all but a few would assume it was an emerald of the finest quality. In fact, it is "clearer," more brilliant, and more durable. There is also a rarer green garnet, called demantoid, which costs slightly more than tsavorite but which, although slightly softer, has more fire. These gems offer fine alternatives to the person desiring a lovely green gem who can't afford emerald. While still rare, expensive gems themselves, they are far less expensive than an emerald of comparable quality. Garnet also occurs in certain shades of red that have been taken for some varieties of ruby. And in yellow it has been confused with precious topaz.

Garnet can be found in almost every color and shade except blue. It is best known in a deep red variety, sometimes with a brownish cast, but it is commonly found in orangish brown shades, and brilliant wine red shades as well. Other colors include orange, red purple, violet, and pink. A nontransparent variety, grossularite, has a jade-like appearance and may be mistaken for jade when cut into cabochons or carved.

❖ *Iolite*

This is a transparent, usually very clean, blue gem, ranging from deep blue to light gray blue to yellowish gray. It is sometimes called dichroite, and in its sapphire blue color is occasionally referred to as water sapphire or lynx sapphire. It is a lovely, brilliant stone but not as durable as sapphire. We are just beginning to see this stone in jewelry, and it is still a good value. It is abundant, still very low priced, and makes a good alternative for those who like blue.

❖ *Jade*

Jade has long been revered by the Chinese. White jade (yes, white) was believed by the early Chinese to quiet intestinal disturbances and black jade to give strength and power. A very early written Chinese symbol for king was a string of jade beads, and jade beads are still used in China as a symbol of high rank and authority. Jade is also an important part of the Chinese wedding ceremony (the "jade ceremony" holds a prominent place here), for jade is considered the "concentrated essence of love."

Jade is a very tough, although not too hard, translucent to opaque gem, often seen in jewelry and carvings. There are really two types of jade—jadeite and nephrite—which are really two separate and distinct minerals differing from one another in weight, hardness, and color range.

Jadeite is the most expensive, more desirable variety. It was the most sought after by the Chinese after 1740. It is *not* found in China, however, but in Burma. Some fine jadeite also comes from Guatemala. It comes in a much wider range of colors than nephrite: green, mottled green and white, whitish gray, pink, brown, mauve, yellow, orange, and lilac. In fact, it comes in almost every color. But with the exception of green (which comes in shades that vary from pale to a beautiful emerald green), colored jade is usually pale and unevenly colored. The most desirable color is a rich emerald green sometimes referred to as imperial jade. Smooth, evenly colored pieces of this jadeite are highly prized. In fact, they can be classed as precious stones today. The mottled pieces of irregular green, often seen carved, are less valuable, but still more rare and valuable than nephrite jade.

Nephrite jade, the old and true Chinese jade, resembles jadeite but is slightly softer (yet slightly tougher and thus less easily broken) and has a much more limited range of color. It is regularly seen in dark green shades (sometimes so dark as to look black: black jade), usually fashioned in cabochon cut, round beads, or in carvings. Nephrite green is a more sober green than the apple green or emerald green color of good jadeite. It is closer in color to a dark, sage green or spinach green. Nephrite may also be a creamier color, as in mutton fat jade. Any fine Chinese carving that is more than 250 years old is carved from nephrite (jadeite was unknown to the Chinese before 1740).

Nephrite has been found in many countries, including the United States, where in the late nineteenth century Chinese miners panning for gold in California discovered large boulders of nephrite jade that they sent back to China to be cut or carved. It is also common in Wyoming, Alaska, and British Columbia.

Nephrite jade is much more common than jadeite and is therefore much less expensive. But it is a lovely, popular stone, and makes lovely jewelry.

One must be careful, however, in purchasing jade. You will often see "imperial" jade that is nothing more than a cheap jade that has been dyed. Much of it is treated (usually this means dyed) to enhance its value. The dyeing, however, may be very temporary. Black jade is either dyed or very dark green nephrite that looks black. There are also numerous minerals that look like jade and are sold as jade under misleading names, such as "Korean jade," or "new jade," both of which are serpentine (another green stone similar to some varieties of jade, but more common and less expensive). Much of the intricately and beautifully carved jade is actually serpentine, which can be scratched easily with a knife.

Soapstone may also look like jade to the amateur, especially when beautifully carved. This stone is so soft that it can easily be scratched with a pin, hairpin, or point of a pen. (But don't scratch it in a noticeable place and, if it doesn't belong to you, seek permission before performing this test!) It is very much less expensive than comparable varieties of jade, and it is softer and less durable.

Jade is a wonderful stone. Imperial jade is breathtaking. It is no wonder it was the emperor's stone. But jade has long been "copied"—misrepresented and altered. Be sure to verify its true identity with a gemologist-appraiser to be sure you are buying what you think you are buying. And then enjoy it!

❖ *Lapis Lazuli*

Lapis, a birthstone for December, has been highly prized since ancient Babylonian and Egyptian times. An amulet of "great power" was formed when lapis was worked into the form of an eye and ornamented with gold; in fact, so powerful that sometimes these eyes were put to rest on the limbs of a mummy. In addition, it was recognized as a symbol for capacity, ability, success, and divine favor.

Genuine lapis is a natural blue opaque stone of intense, brilliant, deep blue color. It sometimes possesses small, sparkling gold- or silver-colored flecks (pyrite inclusions), although the finest quality is a deep, even blue with a purplish tint or undertone and no trace of these flecks. Occasionally it may be blue mottled with white.

Don't confuse genuine lapis with the cheaper "Swiss lapis" or "Italian lapis," which aren't lapis at all. These are natural stones (usually quartz) artificially colored to look like lapis lazuli. Genuine lapis is often represented as "Russian lapis," although it doesn't always come from Russia. The finest lapis comes from Afghanistan.

Lapis has become very fashionable, and the finest-quality lapis is becoming more rare and more expensive. This has resulted in an abundance of lapis that has been "color-improved." It is often fashioned today with other gems—pearls, crystal, coral—that make particularly striking fashion accessories.

Sodalite is sometimes confused with the more expensive, and rarer, lapis and used as a substitute for it. However, sodalite rarely contains the silvery or golden flecks typical of most lapis. It may have some white veining, but more commonly it just exhibits the fine lapis blue without any markings. The lapis substitutes do transmit some light through the edges of the stone; lapis does not, since it is opaque.

Dyed chalcedony (quartz), glass, and plastic imitations are common. A gemologist can quickly and easily separate genuine lapis from imitations.

✤ *Moonstone (Feldspar)*

Moonstone is definitely a good luck stone, especially for lovers. As a gift for lovers the moonstone holds a high rank, for it is believed to arouse one's tender passion and give lovers the ability to foretell their future—good or ill. (But to get this information, the stone must be placed in the mouth while the moon is full.) Perhaps a more important use, however, was in amulets made of moonstone, which would protect men from epilepsy and guarantee a greater fruit-crop yield when hung on fruit trees (it assisted all vegetation).

The name "moonstone" is probably derived from the theory that one can observe the lunar month through the stone—that a small white spot appears in the stone as the new moon begins and gradually moves toward the stone's center, getting always larger, until at full moon the spot has taken the shape of a full moon in the center of the stone.

Moonstone is a member of the feldspar family. It is a transparent, milky-white variety in which can be seen a floating opalescent white or blue light within the stone's body. It is a popular stone for rings because as the hand moves the effect of the brilliant light/color is more pronounced. The bluer color is the finer and more desirable, but it is becoming rare in today's market, particularly in large sizes.

There are some glass imitations of moonstone, but compared to the real thing they are not very good.

❖ *Opal*

The opal has suffered from an unfortunate reputation as being an evil stone and bearing an ill omen. There are several explanations for the ominous superstitions surrounding this wonderful gem, but we'd rather mention some of its good properties and leave you with an assurance that the evil association has never been merited and probably resulted from a careless reading of Sir Walter Scott's *Anne of Geierstein.*

Among the ancients, opal was a symbol of fidelity and assurance, and in later history it became strongly associated with religious emotion and prayer. It was believed to have a strong therapeutic value for diseases of the eye, and worn as an amulet it would make the wearer immune from all such diseases as well as increase the powers of the eyes and the mind. Further, many believed that to the extent the colors of red and green were seen, the therapeutic powers of stones of those colors (ruby and emerald) were also to be enjoyed by the wearer—the power to stop bleeding, etc. (when ruby-red is present); the power to cure kidney diseases, etc. (when emerald-green is present). The black opal was particularly highly prized as the luck stone of anyone fortunate enough to own one!

This stone, whose brilliance and vibrant colors resemble the colors of the fall, is certainly appropriate as a birthstone for October. When we try to describe the opal, we realize how insufficient the English language is. It is unique among the gems, displaying an array of very brilliant miniature rainbow effects, all mixed up together.

Its most outstanding characteristic is this unusual, intense display of many colors flashing out like mini-rainbows. This effect is created by opal's formation process, which is very different from that of other gems. Opal is composed of hydrated silica spheres. The mini-rainbows seen in most opals result from light interference created by these spheres. The arrangement of the spheres, which vary in size and pattern, is responsible for the different colors.

The
following section
of color photographs
provides examples of
antique and contemporary
engagement rings
and wedding bands.
We hope they will help you
in selecting or designing
the "perfect ring"... a ring
to last a lifetime.

Antique Betrothal Rings

Sforza Marriage Ring, 15th c.

Photo: Diamond Information Center

Table-cut Diamond Ring, 15th c.

Photo: Benjamin Zucker, Precious Stones Company, New York

Hogback Diamond Ring, 15th c.

Photo: Diamond Information Center

Fede Ring, 13th c.

Photo: Christie's

Fancy Color Pink Diamond Ring, 17th c.

Fede-type Gimmel Ring, 17th c.

Photo: Christie's

Photo: Benjamin Zucker, Precious Stones Company, New York

from the 15th to the 19th Century

Ring set with
uncut diamond crystals, 15th c.

Bali Ring,
late 19th c.

The Bottom of an
Intricately Enamelled
16th c. Ring

Gimmel Ring, 16th c.

Rose-cut Diamond Ring, 18th c.

Table-cut Ring
17th c.

See chapter
two for
complete
descriptions.

Engagement Ring Styles...

A Selection of Distinctive Rings from Lazare Kaplan, New York City

The various ring designs on the following pages illustrate the many possibilities available today. Some make use of prongs to hold the stones; some are channel-set; some are bar-set; and some combine prongs with other setting techniques.

A Selection of Distinctive Rings from Nova Stylings, Van Nuys, California

Engagement Ring Styles

A Selection of Distinctive Rings from Whitney Boin, New York City.

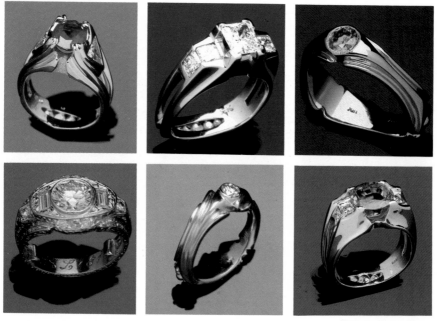

A Selection of Distinctive Rings from Richard Kimball, Denver, Colorado.

Classic engagement ring styles using a colored center stone—

Unusual engagement & wedding rings using the Japanese "mokume-gane" metal technique. Diamonds or colored stones may be used.

From George Sawyer Design, Minneapolis, Minnesota.

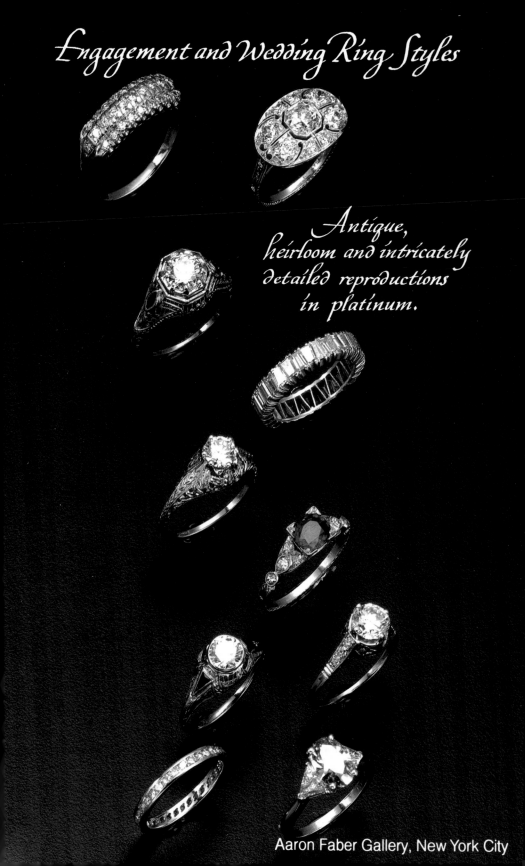

Engagement and Wedding Ring Styles

Antique, heirloom and intricately detailed reproductions in platinum.

Aaron Faber Gallery, New York City

*Diamond
wedding bands
using round diamonds,
emerald cut diamonds,
and round diamonds
alternating with
straight baguettes.*

Engagement Rings and Wedding Band Styles

Diamond bands
using the Quadrillion
or "Princess" cut.
Notice that diamonds
can be used part-way round
or all around.

Ambar Diamonds, Los Angeles, California.

Tri-gold diamond engagment rings

Engagement and Wedding Ring Styles

Engagement rings, wedding bands, and wedding sets using colored stones and diamonds. Notice that the center stone is missing. The individual can choose *either* a diamond or colored gem for the center. Any colored gem may be used, and any color combination. Create your own look!

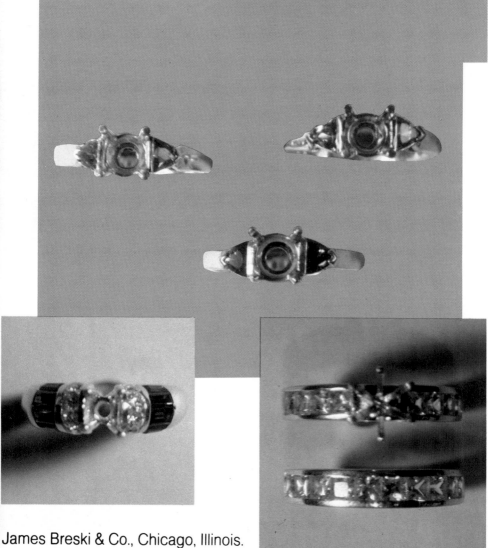

James Breski & Co., Chicago, Illinois.

Gem-studded wedding bands using diamonds and colored gems.

Tiffany & Co.

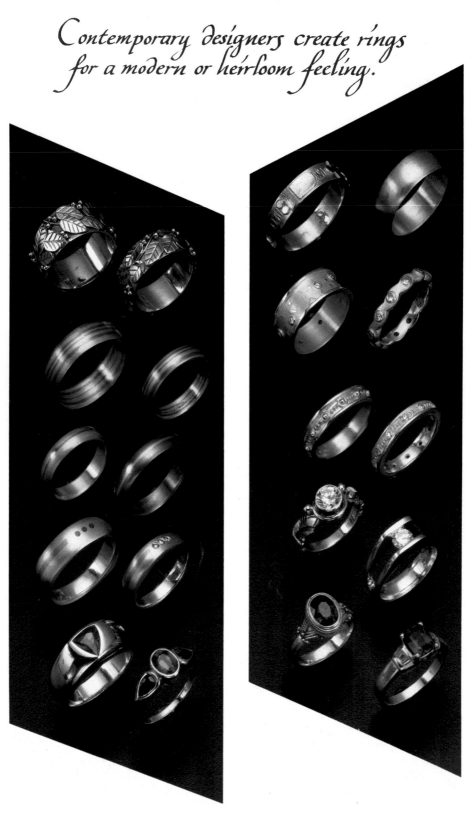

Contemporary designers create rings for a modern or heirloom feeling.

Aaron Faber Gallery, New York City

Opal is usually cut flat or in cabochon, since there is no additional brilliance to be captured by a good faceting job. Color is everything. The more brilliant the color, the more valuable the gem. It is probably truer of opal than any other stone that the more beautiful the stone and its color, the more it will cost.

The finest of all is the black opal. Black opals are usually a deep gray or grayish black with flashes of incredibly brilliant color dancing around within and about the stone as it is turned. One must be careful when purchasing a black opal, however, to ensure that it is not a *doublet* or *triplet*, a stone composed of two or three pieces of stone glued together. There are many such doublets on the market because of the black opal's rarity, beauty, and extremely high cost (one the size of a lima bean could cost $25,000 today). The black opal doublet provides an affordable option to one who loves them but can't afford them. But it also offers another opportunity for misrepresentation that can be very costly to the consumer.

Generally speaking, purity of color, absence of dead spots (called *trueness*), flawlessness, and intensity or brilliance of color are the primary variables affecting value. Opals with an abundance of red are usually the most expensive; those strong in blue and green are equally beautiful but not as rare, so their price is somewhat less. Some opals are very transparent and are classified as "jelly," "semi-jelly," or "water" opals.

While there are imitations, for the most part they are still not worth mentioning. The synthetic opal, however, is being used extensively. Also, the color of black opals can be improved by treatment, and treated opals are encountered frequently. So let us reiterate—make sure you know what you are getting by checking the facts with a gemologist-appraiser. And as we've mentioned many times, before buying shop around. This holds truer for opal, perhaps, than any other stone.

One word of caution must also be offered: Opals require special care because some tend to dry and crack. Avoid exposure to anything that is potentially drying. And, believe it or not, wiping the opal occasionally with oil such as olive oil (moisten a paper towel, wipe the opal, then remove any excess with another paper towel), will help preserve it. But *do not soak it* in oil because soaking can cause some opals to lose some or nearly all of their fire.

❖ *Oriental Pearls*

June's birthstone, the pearl, pure and fair to the eye, has been recognized since the earliest times as the emblem of modesty, chastity, and purity. We will explain the pearl in some detail since it is also the choice of many brides to be worn on their wedding day. Here we will discuss only round pearls.

The Pearl Market Today Is A Cultured Pearl Market

A fine natural or Oriental pearl—the real "genuine pearl"—has always been considered a precious gem because of its rarity. This is even truer today than ever before. Virtually all pearls sold today are *cultured*. But fine cultured pearls are also very expensive, and prices seem to continue to rise.

Natural pearls are produced by oysters (not the edible variety) and by mussels in freshwater lakes and rivers. When a foreign substance accidentally finds its way into the oyster's body, and the oyster can't get rid of it, it becomes an irritant. To soothe the irritation, the oyster produces an iridescent substance called *nacre* (nay-ker) to act as a coating. This substance builds up over the years, creating the pearl.

Cultured pearls are created by the oyster in essentially the same way. However, in the case of the cultured pearl the "irritant" is a mother-of-pearl bead that is *implanted by man* into the tissue of a live oyster. Over time (usually several years), the oyster secretes a coating of nacre over it, approximately ½ millimeter thick, creating the cultured pearl. The thickness depends in part on the length of time the bead remains in the oyster. Sometimes the cultured pearl is removed from the oyster prematurely, so that the nacre coating is too thin and may begin to wear through in only a few years. In other cases, the cultured pearl is so fine as to require an expert to tell it from a fine, genuine natural pearl.

In terms of quality and value, the same factors are used to determine the quality and value of a cultured pearl as for a natural one. But a pearl must always be clearly described as cultured or genuine (Oriental), and this should be stated in writing on your bill of sale.

As with all gems, quality and value vary. The quality and value of the pearl are determined by:

- *Luster*—the pearl's "glow;" its soft shine. Don't confuse this with a surface shine, but rather a quality that seems to emanate from within the pearl itself. Some pearls also show a rainbow-like play of color that produces a shimmering effect (this is called *orient* and can be seen in the finest pearls). As you shop, compare the depth and richness of the luster. This is the most important factor in terms of the pearl's beauty.

- *Color*—the most desirable round pearls are white with a rose overtone, although there are also white pearls with a cream-colored overtone that are highly desirable. Pearls with a strong yellowish or greenish overtone are less expensive. Keep in mind as you shop, however, that it is important to try pearls on to see what color really looks best with the coloring of your own skin, hair and eyes. Some look better in creamier shades, others in whiter shades. You may find you prefer a creamier shade, which may be more affordable.
- *Cleanliness* or perfection (skin texture)—freedom from skin blemishes such as blisters, pits, or spots. Perfectly spotless pearls are rare, but the cleaner, the better.
- *Roundness*—while it is extremely rare to find a strand of perfectly round pearls, the closer they come to being perfectly round the better. Check closely for roundness, and for careful matching of the pearl shape within the strand. Sometimes slightly out-of-round pearls can give the impression of being round when worn, and might be a good alternative. But slightly out-of-round pearls sell for less, so be sure the price reflects this.
- *Size*—natural pearls are sold by weight, which is given in *grains* (there are 4 grains to a carat). Cultured pearls are measured and sold by their *millimeter* size. The larger the pearl, the greater the cost. There is a dramatic jump in price, for example, between 7½ and 8 millimeters, or between 9 and 10 millimeters. An 8 millimeter pearl is considered large; a 9 millimeter, *very* large, both in size and in price. The price jumps upward rapidly with each millimeter once you pass 8.

A fine pearl necklace, or any strung pearl item, requires very careful *matching*—of size, roundness, luster, color, and cleanliness. Graduated pearls—a strand containing larger pearls in the center, with the pearls becoming progressively smaller toward the ends—also require careful sizing. Failure to match carefully will detract from both the appearance of the piece and the value.

Pearls should be handled with care. It is best to keep them in a separate pouch, and to exercise some caution when wearing.

Avoid contact with harsh or acidic substances such as vinegar (when making a salad), ammonia, inks, and certain perfumes, since these can spot the pearl's surface. Also, the frequent application of hair spray while wearing pearls will coat them and make them very dull, but this coating can be removed with a soft cloth moistened with nail polish remover.

Is It Real or Simulated?

Simulated or imitation pearls are sold everywhere. Many of the finest imitations have been mistaken for the real thing. One quick test that normally reveals the fake is to run the pearl gently between your teeth. The cultured or genuine pearl will have a mildly abrasive or gritty feel, while the imitation will be slippery smooth. (This test won't work with false teeth.) Try the test on pearls you know are cultured or genuine, and then try it on known imitations to get a feel for the difference.

But once again, when in doubt, seek out a qualified gemologist. The cost of being wrong may be too great to risk it.

A Final Word on Pearls

There are innumerable differences in quality—if roundness is good, luster may be poor; if luster is good, roundness may be poor; if color and luster are good, there may be poor surface texture from too many skin blemishes, or matching in a strand may be poor. Shopping around can teach you a tremendous amount about pearls. Keeping in mind the factors that affect quality—size, luster, color, roundness, skin blemishes—go shopping and compare. You'll be surprised how quickly you will learn to spot differences that affect cost. Now you can decide which factors are important to you, and which you can juggle to get the pearls that are right for you. For example, you may be able to afford a larger size pearl if you prefer a creamier color; or, if you can't afford a strand of 8-millimeter pearls, you may find a *double* strand in a 6½-millimeter (which will be cheaper than a single strand of 8) creates an equally important—and more versatile—look. And so on.

❖ Peridot

Today's birthstone for August, peridot was also a favorite of the ancients. This lovely transparent yellowish green to deep chartreuse stone was quite a powerful gem. It was considered an aid to friendship and was also believed to free the mind of envious thoughts. (Which is probably why it was an aid to friendship.) Because of its yellowish green color, it was also believed to cure or prevent diseases of the liver and dropsy. And, if that's not enough, if worn on the left arm it would protect the wearer from the evil eye.

It is also popular today, but probably more for its depth of green color than its professed powers. While not particularly brilliant, the richness of its color is exceptional. It comes in shades of yellowish green to darker, purer green colors. It is still widely available in small sizes but larger sizes are becoming scarce, so prices in larger sizes are now fairly high for good quality material.

Some caution should also be exercised in wearing peridot. It is not a very hard stone and may scratch easily. Also, some stones may look like peridot (green sapphire, green tourmaline) and be mistaken for it.

❖ *Quartz*

Quartz is the most versatile of any of the gem families. It includes among its members more variety and a larger number of gems than any other three mineral families together. As someone once said, "If in doubt, say quartz."

The quartz minerals, for the most part, are relatively inexpensive gems that offer a wide range of pleasing color alternatives both in transparent and nontransparent varieties (from translucent to opaque). They are reasonably hard stones, and while not very brilliant in the transparent varieties, still create lovely, affordable jewelry.

Some of these gems have been discussed in separate sections, but we will provide a list here with brief descriptions of most of the quartz family members.

Amethyst (see page 137). Lilac to purple.

Citrine (often called quartz topaz, citrine topaz, or topaz, all of which are misleading; the correct name for this stone is citrine). It ranges from yellow to amber, to amber brown. This is the most commonly seen "topaz" in today's marketplace and is, unfortunately, too often confused with precious topaz because of the careless use of the name topaz. While a pleasing stone in terms of color, and fairly durable, citrine is slightly softer and has less brilliance than precious topaz. It also lacks the subtle color shading, the pinkier yellow or pinkish amber shades, which lend to precious topaz a distinctive color difference. (Much citrine is made by heat-treating purple amethyst.)

Citrine is also much less expensive than precious topaz. It should never be represented as topaz, which technically is "precious" or "imperial" topaz. Unfortunately, it often is. For example, "topaz" birthstone jewelry is almost always citrine (or a worthless synthetic). So ask, "Is this citrine or precious topaz?" (And get the answer in writing if you are told "precious topaz.")

Citrine is plentiful in all sizes, and can be made into striking jewelry, especially in very large sizes, for a relatively small investment (while precious topaz of fine quality is scarce in sizes over 7 carats, and very expensive).

Rock crystal. Water clear. Used in old jewelry for rondelles (a type of small bead resembling a doughnut). Cut (faceted) crystal beads were also common in older jewelry. Today, however, crystal usually refers to glass.

Rose quartz. Light to deep pink. This stone has been very popular for many years for use in carved pieces—beads, statues, ashtrays, fine lamp bases, and pins and brooches. Rarely clear, this stone is usually seen in cabochon cut, rounded beads, or carvings rather than in faceted styles. Once very inexpensive, it is becoming more costly, particularly in the finer deep pink shades. But the color of rose quartz is especially pleasing and offers an excellent choice for use in fashion accessory jewelry. One must be somewhat cautious with rose quartz, however, because it tends to crack more easily than most other varieties of quartz if struck or exposed to a blow (due to the inclusions or internal fractures that are also responsible for the absence of clarity in this stone).

Smoky quartz. A pale to rich smoky brown variety, sometimes mistaken for or misrepresented as smoky topaz or topaz. Also very plentiful and becoming popular for use in very large sizes for beautiful brooches, large dinner rings, etc.

❖ *Ruby*

Prized through the ages, even by kings, as the "gem of gems . . . surpassing all other precious stones in virtue," and today's birthstone for July, ruby is the red variety of the mineral corundum. Historically, it has been symbolic of love and passion, considered to be an aid to firm friendship, and believed to ensure beauty. Its color ranges from purplish or bluish red to a yellowish red. The finest color is a vivid, almost pure spectral red with a very faint undertone of blue, as seen in Burmese rubies, which are considered the finest. The ruby is a very brilliant stone and is also a very hard, durable, and wearable stone. Because of these characteristics, ruby makes an unusually fine choice for rings.

Translucent varieties of ruby are also seen, and one variety exhibits a six-ray star effect when cut as a cabochon. This variety is called star ruby and is one of nature's most beautiful and interesting gifts. But, as with so many other beautiful gifts once produced only in nature, today man has also learned to make synthetic star ruby.

Here again, remember that the greater the value and demand, the greater the use of techniques to "improve" or simulate. Again, examples of almost every type of technique can be found—color enhancement, synthesis, substitutes, doublets, triplets, misleading names, etc. The newest synthetic rubies—the Kashan ruby and Chatham ruby—are so close to natural ruby in every aspect that many are actually passing for genuine, even among many gemologists. When verifying the identity and quality of a fine ruby, make every effort to select a gemologist with both many years' experience in colored gems and an astute knowledge of the marketplace today.

Here again, be especially cautious of bargains. Deal with reputable jewelers when planning to purchase, and have the purchase double-checked by a qualified gemologist-appraiser.

❖ *Sapphire*

The "celestial" sapphire, symbol of the heavens, bestower of innocence, truth, good health, and preserver of chastity, is reserved today as the birthstone of September. Sapphire is corundum. While we know it best in its blue variety, which is one of the most highly prized varieties, it comes in essentially every color (the red variety is ruby). As we mentioned when discussing ruby, sapphire's hardness, brilliance, and availability in so many beautiful colors make it probably the most important and most versatile of the gem families. The finest sapphires are considered to be the blue variety—specifically those from Burma and Kashmir, which are closest to the pure spectral blue. Fine, brilliant, deep blue Burmese sapphires will surely dazzle the eye and the pocketbook, as will the Kashmir, which is a fine velvety-toned deep blue. Many today tend to be too dark, however, because of the presence of too much black and poor cutting (cutting deep for additional weight).

The Ceylon sapphires are a very pleasing shade of blue, but are a less deep shade than the Burmese or Kashmir, often on the pastel side.

We are also seeing many Australian sapphires. These are often a dark blue, but have a slightly green undertone, as do those from Thailand, and sell for much less per carat. They offer a very affordable alternative to the Burmese, Kashmir, or Ceylon, and can still be very pleasing in their color. Blue sapphires also come from Tanzania, Brazil, Africa, and even the U.S.A. (Montana and North Carolina).

With sapphire, country of origin can have a significant effect on price, so if you are purchasing a Burmese or Ceylon sapphire, that should be noted on the bill of sale.

Like ruby, the blue sapphire may be found in a translucent variety that may show a six-rayed star effect when cut into a cabochon. This variety is known as star sapphire, of which there are numerous synthetics (often referred to in the trade as "Linde" (pronounced Lin'dee).

In addition to blue sapphire, we are now beginning to see the appearance of many other color varieties, especially yellow and pink, and in smaller sizes some beautiful shades of green. These are known as fancy sapphires. Compared to the cost of blue sapphire and ruby, these stones offer excellent value and beauty.

Inevitably, one can find evidence of every technique known to improve the perceived quality and value of the sapphire—the alteration of color, synthesis, composites, misleading names. Yet again, we urge you to be especially cautious of bargains, deal with reputable jewelers, and have your stone double-checked by a qualified gemologist-appraiser.

❖ *Spinel*

Spinel is one of the loveliest of the gems but hasn't yet been given due credit and respect. It is usually compared to sapphire or ruby, rather than being recognized for its own intrinsic beauty and value. There is also a common belief that spinel (and similarly zircon) is synthetic rather than natural, when in fact it is one of nature's most beautiful products (although synthetic spinel is also seen frequently on the market).

Spinel commonly occurs in red orange (flame spinel), light to dark orangy red, light to dark slightly grayish blue, greenish blue, grayish green, and dark to light purple to violet. It also occurs in yellow and in an opaque variety—black. When compared to the blue of sapphire or the red of ruby, its color is considered less intense, but its brilliance can be greater. If you appreciate these spinel colors for themselves, they are quite pleasing. The most popular are red (more orange than the ruby red) and blue (a strong Bromo-Seltzer-bottle blue).

Spinel may be confused with or misrepresented as one of many stones—ruby, sapphire, zircon, amethyst, garnet, synthetic ruby/sapphire or synthetic spinel—as well as glass. The synthetic is often used to make composite stones such as doublets. Spinel is a fairly hard, fairly durable stone, possessing a nice brilliance, and still a good value.

This stone is becoming more and more popular today, and may, therefore, become more expensive if current trends continue.

❖ *Spodumene (Kunzite and Hiddenite)*

Spodumene is another gem relatively new to widespread jewelry use. The most popular varieties are kunzite and hiddenite.

Kunzite is a very lovely brilliant stone occurring in delicate lilac, pink, or violet shades. Its color can fade in strong light, and so it has become known as an "evening" stone. Also, while hard, it can break easily if it receives a sharp blow from certain directions. It is not recommended for rings for this reason unless set in a protective mounting. But it is a lovely gem, whose low cost makes it attractive in large sizes, and an excellent choice for lovely, dramatic jewelry design.

Hiddenite is rarer. Light green or yellow green varieties are available, but the emerald green varieties are scarce. As with kunzite, it is hard but brittle, so care must be exercised in wear.

Spodumene also occurs in many other shades of color, all pale but very clear and brilliant. Only blue is currently missing (but who knows what may yet be discovered?).

Spodumene is still fairly inexpensive and is an excellent choice for contemporary jewelry design. Be careful, however, as it can be confused with topaz, tourmaline, spinel, or beryl. Also, synthetic corundum or spinel, doublets, and glass can be mistaken for this gem.

❖ *Topaz*

True topaz, symbol of love and affection, aid to sweetness of disposition, and birthstone for November, is one of nature's most wonderful and least-known families.

The true topaz is rarely seen in jewelry stores. Unfortunately, most people know only the quartz (citrine) topaz, or glass. In the past almost any yellow stone was called topaz. True topaz is very beautiful and versatile.

Topaz occurs not only in the transparent yellow, yellow brown, orangy brown, and pinky brown colors most popularly associated with it, but also in a very light to medium red (now found naturally in fair supply, although many are produced through heat treatment), very light to light blue (also often the result of treatment, although it does occur naturally), very light green, light greenish yellow, violet, and colorless.

Topaz is a hard, brilliant stone with a fine color range, but it is much rarer and much more expensive than the stones commonly sold as topaz. It is also heavier than its imitators.

There are many misleading names to suggest that a stone is topaz when it is not. For example, "Rio topaz," "Madeira topaz," "Spanish topaz," and "Palmeira topaz" are types of citrine (quartz) and should be represented as such.

Blue topaz has become very popular in recent years, but most of it is treated (there is no way yet to determine which have been treated and which are natural). It closely resembles the finest aquamarine (which is very expensive today) and offers a very attractive, and much more affordable, alternative to it. *Caution: Some of the fine, deeper blue treated topazes have been found to be radioactive and, according to the Nuclear Regulatory Com-*

mission, may be injurious to the wearer. While this is not a major problem in the United States because of regulations here, blue topaz purchased in other countries may be radioactive.

The true topaz family offers a variety of color options in lovely, clear, brilliant, and durable stones.

❖ *Tourmaline*

Tourmaline is a gem of modern times, but nonetheless has found its way to the list of birthstones, becoming an "alternate birthstone" for October. Perhaps this honor results from tourmaline's versatility and broad color range. Or perhaps from the fact that red-and-green tourmaline, in which the red and green occur side by side in the same stone, is reminiscent of the turning of October leaves.

Whatever the case, tourmaline is one of the most versatile of the gem families. It is available in every color, in every tone, from deep to pastel and even with two or more colors appearing in the same stone, side by side. There are bicolored tourmalines (half red and the other half green, for example) and tricolored (one-third blue, one-third green, and one-third yet another color). The fascinating "watermelon" tourmaline looks just like the inside of a watermelon—red in the center surrounded by a green "rind." Tourmaline can also be found in a cat's-eye type.

It is indeed surprising that most people know of tourmaline simply as a common "green" stone. Only today are we beginning to see other lovely varieties of this fascinating gem used in jewelry:

- Chrome—A particular rare green hue
- Dravite—Yellow to brown
- Indicolite—deep indigo blue, usually with a green undertone
- Rubellite—Deep pink to red (as in ruby)
- Siberite—purple
- Verdelite—green varieties

While tourmaline is still a very affordable gem, even in large sizes, the chrome, indicolite, and rubellite varieties are priced (depending on size and quality) anywhere from $300 to $1,000 per carat wholesale. So much for the "common and inexpensive" myth!

Tourmaline is a fairly hard, durable, brilliant, and very wearable stone with a wide choice of colors. It makes an excellent choice for rings.

❖ *Turquoise*

A birthstone for December, and ranking highest among all the opaque stones, turquoise—the "Turkish stone"—is highly prized throughout Asia and Africa, not only for its particular hue of blue (a beautiful robin's-egg or sky blue), but more important for its prophylactic and therapeutic qualities. The Arabs consider it a lucky stone and have great confidence in its benevolent action. Used in rings, earrings, necklaces, head ornaments, and amulets, it protects the wearer from poison, reptile bites, eye diseases, and the evil eye. It was also believed capable of warning of impending death by changing color. Also, the drinking of water in which turquoise has been dipped or washed was believed to cure bladder ailments. Buddhists revere the turquoise because it is associated with a legend in which a turquoise enabled Buddha to destroy a monster. Even today it is considered a symbol of courage, success, and love. It has also long been associated with American Indian jewelry and art.

Turquoise is an opaque, light to dark blue or blue green stone. The finest color is an intense blue, with poorer qualities tending toward yellowish green. The famous Persian turquoise, which can be a very intense and pleasing blue, is considered a very rare and valuable gem.

All turquoises are susceptible to aging and may turn greenish or possibly darker with age. Also, care must be taken when wearing, both to avoid contact with soap, grease, or other materials that might discolor it, and to protect it from abuse, since turquoise scratches fairly easily.

Exercise caution when buying turquoise. This is a frequently simulated gem. Very fine glass imitations are produced that are difficult to distinguish from the genuine. Very fine imitations and *reconstructed* stones (made from turquoise powder bonded in plastic) saturate the marketplace, as does synthetic turquoise. There are techniques to quickly distinguish these simulations so, if in doubt, check it out (and get a complete description on the bill of sale: "genuine, natural turquoise").

❖ *Zircon*

Known to the ancients as "hyacinth," this gem had many powers, especially for men. While it was believed to assist women in childbirth, for men it kept evil spirits and bad dreams away, gave protection against "fascination" and lightning, strengthened their bodies, fortified their hearts, restored appetite, suppressed fat, produced sleep, and banished grief and sadness from the mind. If looking for the right stone for the groom, this may well be it!

Zircons are very brilliant transparent stones available in several lovely colors. Unfortunately, zircon suffers from a strange misconception that it is a synthetic or man-made stone rather than the lovely natural creation that it is. Perhaps this is because they are frequently, if not usually, treated.

Zircons are regularly treated to alter color, as in the blue and colorless zircons so often seen (many might mistake the colorless zircon for diamond because of its strong brilliance), but zircons also occur naturally in yellow, brown, orange, and red.

Colorless zircons, because of their intense brilliance and very low cost, offer an interesting alternative to diamonds as a stone to offset or dress up colored stones. But care needs to be exercised because zircon is brittle and will chip or abrade easily. For this reason, zircon is recommended for rings only if set with a protective setting.

❖ *Zoisite (Tanzanite)*

Zoisite was not considered a gem material until 1967, when a beautiful, rich, blue to purple blue, transparent variety was found in Tanzania (hence tanzanite). Tanzanite can possess a rich, sapphire blue color (possibly with some violet red or greenish yellow flashes).

This lovely gem can cost over $2,000 per carat today in larger sizes. But one must be cautious. It is relatively soft, so we do not recommend tanzanite for everyday wear in which it would be exposed to knocks and other abuse, or for rings unless set in a very protected setting.

PART FOUR

DESIGN AND STYLE:
GETTING THE LOOK
YOU WANT

Photo: Diamond Information Center

CHAPTER 16

Choosing the Shape

*T*oday's bride-to-be has more choices in engagement ring design and style than ever before. But the first step in creating the look you want is selecting the shape of the stone—the shape that's right for you. There are many shapes from which to choose, but it's important to choose the right shape because it will affect the overall design and look of your ring.

Uncut *diamond in its* **natural crystal state,** *mounted in gold shank.*

Photo: Diamond Information Center, copied by Julie Crossland, London.

Ring, centering a **table-cut** *diamond—15th century.*

Photo: Benjamin Zucker, Precious Stones Company, New York

Ring, containing a pear-shaped **rose-cut** *diamond—17th century.*

Photo: Courtesy The Browning Institute, New York City, and the Diamond Information Center

Modern **brilliant-cut.**

Photo: Diamond Information Center

Diamond cuts—from the 15th century to the present.

❖ The Evolution of Diamond Shapes

Indeed, today there are a variety of diamond shapes to choose from. But it wasn't always so. The evolution of diamond shapes actually dates back to the fifteenth century when the first cut diamonds appeared.

In the fifteenth century a remarkable technological breakthrough occurred, probably originating in Europe (although some

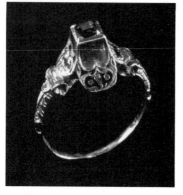

A table-cut diamond. Note the table-like flat surface on the top where the crystal point was polished off. The remainder of the crystal is left unchanged.

Photo: Benjamin Zucker, Precious Stones Company, New York

think it began in the East) which enabled stone-cutters finally to cut the "invincible" diamond crystal. For the first time, by placing the pointed end of the diamond crystal against a turning wheel that held another diamond, the stone cutter could actually grind off the point of the diamond, creating a large, flat surface. This flat-topped diamond resembled a squarish or rectangular shape or "table top." And so this early cut came to be called the table-cut diamond. (Today the large, flat facet on top of the diamond is still called the "table.") The early table-cut diamond represents man's first effort at releasing the potential fire and brilliance that otherwise lies dormant within the diamond crystal.

As man learned more and more about the diamond, he began to experiment with new cuts and shapes. During the sixteenth century, the gem-cutters of Amsterdam perfected a new cut, a rosette or rose-cut, which is still often seen in antique jewelry. Its base is flat and its facets, which are in multiples of six, give it a flower-like appearance, like an "opening rose-bud." The rose-cut quickly replaced the table-cut during the Renaissance. While it required more faceting than the table-cut, the finished product revealed more beauty and more brilliance than had ever been seen. The rose-cut can be seen in round, oval, or pear-shapes.

A ring containing a pear-shaped rose cut diamond.

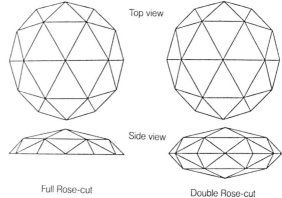

Top view

Side view

Full Rose-cut   Double Rose-cut

Photo: Courtesy The Browning Institute, New York City, and the Diamond Information Center

By the eighteenth century, cutting had progressed even further and what is now called the "old mine-cut" became popular. The old mine-cut is really the precursor to today's popular round, brilliant cut. The old mine-cut had more brilliance and fire than was ever imagined. Some are quite beautiful, even by current standards. It differs from contemporary cuts in several ways, however: the shape was normally not truly round, but "cushion" shaped (more like an oval with squarish corners); the crown was much higher; the table facet on top was much smaller in diameter; and the culet was "open" (the culet looks like a point in modern stones, whereas in the old mine-cut, instead of a point, there was another small, flat facet). We also find a variation on the pear-shape and oval during this period.

The next stage in the increasing sophistication of diamond cutting resulted in the "old European-cut," which appeared in the mid-1800s. Like the old mine-cut, it had a higher crown, small table facet and "open" culet. However, the old European-cut was round in shape, the crown wasn't quite so high nor the table quite as small as in the old mine-cut. As a result, it exhibited even more beauty and a better balance of fire and brilliance. Again, the pear-shape is improved, along with the oval, and we see other "fancy" shapes emerging.

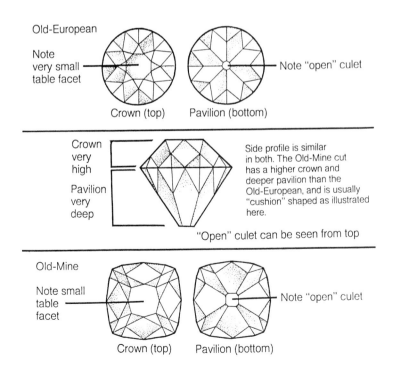

Old-European

Note very small table facet

Crown (top)   Pavilion (bottom)

Note "open" culet

Crown very high

Pavilion very deep

Side profile is similar in both. The Old-Mine cut has a higher crown and deeper pavilion than the Old-European, and is usually "cushion" shaped as illustrated here.

"Open" culet can be seen from top

Old-Mine

Note small table facet

Crown (top)   Pavilion (bottom)

Note "open" culet

Both the old European-cut and the old mine-cut have fifty-eight facets as in today's modern brilliant cut. And both have tremendous fire (the rainbow colors one sees—actually, more fire than today's modern cuts. But they lacked the tremendous brilliance or liveliness of modern stones.

Each stage in the development of diamond cutting came closer to revealing the beauty of the diamond to its fullest potential. The real breakthrough came in 1919 when Marcel Tolkowsky, a mathematician and engineer who grew up in Antwerp, Belgium, developed a new formula for cutting round diamonds that would reveal the stone's fullest beauty, its full potential, by providing the ideal balance between the fire exhibited and the degree of brilliance. The Tolkowsky cut serves as the basis for the modern American ideal cut.

Are Older Cut Diamonds as Valuable as Modern Cut Diamonds?

If you are considering an antique or estate piece for your engagement and/or wedding ring or are lucky enough to be receiving a diamond that has been passed down through the family, it is important to understand some of the earlier cuts and how they differ from modern cuts, since they are still frequently seen. In addition to differences in brilliance and fire (although many of these older stones have plenty of sparkle and lots of fire—we've even seen some we prefer to some modern cut stones), they are valued at less than modern cuts.

Old mine- and old European-cuts, when appraised, are evaluated by comparison to modern cuts. The appraiser will calculate how much weight loss would be incurred if the stone were recut into a modern cut, and adjust the appraised value by the same amount—even if you have no plans to recut it. For example, if you have a 1-carat old European-cut diamond, and you take it to be appraised, the appraiser would grade the color and clarity and calculate how much a 1-carat, well-cut modern stone of the same color and clarity would sell for today. The appraiser would then determine how much weight would be lost to recut the stone into a well-cut modern stone. If he estimates a weight loss of 15%, he would reduce the value by 15%. If a modern cut stone comparable to your 1-carat stone would sell for $10,000, the appraiser would value the stone at $8,500 (15% off of $10,000). Some old mine- or old European-cut stones can lose 20-30% of their weight, if recut, and their value would be adjusted accordingly.

If a stone is well cut for its period, and has liveliness and sparkle, we do not recommend recutting it—especially if you plan to leave it in a period or antique ring. Keeping the stone(s) as originally cut will preserve the integrity of the piece and may actually enhance the value of the *ring*. However, if you personally prefer a modern cut, or if the older cut was not well done, recutting may be a desirable option. It is not very expensive and an appraiser or fine jeweler should be able to give you an estimate based on how much labor would be involved in the recutting.

❖ *Modern Diamond Shapes*

In choosing a design and style that suits your taste, budget, and personality, one of the first steps is to decide on the diamond shape you want. Today there are eight shapes that have become very popular, all variations on the round, brilliant-cut developed by Tolkowsky. They include:

Round   Photo: Diamond Information Center

Pear-shape   Photo: Diamond Information Center

Marquise   Photo: Diamond Information Center

Oval   Photo: Diamond Information Center

Emerald   Photo: Diamond Information Center

Heart-shape   Photo: Diamond Information Center

Photo: Radiant Cut Diamond Corporation   *Radiant*   Photo: John Farrell, New York City

Ring by Richard Kimball, photo by Stephen Ramsey   *Princess*   Photo: Ambar Diamonds, Inc.

A Word About "Fancy" Cuts

Fancy cuts—any shape other than a round, brilliant-cut—can vary in their width and length and basic proportioning. To some extent, the choice of shape is a very personal matter—some people prefer a long, thin pear-shape, while others like a more triangular pear-shape. Although there is no "ideal" make for fancy shapes as there is for the round, brilliant-cut, one must be careful that the stone is not cut in such a way that its liveliness and brilliance is reduced or adversely affected. (see Chapter 4).

Popular Cuts Frequently Used As Side Stones For Accent

In addition to the eight fancy shapes described in the preceding section, there are several cuts that are frequently used as side accents. The most popular include straight baguettes, tapered baguettes, and two new shapes—the trilliant and princess (also called quadrillion).

Baguettes have been popular for many years and create a very traditional look. In both straight and tapered shapes, they are understated and serve simply to lead the eye to the important center-stone.

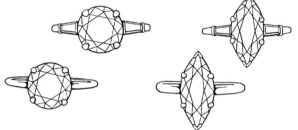

Solitaire diamond rings mounted with and without tapered baguettes. Tapered baguettes can be used to accent any shape diamond.

The trilliant is a relative newcomer that has quickly become one of the most popular choices to create an elegant and classic look. It is a triangular shape that has been cut with extra facets to create tremendous brilliance and liveliness. The trilliant, because it is cut from a very flat piece of diamond rough, also gives a very large look for its actual weight. It provides an important look to balance a large center-stone, within a reasonable budget.

The princess cut, shown on the preceding page, is also very popular as a choice for side stones.

Again, the use of side stones to accent a center-stone, and the shape of the side-stone, is a matter of personal choice. In addition to baguettes and trilliants, almost any of the other popular shapes can be found in small sizes and can be used to create an interesting and distinctive ring.

Photo: John Farrell, New York City.

A radiant cut solitaire and a marquise solitaire, each flanked on either side by a trilliant-cut. The center can be a diamond or colored gem; the side stones can be diamond or colored gems.

Photo: James Breski & Co., Chicago, Illinois

A *pair of cushion-cut sapphires. Notice they are neither round nor oval, but a pleasing shape in-between.*

Photo: Benjamin Zucker, Precious Stones Company, New York

❖ *Popular Shapes in Colored Gems*

Colored gems can be found in any of the shapes described for diamonds. In addition, they are often seen in the "cushion-cut," a modified oval.

Keep in mind that some gems are more easily found in particular shapes than in others. For example, emeralds are most often seen in a rectangular shape (actually called "emerald cut") because this is the shape that tends to present emerald to its best advantage. In addition, the natural crystal shape of emerald lends itself particularly well to a rectangular shape.

Rubies and sapphires are often seen in the cushion-cut, as pictured above. This cut seems to exhibit the rich, lush color of these stones more fully than other cuts. On the other hand, one rarely sees sapphire or ruby in an emerald-cut. Once again, your choice is very much a personal matter. But be sure to select a shape that is readily available in the stone of your choice.

CHAPTER 17

Choosing Your Setting

The setting you choose will be determined primarily by your personal taste. Nevertheless, it is a good idea to be familiar with a few of the most common settings so that you have a working vocabulary and some idea of what is available.

Bezel setting. With a bezel setting, a rim holds the stone and completely surrounds the gem. Bezels can have straight edges, scalloped edges, or can be molded into any shape to accommodate the stone. The backs can be open or closed. One advantage of the bezel setting is that it can make a stone look larger. The bezel setting can also conceal nicks or chips on the girdle. It can also protect the girdle from becoming chipped or nicked.

Keep in mind that if you use yellow gold in a bezel setting, the yellow of the bezel surrounding the stone will be reflected into the stone, causing white stones to appear less white. On the other hand, a yellow gold bezel can make a red stone such as ruby look even redder, or an emerald look greener.

A variation on the bezel setting is the *collet* setting. The collet setting has a similar appearance to the bezel setting but involves the use of gold tubing.

Prong setting. Prong settings are perhaps the most common type of setting. They come in an almost infinite variety. There are four-prong, six-prong, and special styles, such as Belcher, Fishtail, and six-prong Tiffany. In addition, prongs can be pointed, rounded, flat, or V-shaped. Extra prongs provide added security for the stone and can make a stone look slightly larger. However, too many prongs holding too small a stone can over-power the stone and make it look heavy. When setting a marquise,

Flat-top or bead setting   Bar settings   Channel setting

Pave setting   Cluster setting

Bezel settings   Four-prong setting   Six-prong setting

Prong setting for an emerald-cut stone   Fishtail setting   Belcher setting

Gypsy setting   Illusion setting

heart-shape, or pear-shape stone, we recommend that the point or points be held by a V-shaped prong, which will best protect the point(s). For emerald-cut stones which have canted corners, straight, flat prongs are the best choice.

A pear-shaped diamond showing a V-shaped prong holding the point *and two normal prongs holding the upper portion.*
Photo: Diamond Information Center

Notice the collet setting of the top ring. The other rings are bezel-set and channel-set.
George Sawyer, Minneapolis, Mn. Photo by Jos. Giannetti, Minneapolis

Gypsy setting. In this type of setting, the metal at the top of the ring (around the stone) is much heavier than the shank. The stone is set flush into a hole at the top.

Illusion setting. The illusion setting is used to make the mounted stone appear larger.

Flat-top and bead settings. In a flat-top setting a faceted stone is placed into a hole in the flat top of the metal and then held in place by small chips of metal attached at the stone's girdle. Sometimes these metal chips are worked into small beads, so this setting is sometimes called a bead setting.

Channel setting. This setting is used extensively today, especially for wedding bands. The stones are set into a channel with no metal separating them. In some cases the channel can continue completely around the ring, so that the piece has a continuous row of stones.

Bar setting. This setting, which resembles a channel setting, combines the contemporary and classic look. It is used in a circular band and, rather than using prongs, each stone is held in the ring by a long thin bar, shared between two stones.

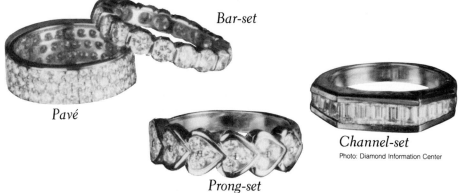

Bar-set

Pavé

Channel-set
Photo: Diamond Information Center

Prong-set
within a heart-shaped outline

Pavé setting. This setting is used for numerous small stones set together in a cluster with no metal showing through. The impression is that the piece is entirely paved with stones. The setting can be flat or dome-shaped, and can be worked so that the piece almost appears to be one large single stone. Fine pavé work can be very expensive.

Cluster setting. A cluster setting usually consists of one large stone and several smaller stones as accents. A cluster setting is designed to create a lovely larger piece from several small stones.

❖ *A Few Popular Ring Designs*

Solitaire. The solitaire is precisely what its name denotes: a *single* (solitary) stone mounted in a setting. The stone can be any shape (brilliant, emerald, pear, etc.), and the setting can be any style that sets off the stone to its best advantage (prong, illusion, fishtail, etc.).

A solitaire can also have small side stones that enhance the important center stone. The most classic solitaire look using side stones normally has a tapered baguette on each side or, for a newer look, the trilliant. This style is equally beautiful whether you use a diamond or colored center stone. Today, we are also seeing diamond center stones with *colored side stones*.

Traditional solitaire settings.
Photos: Diamond Information Center

Some contemporary solitaire styles
Courtesy: Lazare Kaplan International Inc.

Multi-stone Rings. Multi-stone rings usually contain several stones of comparable size, each one being important. This ring style almost always contains an odd number of stones—3, 5, or 7—which creates the most pleasing aesthetic balance. Some people however, prefer the center stone slightly larger to achieve a slight tapering in the shape of the ring. Multi-stone rings offer many creative alternatives. One can use diamonds alone, colored stones alone, a mixture of colored stones and diamonds, and/or a mixture of shapes.

Multi-stone rings can create a very important look that will also be more affordable than a single, larger stone. Today's designers and jewelry manufacturers are showing some of the most exciting multi-stone designs ever. A wide variety is available so be sure you take the time to shop around to see what is right for you.

A three-stone ring with a ruby in the center and a diamond on each side.

Ring: Maurice Shire.
Photo: John Farrell,
New York

Distinctive Contemporary Settings

There are an increasing number of engagement and wedding ring designs that appeal to the more independent woman who seeks to make a more personal statement. There are also an increasing number of custom jewelry designers catering to the market. The result is an almost limitless choice, ranging from wide, sculpted gold and platinum combinations containing unusual fancy cut stones, to intricate antique reproductions.

A three-stone diamond ring.
Photo: Diamond Information Center

Wedding Ring Sets

Many couples prefer wedding ring sets. There are many lovely designs, textures and shapes from which to choose. Wedding ring sets offer the benefit of an interlocking or perfectly fitting wedding band, often with a matching band for the groom. In addition, sets usually offer distinctive styling at a more affordable price than custom design.

Settings To Suit Your Lifestyle

It is important to consider your lifestyle when selecting the shape of the stone and the design of your ring. Be realistic about the wear-and-tear your ring must take and realize that while "diamonds are forever," no piece of jewelry is indestructible. Remember, even diamond, the hardest natural substance known, can chip or break if exposed to a sharp accidental blow.

Active outdoor types, for example, might be better off avoiding the marquise or pear-shape. The pear-shape has a point at one end and the marquise has two points, one at each end. Points are more vulnerable to chipping or breaking, which could result from a sudden or sharp blow to which a very active person might be more vulnerable.

The shank as well as the prongs of a ring worn daily by a very active person will also show the effects of wear; any detailing on your ring will blur over time, as the result of gardening, playing on the beach, mountain-climbing, handling ski equipment or bicycles, etc.

The classic four- or six-prong setting served a less active generation well, but may not be as well suited to today's woman. If your daily schedule features a great deal of activity, you would be wise to consider a sturdier engagement ring and wedding band. *Remember:* sturdy and graceful are not mutually exclusive. Bezel settings do not detract from a gemstone's brilliance, yet they will afford you greater security.

Note: It is important to have a reputable jeweler check mountings and settings once every six months. Chlorine attacks soldering links and stress points, so if you swim regularly in a chlorinated pool, take your ring off when you swim and/or have it checked frequently.

In terms of design, rings are usually round, fingers aren't. Top-heavy rings will turn on the finger unless the diameter, or outline, is square or stirrup-shaped to conform to the shape of the finger. Also, remember that rings worn together side by side quickly begin to wear on each other.

In considering which metal is best, remember that color is a personal choice. The higher the gold karatage, the richer the color; but the higher the karatage, the softer the metal. Also, white gold is stronger than yellow. Platinum is expensive, but it is also tougher than gold—rather than abrading easily, platinum tends to "roll over itself" much like warm wax does when you roll it between your fingers. This tends to make a platinum setting more durable than a gold setting, but both metals dent and scratch equally.

❖ *Shopping Tips*

- *Set a realistic budget* range to eliminate confusion and temptation that can result in disappointment.
- *Shop around and familiarize yourself with current styles* to educate your eye and learn what really appeals to you.
- *Try on different styles*—rings look different on the hand than they do in the window. We know of women who really disliked a ring seeing it in the showcase and then loved it on their hand.
- *Decide what is important to you.* Is size important? Do you prefer size to other qualities? Do you feel you need a smaller stone because you have very tiny fingers; or if you have very long fingers, do you feel you must have a larger stone so that it won't look lost? What shape looks best? If you're considering a colored gem, do you prefer lighter or darker shades of color? Do you prefer yellow gold or white gold/platinum? Will yellow gold or white gold provide the best setting for your stone? What width should the ring be for your finger?
- *Consider the wedding band when you select your engagement ring.* As you select your engagement ring, remember that you will also be wearing a wedding band. Be sure to select a style that will complement the type of wedding band you are considering.

CHAPTER 18

The Heirloom Ring

*I*f you are thinking of giving an heirloom or estate piece as an engagement or wedding ring, or are considering taking stones out of an heirloom piece, the first step is to have the piece appraised by a qualified gemologist-appraiser. The appraisal will verify that the ring is what you believe it to be, will fully describe its quality, and identify whether or not there are any problems— that is, if the stone is chipped or cracked in such a way that it may be vulnerable to breakage. With full knowledge of the stone, you can take any necessary precautions when wearing or resetting it. For example, if a diamond has been chipped from wear over the years and the chip has resulted in a small fracture that penetrates the stone, when resetting it you have to consider what kind of setting is best. Can a prong conceal and protect the stone? Possibly a bezel setting will be most advantageous.

One point to keep in mind when updating or resetting an heirloom: Some require custom-made settings that are more expensive than settings already made. Today, there are many styles of rings that can accommodate almost any stone.

It is much easier and less expensive to find a desirable setting if you are using a round stone. A stone other than a round may require custom setting or a jeweler who can customize part of the setting to suit the shape of your stone.

Take extra precaution with antique settings. Chances are the setting has been repaired over the years, and may well have been improperly fixed. This is frequently the case with platinum pieces. Often platinum settings have been restored or repaired with white gold solder, which is actually a different color from the original piece.

It is a good idea to closely examine any antique platinum piece for minute cracks that may have formed around open work or bridge work. A jeweler may have inadvertently damaged the platinum in the process of doing a minor repair (a jeweler unaccustomed to working with platinum may immerse the piece in sulphuric acid after soldering—this breaks down the molecular structure of the metal, causing it to begin to crack and deteriorate). A platinum piece that has begun to crack as a result of sulfuric acid cannot be restored and is unstable. Be sure to check for signs of deterioration in the prong areas and other thin places.

❖ *Tips on Updating an Heirloom or Older Piece*

When To Redesign

- *When you don't like the style of the ring,* whether it looks outdated or is simply not your taste.
- *When the setting is in need of repair,* but the techniques involved are too expensive to make it worthwhile. Take, for example, a ring with extensive damage to the enameling, or a ring with delicate granulation or extensive filigree.
- *When the overall piece is too small for your taste.* A new setting using a bold gold or platinum design can add size and importance to a smaller stone.
- *When you wish to use just the stone(s)* from another piece of jewelry, such as a pendant or brooch.

❖ *How to Create Something New from Something Old*

Getting Started

The first step in creating a new look out of an antique or old piece is to know exactly what you have and what condition it is in. Have the piece examined and evaluated by a qualified gemologist-appraiser. The examination should include:

1. *Verification of what the stone is.* Is it what you believe it is or something else? Is it genuine, synthetic, or imitation? Just because it has been in the family is no guarantee of its true

identity. For your protection *and* the jeweler's, check it out first. For more information on the use of enhancement techniques used in antique and estate jewelry, *Gem Identification Made Easy* (GemStone Press, South Woodstock, VT., 1989) describes them in a chapter devoted to this subject.

2. *Full description of the stone.* (The 4C's discussed in Chapters 4–7).

3. *Notation of condition and any problem areas,* including any scratches, chips, cracks, etc.. It is helpful if these are indicated on a sketch, showing their positions on (or in) the stone. If there is anything else that the jeweler should know about your stone before beginning work on your ring, have the appraiser make a notation. For example, some stones can't take high temperatures and any jewelry technique using intense heat could damage the stone.

Be sure to give the jeweler who will be making the ring a copy of this information so proper precautions can be taken.

Selecting the Jeweler

Be sure to select a fine jeweler who has experience working with stones as well as metal. A jeweler who creates beautiful gold or silver jewelry is not necessarily skilled at making jewelry that uses stones. Also, if you are using a stone other than a diamond for your ring, the jeweler should be experienced in colored gems as well—they are more difficult to work with than diamonds.

Ask for recommendations from friends or acquaintances who have had pieces remade.

Ask your appraiser for recommendations. If you don't know anyone who can offer a recommendation, ask your appraiser— they are often aware of good jewelers in the community and familiar with their work.

Meet with the jeweler and look at his work. Jewelry design is like art . . . what appeals to someone else may not appeal to you; what is considered "great" by someone else may not be to your own personal liking. Try to find someone whose work excites you.

Working with the Jeweler To Design the Ring

When you find someone whose work you like, give them as much information as you can about what you like and what you're looking for. Look through magazines and catalogues and clip pictures of rings you admire, even if there are little details you would want to change. Give these to the jeweler and discuss the details you like or don't like. Do your best to help the jeweler clearly understand what you want.

Have the jeweler provide sketches, if possible, showing both top and side views. Some jewelers won't do this, but will be happy to make a wax model. Always request a model so that you can have a clearer view of what the finished piece will look like. This way alterations can be made before the ring is cast and stones are set. Do keep in mind, however, that the wax models have a heavier, clunkier look than the finished piece. A little imagination is required to get a real sense of the ring. Even so, important details can be refined and altered at this stage more easily than after the ring is completed.

Remember: Jewelers are not mind readers. You may have an idea in mind that you think you can describe in words. Most people can't. It is difficult to communicate with words alone an image that only you can see. All too often the big day arrives, you go to get your ring, and your heart sinks upon seeing it. This is why it is so important to take the extra time to work with sketches and models—to help ensure that your heart will soar when you see the ring you will treasure forever!

CHAPTER 19

Tips on Getting The Diamond You Really Want Within Your Budget

*I*f you have an unlimited budget, you may feel it's important to have a large stone of the finest quality available—a "D" Flawless with an "ideal make," or a rich velvety blue Kashmir sapphire or fire-engine red Burma ruby. But for most of us who must work within a limited budget, selecting the correct stone and the correct ring is a matter of learning how to juggle, and discovering what factors will best meet our needs, emotional as well as financial.

• *Go for color and sparkle first.* If you have a limited budget, you have to compromise on something—either the size, color, clarity grade (flaw grade), or liveliness. Of these four factors, one can see size, color and liveliness. In terms of what most people notice on the finger, the clarity grade is the *least* important in our opinion. Personally, on a limited budget we would choose a stone with the best possible color and the liveliest personality.

What most people don't understand is that even in SI_2 stones, flaws are not really noticeable when the stone is being worn, and, in most cases, can't be seen at all without using a magnifier. In fact, if you take a well-cut 1-carat D/Flawless diamond and hold it next to a well-cut 1-carat D/SI_2 diamond, you will not see any difference with the naked eye. Contrary to what many think, it is not the clarity grade that determines how lively and brilliant a diamond will be, but its cut and proportioning. And you may feel much more sparkling yourself if you can spend $8,000 for a diamond (D/SI_2) that could look like a $30,000 (D/ IF) diamond to anyone without a magnifier!

The stone's brilliance and liveliness is as important as its color.

After all, that's what sets the gem apart from glass and cheap imitations. A well-cut diamond has more sparkle—more brilliance and "fire"—than any other gem. But the key to the sparkle is in its being well cut. We have seen diamonds that were so badly cut that they had no life at all. In fact, one might just as well be looking at a piece of glass.

For this reason, we prefer stones with "ideal" makes, or makes that come close to ideal. Stones that are cut to look a little larger than they actually are can also be pretty, but when they are cut *too spread*, they will be lifeless. In our opinion, we'd rather buy a stone that's cut exceptionally well—a stone that really dances before the eye—even though it costs more. Because it does cost more, we would consider lowering the color grade a little in exchange for the best possible "make," or coming down in size a little. As you shop around, be sure to pay attention to the way a stone is cut. Ask to see stones with "ideal" makes. You'll soon be able to spot differences in brilliance and liveliness. Then your eye will help you find the right balance for your own budget.

• *A small difference in points can make a big difference in dollars.* The cost of a diamond increases significantly when it reaches the full, 1-carat weight. However, try to find a diamond that weighs 90 points (there are 100 points to a carat, so a 90-pointer is 9/10 of a carat). When set, few can see the difference between a 90-point diamond and one that is a full 1-carat stone. The difference, however, is very noticeable in dollars. Where a fine 1-carat diamond (G/VS$_1$ quality) might sell for $9,000, the same quality stone weighing 90 points might cost only $7,500. The money you save could pay for a beautiful diamond-studded wedding band!

If you are considering a diamond in the 2-carat range, the difference is even greater. While a full 2-carat diamond in the quality described above might cost $30,000, a diamond weighing 1.90 carats might cost only $24,000—saving you $6,000.

One word of caution: Be careful that you aren't sold a stone that is too "spread" (a term used to describe a stone that is cut to look larger than its real weight). We've seen stones weighing 90 points that are actually LARGER in dimension than a full 1-carat stone that is cut well; we've seen stones weighing 1.90 carats that are actually larger in dimension than a well-cut 2-carat stone. These stones usually lack the brilliance and sparkle of a well-made stone. You may be pleased with their size, but make sure you are pleased with the sparkle. After all, if you're paying for a diamond, you deserve a stone that shows its full beauty.

• *What to consider when selecting the color grade.* "D" color is the rarest and most expensive color in white diamonds. There are very few diamonds that receive this very high grade. Diamonds graded from D through H on the GIA scale are graded in the "white" range by other grading systems and, when mounted, will appear white. I and J colors are called "slightly tinted" by other systems and you may see some yellowish or brownish tint in the stone's body color. K and L may also be called "tinted white" and you can more easily see the tint. M through Z may also be called "tinted color" or "off-white" and appear yellowish- or brownish-white.

The difference in cost between D and E color, however—even though both are considered "white" diamonds—can be significant. In a 1-carat diamond, the cost of a D/Flawless could be $30,000, while the same stone if it were E color might only be $20,000; a one-carat stone D/VS$_1$ might retail for $14,000 while the same stone in E color might cost only $11,000.

It is important to remember that when a diamond is set, it is extremely difficult to tell the difference between D, E, and F color without comparing them immediately next to each other. For those on a budget, selecting a diamond with an E, F, or G color rather than D might enable you to best meet all your expectations—a "white" diamond with lots of sparkle in a pleasing size.

• *The color of your setting can make your diamond appear whiter.* If you are on a limited budget, keep in mind that if you feel you can't afford a diamond as white as you would like and still have the size and sparkle that's important, setting the stone in white gold or platinum may make the stone appear whiter than it really is. Less-white diamonds (through L-M color) can actually look whiter in a white gold or platinum setting—the whiteness of the metal is reflected into the diamond and masks the yellow, making the stone appear whiter. Yellowish tinted diamonds (M-Z) usually look whiter in a yellow gold setting, where the contrast with the bright yellow of the setting masks the yellowish tint of the diamond, and often makes it appear whiter.

• *Flaws may mar the beauty of your diamond ring less than you think.* On a budget, they may add beauty! As we discussed in

Chapter 6 on flaw grading, flaws cannot normally be seen in a mounted diamond with the naked eye until the classification I_1! And even in stones classified as "I_1" flaws are normally not immediately visible when the stone is set, especially when being worn. So, while it's important to know what the flaw grade is to be sure you are paying the correct price, this is the factor one can stretch the farthest without affecting the beauty of the stone you select. It's one area in which juggling can dramatically affect the budget while not affecting the sparkle. Therefore, we normally recommend trying to meet your personal preferences regarding the other three factors first. The price difference between Flawless or Internally Flawless, and each successive grade, can be dramatic. As we mentioned earlier, a one carat D/IF might well cost $30,000 and a 1-carat D/SI_2 only $8,000. Looking at the stones without using a loupe, the D/SI_2 would appear exactly like the D/IF! (All else being equal, of course.)

• *Consider shapes other than round.* While the round, brilliant-cut diamond is considered by most to be the cut that exhibits the diamond's maximum beauty, it normally looks smaller than diamonds cut in other shapes. Today women are showing an increased interest in other shapes. In comparison to the round, pear-shaped diamonds and marquise-shaped diamonds look larger.

• *Consider a design that uses several small stones rather than one large diamond.* As we discussed in greater depth in the preceding chapter, many beautiful designs use several small diamonds rather than one large diamond. These designs offer a beautiful way to keep the budget down. The smaller the diamond, the lower the price per-carat. For example, a 1-carat round, brilliant-cut diamond set in a solitaire ring might cost $5,000, while a ring containing three stones having a total weight of 1-carat (each stone weighing ⅓ carat) might sell for only $2,500; or a diamond band containing seven diamonds (with each stone weighing only ⅐ carat) with a total weight of 1-carat might cost only $1,500. As you can see, the solitaire, while it is the most popular style among brides-to-be, is also the most expensive.

Look around at the innovative designs available in multi-stone rings. These offer an alternative that can create a very important and individual look.

• *Illusion settings.* Certain settings create an illusion that the diamond is larger than it is. (See preceding chapter.)

• *Bold designs in gold and platinum add importance* and distinctiveness to smaller diamonds. New designs reflecting today's more independent woman have had a major impact on the engagement ring and wedding band market. Using wider, innovative designs in metal can create a very impressive look, using a smaller diamond (under 1-carat) as well as larger stones.

• *Listen to your heart as well as your head.* The most important consideration in the selection of your ring is how you *feel* about it. You want to feel a thrill; you want to feel excited; you want it to be *your* choice. If you really prefer yellow gold, don't let someone talk you into platinum; if you really prefer the pear-shape, don't let someone talk you into round.

One of our clients was torn between two diamonds—one had the finest possible color (D) and she knew it was the "better" stone. The other was a little larger and it wasn't quite as white (F color), but it had a magnificent make and the sparkle was really dazzling. She decided on the slightly larger stone, even though it was F color, because she was honest with herself and her fiancé—she really preferred a stone that was a little larger, and she was constantly drawn back to that stone because of its "personality." The other diamond was really a "better" stone, but it wasn't the one she really felt excited about. She made the right choice in going with her heart and not her head!

PART FIVE

THE WEDDING BANDS

Ring: Reinstein Ross

Ring: Wedding Rings Inc.

Ring: Diamond Essence

Ring: Cartier

Ring: Fortunoff

Photos: David Tomono

Ring: Reinstein Ross

CHAPTER 20

Choosing the Wedding Bands

There are virtually hundreds of styles of wedding bands from which to choose, for both the bride *and* the groom. While the traditional band for both is a simple, round gold ring, today they can be simple or elaborate, wide or thin, gem-studded or not. It is not unusual, even in the groom's ring, to find gemstone accents.

Traditionally, the woman receives two rings—one upon consenting to marriage and the second at the wedding ceremony. Today, this tradition continues to be the most popular choice. However, couples sometimes opt for a more important wedding band that incorporates the gem of choice and eliminates the need for an engagement ring, as such. For example, rather than purchasing an engagement ring with a 1-carat diamond followed by a simple wedding band, one might purchase for the same price a diamond wedding band that contains 4-carats total weight of diamonds encircling the finger.

The diamond wedding band then becomes the single focal point and combines the symbolism of the simple round ring with the symbolism of the diamond or other stone of choice. It can create an important and classic look. Another example might involve the purchase of a single diamond that is then set within a very wide, gold wedding band, again combining the gem traditionally received at an earlier moment within the wedding band itself.

The choice as to whether to have one or two rings is largely personal, but keep in mind that the length of the engagement may affect your decision. If the engagement is going to be long, rather than waiting for the wedding day the bride-to-be may prefer to have an engagement ring to announce the change in her status and the upcoming event.

Wedding
Band
Widths

❖ *Important Considerations*
Before You Make the Choice

To help you make the right choice for the wedding ring, here are some important factors to consider.

2

How does the wedding band look with the engagement ring? If an engagement ring is given, it is very important to consider how the wedding band will look with it on the hand. (We hope that before making the final decision on your engagement ring, you also give some thought to your wedding band.) It's a good idea to try on different styles of wedding bands with the engagement ring to see how they look together. The width of the band can dramatically affect the way it works with the engagement ring. Remember also that certain details such as milgraining (see Chapter 21) or a particular type of finish may look great when worn alone, but could detract from the overall appearance when worn together with the engagement ring.

3

4

5

What width looks best? The width of the wedding band is measured in millimeters. The standard lady's simple gold or platinum band ranges from 2 millimeters to 4 millimeters; the man's ranges from 3½ millimeters to 6 millimeters. Stock sizes can go as wide as ten millimeters. It is important to try the same style band in different widths because you will be surprised to see how different the effect created by width alone can be. Avoid very wide rings that feel uncomfortable when you try them on. You will *not* get used to them. While a very wide band may be beautiful from a design standpoint, keep in mind that it may be less comfortable in very hot climates.

6

8

Do you prefer a "flat" band or a "half-round" band? A flat band is flatter on the finger, while a half round has a somewhat curved or dome-like shape to it. The decision is purely a matter of personal taste.

10

ACTUAL WIDTH
IN MILLIMETERS

Do you prefer "matching" bands? Most wedding ring manufacturers today offer a wide selection of matching ladies' and men's wedding bands.

Do you plan to wear the wedding band without the engagement ring? If you think you may frequently wear your wedding band without your engagement ring, you may prefer a different type of band. For example, some women prefer to wear only their wedding band at the office; some prefer to wear their engagement ring only in social situations. If you think this might be the case with you, you may prefer a larger or more important looking band, one that will stand on its own.

A half-round band

A flat band

For gem studded-bands

Should the stones completely encircle the ring? This is a decision that depends on personal taste, budget, comfort, and fit. Many prefer that the stones continue around the entire ring, while others want the stones set only across the top. The primary benefit in having stones all around is that you never need to worry about the ring twisting on your finger. A significant disadvantage is that some of the stones are subjected to strenuous wear which can result in breakage and loss. The choice is really not an economic one—by juggling the size and quality of the stones and the width of the ring, you can get either look on any budget.

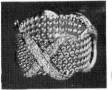

Some diamond-studded wedding or anniversary bands designed by Schlumberger.

Photo: Tiffany & Co.

Does the ring fit properly? When selecting a gem-studded style, be sure to try rings that actually fit your finger properly. Otherwise you may find that a ring feels very uncomfortable on your finger when, in fact, it would be very comfortable if it fit properly. This is particularly true for rings with larger stones held by prongs. Also, for rings with stones going part way around, proper fit is critical to comfort because it affects the contour of the top portion of the ring.

We will not discuss the many different styles of wedding bands here since the selection is truly limitless. We have provided photographs of a variety of the most popular styles in the color insert section, and we encourage you to use your own imagination. In the following chapter we will focus on what you need to know to understand gold and platinum.

CHAPTER 21

Gold and Platinum Wedding Bands

❖ The Gold Wedding Band

Since primitive times, brides and bridegrooms have sealed their wedding vows with a symbolic exchange of rings. As illustrated in folklore and fantasy, once this exchange takes place, the marriage begins.

The history of the gold wedding band is indeed long and illustrious. Before the introduction of coinage, gold rings were circulated as currency. A man would give his bride a gold ring as a sign that he trusted her with his property. Under Roman law, a bridegroom would furnish a ring as a sign of security, a form of collateral to protect the interests of the bride-to-be. Some believe that the idea of using a ring to seal the pact dates back to the time in Iceland when a marriage pledge was made by a man passing his hand through a large iron ring to clasp the hand of his beloved.

During the engagement period in Elizabethan times, three rings were distributed: one to be worn by the groom, one to be worn by the bride, and one to be worn by a witness. At the time of the wedding, all three would be united on the bride's finger!

The pharaohs of Egypt wore their wedding ring on the third finger of the left hand because of the *vena amoris*, a vein that they believed ran from that finger directly to the heart. In many cultures, the wedding ring is worn on another finger, but the pharaoh's finger remains the choice of most American brides and grooms.

To the ancients, the circular shape of the ring symbolized eternity. Even today, in some religious ceremonies, the couple is married with rings that have no stones or other "interruptions" that might affect the heavenly circle—the circle of life and happiness that has no beginning and no end.

In modern times, millions of couples exchange gold bands at their wedding ceremony. The circlet of gold has become the universal symbol of trust and commitment between two loving people. The simple gold wedding band probably uses more of the world's gold than any other single type of jewelry.

❖ *What Is Gold?*

Gold is one of the world's most precious metals. It combines four basic characteristics that have made it since earliest times a treasured possession: lustrous beauty, easy workability, rarity, and virtual indestructibility. Gold is so soft and malleable that one ounce can be stretched into a wire five miles long, or hammered into a sheet so thin it covers 100 square feet. Gold is so rare that only an estimated 102,000 tons have been taken from the earth during all of recorded history. More steel is poured in one hour than gold has been poured since the beginning of time. Since it does not rust, tarnish, or corrode, gold virtually lasts forever. Coins found in sunken galleons centuries old are as bright and shiny as the day they were cast.

Through the years, gold has held a preeminent position as the metal most desired for jewelry. In many parts of the world, the finest pieces of jewelry are fashioned in 18- or 22-karat gold. In the United States, 14- or 18-karat gold is preferred for fine jewelry because it is more durable than higher karat gold.

Although gold is everywhere around us—in the earth's crust, in our seas, rivers, and plants—it is difficult and expensive to extract. Two-and-a-half to three tons of ore are required to extract just one ounce of the precious metal. It is a small wonder that gold remains so rare and valuable, and is therefore an appropriate symbol commemorating the rarity and value of a good marriage. The leading producers of gold today include Australia, Brazil, Canada, USSR, Union of South Africa, and the United States.

What Is A Karat?

A karat is the measure of the actual amount of pure gold present. Pure gold (also called "fine gold") is 24 karats. But gold in this pure state is really too soft for use in jewelry. We would never recommend a metal so soft as pure gold for the wedding band, a ring that will be worn for a lifetime. By mixing or alloying it with other metals, however, its hardness can be increased. The term karat is used to designate the proportion of pure gold in an alloy. The word karat derives from the Italian *carato*, the Arabic *qirat*, or the Greek *keration*, all signifying the fruit of the carob tree. The seeds of the fruit were used in ancient times for weighing gems. As applied to gold, the 1/24th measurement stems from the weight of the *solidus*, a gold coin used in Byzantium from 312 A.D. to 1453 A.D.

Pure or fine gold is 24 karats. Eighteen karat gold consists of 18 parts of pure gold mixed with 6 parts of other metals. Fourteen karat gold is 14 parts pure gold, combined with ten parts of other metals.

American Marking (Karatage)		Pure Gold Content		European Marking (Fineness)
24K	=	100%	=	999
18K	=	75%	=	750
14K	=	58.5%	=	585
10K	=	41.6%	=	416

The law is very strict with regard to tolerances allowed for gold jewelry. A karat mark along with a registered trademark will assure you that tolerances are being met and the gold is of the specified quality. Any suspected violation should be reported in writing to: Jewelers Vigilance Committee, 1185 Avenue of the Americas, Room 2020, New York, New York 10036.

Legally, to be called "gold," minimum standards have been established in most countries. Metals containing anything less than these minimum requirements cannot be called gold.

Minimum Gold Standards

Canada	9KT
England	9KT
France	18KT
Italy	18KT
United States	10KT

❖ *The Colors of Gold*

Pure or 24-karat gold is always yellow. But because pure gold is too soft for use in jewelry, mixing it with other metals not only increases its hardness, but allows modifications in color. The natural beauty of gold is enhanced by the lovely, soft shades of color achieved by combining it with small amounts of other precious metals. Alloys most commonly used in gold jewelry manufacturing are: copper, zinc, silver, and nickel.

Recently it has become very fashionable to mix different colors of gold in the same item of jewelry. "Tricolor" wedding rings that combine yellow, white, and pink gold are very popular because of their increased versatility.

How Alloys Affect Color

Color	Elements
Yellow Gold	Gold, Copper, Silver
White Gold	Gold, Nickel,* Zinc, Copper
Green Gold	Gold, Silver, Copper, Zinc
Pink Gold	Gold, Copper

*Some people are allergic to nickel and should not wear white gold.

Gold Finishes

Gold has excellent working qualities that make it particularly desirable for fine jewelry. As you will see as you shop for your gold wedding bands, it is available in a wide range of finishes and styles to suit individual tastes.

Popular Finishes and Techniques

Appliqué:	Soldering a design worked in gold to another piece of gold; soldering one color gold to another.
Chasing:	Accent technique, outlining the detail of repoussé.
Diamond cut:	Sections of the surface are cut to achieve bright reflections; can create interesting design effects.
Embossing:	Ornamentation to create a bas-relief-like impression.
Enameling:	Fusing colored glass onto metal surface.

Popular finishes and techniques used in wedding bands:

Florentine finish with milgraining

Polished gold

Polished gold with milgraining

Engraving:	Cutting a design into the surface.
Filigree:	Gold wire twisted and soldered onto other metal in intricate patterns; also used to describe any intricate openwork.
Florentine:	A finish created by texturing the surface with a special tool.
Granulation:	Tiny round balls fastened to another metal by a heating process.
Hammering:	Forming indentations in metal to create interesting patterns and texture.
High polish:	Mirror-like.
Matte:	Soft, flat, non-reflective finish.
Milgraining:	A detail that resembles a string of tiny beads applied as an ornamental border.
Repoussé:	Forming a design by punching or pressing out portions from inside the ring.
Satin:	Grained texture of satin cloth; has a softer shine than "high polish."

Hallmarking

The systematic marking of gold wares began in 1300 in London when a law was introduced to protect the public against the fraudulent use of adulterated gold and silver by dishonest goldsmiths. Actually, hallmarking is one of the earliest forms of consumer protection. On March 30, 1327, London goldsmiths received a Royal Charter, forming them into the Worshipful Company of Goldsmiths and giving them powers to enforce the assay and hallmarking laws, which created a standard for the fineness of gold. The word "hallmark" is derived from "Goldsmiths Hall," the company's headquarters.

A hallmark is a stamp applied to an article of precious metal after it has been tested by assay, by an official Assay Office, to denote fineness of quality. No article or part of an article is marked unless it is first tested and found to be of the standard of quality required by law. While the assaying and marking authorities are not government officials, they operate under full legal powers. The British Hallmark, therefore, is of unquestioned integrity as a guarantee of quality, and is accepted as such in every part of the world.

A complete Hallmark consists of four punch marks that include the makers' mark, the gold-standard mark, the assay mark, and a letter designating a date.

Gold Look Alikes

There are several manufacturing methods that result in jewelry that may look like gold, but actually cannot be considered within the quality range of fine or karat gold. Beware of gold look-alikes and remember that the following terms are used for metal products that are *not* gold in the legal sense: gold filled, gold overlay, double d'or, gold plate, rolled gold plate, plaque d'or lamine, gold electroplating, gold wash or gold flash, vermeil.

❖ *The Platinum Wedding Band*

Platinum is even more rare and valuable than gold. The platinum family is composed of six elements—platinum, palladium, iridium, osmium, rhodium, and ruthenium. The six silvery-white colored metals are generally found together in nature, with platinum and palladium the most abundant, and osmium, rhodium and ruthenium, the rarest. Platinum is rarer and heavier than other precious metals and is the purest metal—often referred to as the "noblest." Most platinum jewelry also contains small amounts of the rarer and more expensive elements iridium or ruthenium for added strength. Because platinum is so pure, it rarely causes allergic reactions. This is greatly appreciated by those sensitive people who experience reaction or skin discoloration to jewelry containing base metals. In addition, platinum is somewhat stronger than other precious metals. Because of its many excellent qualities, platinum makes an excellent choice for fine jewelry. Platinum prongs are preferred by many jewelers because they can be maneuvered around a fragile stone with less risk of damaging the stone.

Unlike gold, platinum is not described in karats. In the United States, abbreviations such as PT, or plat, indicate platinum; in Europe the numerical marking 950 or PT950 indicates platinum. The finest jewelry often uses platinum mixed with 10% iridium or ruthenium for added strength. This also adds somewhat to the cost since iridium and ruthenium are rarer and more expensive members of the platinum family.

Rhodium Plating

Rhodium, another member of the platinum family, is the brightest and most reflective of all the platinum metals. Because of these qualities it is frequently used to coat silver, gold, platinum, and palladium jewelry, and as an electroplate finish. Rhodium is harder and whiter even than platinum, and highly resistant to corrosion. Because rhodium is so hard, it does not wear off as quickly as yellow gold plating.

Rhodium plating is especially helpful for people who are allergic to the alloys in 10K or 14K gold. Rhodium plating can eliminate allergic reaction caused by the alloys and is also used to change the color of yellow gold to white for those people with an allergy who prefer white but can't afford platinum.

❖ *Yellow Gold, White Gold, or Platinum— Which One?*

The first choice you must make is one of color. This selection usually depends on personal preference, skin tone, and the color of other jewelry you may own. Remember when considering yellow gold that it is available in several different hues, which include a greenish-yellow and a pinkish-yellow.

If your choice is yellow, the only decision you must make is whether you prefer 14-karat or 18-karat gold. On a limited budget, 14-karat is more affordable. It is also harder than 18-karat. One noticeable difference is that 18-karat yellow gold is a brighter gold. If you prefer the brighter yellow, ask for 14-karat gold with an 18-karat *finish*. After several years, the finish may wear, but you can have a jeweler restore it at a modest cost.

If you prefer a white metal, your choice may be more difficult. While white gold and platinum may look quite similar, they are distinctly different metals. As we have mentioned, platinum is much more expensive, so if you have a limited budget, white gold is the better choice. In addition to being more affordable, 18-karat white gold is harder and more resistant to scratches. We prefer 18-karat white gold to 14-karat white because the color is whiter and it does not need to be rhodium-plated. Fourteen karat white gold usually exhibits a brownish or yellowish cast which must be covered by rhodium-plating. Rhodium-plating, however, will wear off over time and must be re-plated.

One significant disadvantage of white gold is that it is more brittle than both platinum and yellow gold. Because of this, be sure to have your jeweler check the prongs of a white gold setting at least once a year.

Platinum is somewhat softer, but this makes it easier to work with, so that a fine jeweler can create more intricate and detailed settings with it. It is much easier to do pavé work in platinum. In terms of prongs, platinum enables the jeweler to use a larger prong because the metal can conform more easily to the shape of the stone, with minimal risk of damage. The most important benefit of platinum is that, while it is softer than white gold and can scratch, it is more durable and does not wear down or abrade like gold. Therefore, over time, platinum settings hold up and last longer than gold ones.

One disadvantage to platinum is that many jewelers do not have the proper equipment to work with it. This fact, combined with the higher cost of platinum, results in a more limited variety of available styles. And if custom work is required to get the look you want, it can add substantially to the cost.

In the final analysis, it is up to you to weigh the advantages and disadvantages of each in terms of your own needs. Whichever precious metal you choose, you can find many beautiful styles and designs. With proper care, whatever choice you make should last a lifetime.

PART SIX

IMPORTANT ADVICE
BEFORE YOU BUY

CHAPTER 22

What to Ask When Buying the Stone

Asking the right questions is the key to knowing what you're getting. It is also the only way you will know what you are comparing when considering stones from different jewelers. Be sure the jeweler can answer these questions, or is able to get the answers for you. Then, be sure the jeweler is willing to put the answers *in writing* on your bill of sale. Finally, verify the facts—double-check that the stone is as represented—by having it examined by a qualified gemologist-appraiser (see Appendix). In this way you will know what you're getting, be able to make an informed choice about quality and value, and begin to develop a solid relationship with the jeweler from whom you make the purchase based on confidence and trust. And, in the event the stone is not as represented, you'll have what you need to try to get your money back.

❖ Questions to Ask When Buying a Diamond

You should always ask the following questions before purchasing a fine diamond. But, be aware that most jewelers don't take the time to grade small stones, although .50- and .75-carat stones are now beginning to appear with information designating color and flaw grades. A knowledgeable jeweler should be able to provide this information for stones .50 carats and up, or offer to find out for you.

Here are the basic questions:

- *What is the exact carat weight?* (Be sure its *weight* is given, not its *spread*.)
- *What is its color grade?* (And what grading system was used?)
- *What is its clarity (flaw) grade?* (Again, ask what system was used.)
- *What shape is it?* (marquise, brilliant, emerald?)
- *What are the exact millimeter dimensions of the stone?*
- *Is this stone accompanied by a grading report or certificate?* Ask for the full report.

Be sure to find out what system was used to grade the stone, such as GIA.

Also get the *exact* millimeter dimensions of the stone in addition to its exact carat weight. (The dimensions can be approximated if the stone is mounted.) For a round stone, make sure you are given *two* dimensions for the girdle diameter. For fancy shapes, get the dimensions of the length and width. Also, get the dimension from the table to the culet.

Be especially careful if the diamond is being taken out on consignment, on a jeweler's memorandum or sales slip, or on a contingency sale. Having the measurements on a jeweler's memorandum helps protect you from being accused of switching should you have to return the stone for any reason.

Always ask if the stone has a certificate or diamond grading report, and, if so, make sure it accompanies the stone you are considering. If you are unable to obtain the certificate or a copy, find out who determined the color and flaw grades, and make sure that the sale is contingent upon the stone's having the grades represented by the salesperson.

Some Additional Questions

Does This Stone Have a Good Make? What are the proportions of the stone? How do its proportions compare to the ideal stone? Remember, much variance can exist and a stone can still be a beautiful, desirable gem even if it does not conform to the "ideal." If you have any question about the stone's brilliance and liveliness, you should ask specifically about the proportioning of the cut.

Does This Stone Show Any Fluorescence? If a diamond fluoresces blue when viewed in daylight or under daylight-type fluorescent light, it will appear to have better color than it actually has. This can be a desirable quality so long as the stone has not been graded or classified as having finer color. A diamond may also fluoresce yellow, which means that in a certain light its color could appear worse than it actually is. If the stone is accompanied by a grading report from GIA or other respected lab, any fluorescence should be indicated on the report or certificate. If it has no report, the jeweler may not know its true color.

Special Tips When Buying a Diamond

Ask the Jeweler to Clean the Stone. Don't hesitate to ask to have the stone cleaned before you examine it. Cleaning will remove dirt, grease, or indelible purple ink. For diamonds, cleaning is best done by steaming or in an ultrasonic cleaner.

View the Stone Against a Dead White Background. When looking at unmounted stones, look at them only against a dead-white background such as white blotter paper or a white business card, or on a grading trough. Look at the stone against the white background so that you are observing it through the side, not down through the table. (See Chapter 5.) Tilt the stone toward a good light source (daylight fluorescent lamp is best). If the stone shows any yellow body tint when viewed through the girdle, if it is not as colorless as an ice cube, then the diamond is not "white" or "colorless."

Get the Facts on a Bill of Sale. Ask that all the facts concerning the stone be put on the bill of sale. These include the carat weight, the color and flaw grades, the cut, and the dimensions. Also, be sure you obtain the report on any certificated stone.

Verify Facts with a Gemologist. If a stone is 1 carat or larger and not accompanied by a respected laboratory report, make the sale contingent on verification of the facts by a qualified gemologist, gem-testing lab, or GIA. (GIA will not estimate dollar value, but they will verify color, flaw grade, make, fluorescence, weight, and other characteristics.)

Weigh the Facts. Color is the most important consideration when buying a diamond. If the color is good, then consider its "make" (precision of cutting and proportioning), flaw grade, shape, and weight, in that order.

What to Ask When Buying a Colored Gemstone

Is this a genuine, natural stone, or a synthetic?

Is the color natural? As opposed to irradiated, heat-treated, dyed.

What's in a name? Be particularly careful of misleading names (see page 131). When a stone is described with any qualifier, such as *Rio* Topaz, ask specifically whether or not the stone is genuine, and its color natural. Ask why a qualifier is being used.

What is the carat weight of the main stone(s)? And what is the total weight (if there is more than one stone)?

What is the clarity grade? Are there any flaws, inclusions, or natural characteristics in this stone that might make it more vulnerable to breakage with normal wear? This is a particularly important question when considering a colored stone. As we have mentioned, certain types of flaws or inclusions are characteristic of certain gems. An emerald without an inclusion would be immediately suspect, since it is so rare to encounter a flawless emerald. The existence of the flaw or inclusion isn't necessarily important, so long as it doesn't significantly mar the overall beauty or durability of the stone. The total number of flaws and their positioning, however, is very important. Any flaw that breaks the surface of the stone has weakened the stone significantly, particularly if the flaw is in a position that is normally exposed to wear—in the top, center portion of the stone. On the other hand, if the vulnerable area is on the side of the stone, protected by the setting, it *may* not ever pose a problem. Also, the number of flaws is important to note. Usually, a large number will detract noticeably from the beauty (especially the liveliness), and it will also generally weaken the stone and make it more susceptible to damage from any blow or knock, and so should be avoided as a choice for an engagement or wedding ring.

Also, certain gems, as we've mentioned, are more brittle than others, and may break or chip more easily even without flaws. These stones include opal, zircon, and some of the new and increasingly popular gems, such as iolite (water sapphire) and tanzanite. This does not mean you should avoid buying them, but it does mean you should give thought to how they will be worn and how they will be set. Rings are particularly vulnerable, since they are more susceptible to blows or knocks.

Is the color permanent? Another consideration should be permanence of color. For some inexplicable reason, the color in certain stones seems prone to fading. Two examples are amethyst and kunzite (one of the new and increasingly popular gems). Just which ones will and which ones won't, and over how long, no one can know. This phenomenon has never affected the popularity of amethyst and we see no reason for it to affect kunzite's popularity, but we feel the consumer should be aware of it. And perhaps some protection from too much exposure to strong sunlight, or usage restricted to evening wear, would be wise to consider.

Does the stone need a protective setting? The setting may be of special importance when considering a stone such as tanzanite, opal, or emerald. They require a setting that will offer some protection to the stone (for example, one in which the main stone is surrounded by diamonds). A design in which the stone is unusually exposed, such as in a high setting or one with open, unprotected sides, would be most undesirable.

Is the stone well-cut? Do you feel this is a well-cut stone? This is an important question to ask if the stone seems dull or lifeless, even after cleaning. If this is the case, ask if the jeweler has something that is cut better and exhibits a little more brilliance. Now you can compare it in terms of what you like and what you can afford. Remember that if a colored stone (especially one that is a pastel shade) is cut too shallow (flat), it will lose its appeal quickly because of the accumulation of grease and dirt on the back. This can be immediately remedied by a good cleaning.

What are the colorless stones? In a piece of jewelry where a colored main stone is surrounded by colorless stones to accentuate it or highlight its color, ask, "What are the colorless stones?" *Do not assume they are diamonds.* They may be diamonds, zircons, man-made diamond imitations such as CZ or YAG, or synthetic white spinel.

Information That Should Be Included On the Bill of Sale

Always make sure that any item you purchase is clearly described in the bill of sale as represented to you by the salesperson or jeweler. Essential information includes the following.

- Whether or not the stone(s) is genuine or synthetic, and not in any way a composite (doublet, triplet).
- That the color is natural if it has been so represented.
- A statement describing the overall color (hue, tone, and intensity).
- A statement describing the overall flaw picture. (This is not always necessary with colored stones. In the case of a flawless or nearly flawless stone it is wise to note the excellent clarity. Note any unusual flaw that might prove useful for identification.)
- A statement describing the cut or make. (This is not always necessary, but may be useful if it is especially well cut, or an unusual or fancy cut).
- The carat weight of the main stone(s) plus total weight if there is a combination of main stone(s) and smaller stones.
- If the piece is being represented as being made by a famous designer or house (Van Cleef and Arpels, Tiffany, Caldwell) and the price reflects this claim, the claim should be warranted on the bill of sale and the location of the mark of the designer or house should be indicated.
- If the piece is being represented as antique (technically, an antique must be at least 100 years old) and you are paying a premium for its age, the period should be stated on the bill of sale: "dating from approximately 1850," etc.
- If the stone (piece) is to be taken on approval, make sure millimeter dimensions—top to bottom, as well as length, width, or diameter—are provided, as well as a full description of the stone or piece. Also, check that a time period for acceptance or return is indicated, such as "2 days," and before you sign anything be sure that you are signing an approval form and not a binding contract for its purchase.

Special Tips to Remember When Buying a Colored Stone

Ask the jeweler to clean the stone to remove dirt and grease or color enhancers before you examine it. Because of the more fragile quality of many colored stones, it is wise not to use an ultrasonic cleaner for colored stones. (This may be the jeweler's worry if it's his stone; but if he offers to clean your lovely ring, etc., keep this in mind.)

When looking at unmounted stones, view them through the side as well as from the top. Look for evenness of color versus color zoning—shades of lighter or darker color creating streaks or planes of differing color.

Remember to give special attention to wearability. You want your engagement and wedding rings to wear for a lifetime. If you are considering one of the more fragile stones, pay special attention to the setting and be sure the stone is set in a way that will add protection.

Get the facts on the bill of sale. If a stone is an expensive 1 carat or larger, make the sale contingent on verification of the facts by a qualified gemologist, appraiser, or gem-testing lab (see Appendix).

Remember that color is the most important consideration. The presence of flaws or inclusions doesn't detract from the stone's value as significantly as with diamonds. (If the overall color or beauty is not seriously affected, the presence of flaws should not deter a purchase. But, conversely, flawless stones may bring a disproportionately higher price per carat due to their rarity, and larger sizes will also command higher prices.)

CHAPTER 23

How to Select a Reputable Jeweler

*I*t would be very difficult to give any hard-and-fast rules on this matter since there are so many exceptions. Size and years in business are not always absolute indicators of reliability. Some one-person jewelry firms are highly respected; others are not. Some well-established firms that have been in business for many years have built their trade on the highest standards of integrity and knowledge; others should have been put out of business years ago.

One point worth stressing is that for the average consumer, price alone will not be a reliable guide as an indicator of integrity or knowledge. Aside from the basic differences in quality that affect price, and which usually will not be readily discernible to the consumer, there are cost differences resulting from differences in jewelry manufacturing processes. There are many jewelry manufacturers selling mass-produced lines of good quality jewelry to jewelers all across the country. Mass-produced items, many of which are beautiful, classic designs (and sometimes knockoffs of work from a famous designer), are usually cheaper than items having a more limited production. Then there are designers who create unique pieces or limited quantities of their designs, which are available in only a few select establishments. A premium is always charged for handmade or one-of-a-kind pieces, since the initial cost of production is being paid by one individual rather than being shared by many, as in mass-produced pieces.

And jewelers do not all use the same retail markup. Markup depends upon operating costs and credit risks, among other things. The best way to select wisely is by shopping around. Go to several fine jewelry firms in your geographic area and compare items and the prices being asked for them to get a sense of what is fair in your market area. But as you do, *remember to ask the right questions to be sure you're comparing stones of comparable quality, and pay attention to design and manufacturing details.* Also as part of this process, it may be helpful to consider these questions.

- *How long has the firm been in business?* A quick check with the Better Business Bureau may reveal whether or not there are significant consumer complaints.
- *What are the gemological credentials of the jeweler, manager, or owner?* Is there a gemologist on staff? Does the store have its own laboratory?
- *How would you describe the store window?* One of jewelry nicely displayed? Or incredible bargains and come-on advertising to lure you in?
- *How would you describe the overall atmosphere?* Professional, helpful, tasteful? Or hustling, pushy, intimidating?
- *What is their policy regarding returns?* Full refund or only store credit? How many days? What basis for return?
- *Will they allow a piece to be taken "on memo"?* It won't hurt to ask. Some jewelers will. However, unless you know the jeweler personally this is not often permitted today—too many jewelers have suffered from stolen, damaged, or switched merchandise.
- *To what extent will they guarantee their merchandise to be as represented?* Be careful here. Make sure you've asked the right questions and *get the right information on the bill of sale,* or you may find yourself stuck because of a technicality. And, if you're making the purchase on a contingency basis, put the terms of the contingency on the bill of sale. If they can't or won't provide the necessary information, we recommend you go to another jeweler.

Never allow yourself to be intimidated into "trusting" anyone. Beware of the person who says "Just trust me" or who tries to intimidate you with statements such as "Don't you trust me?" A trustworthy jeweler will have no problem giving you the information you request—in writing.

• *What is their repair or replacement policy?* Be sure they give you a receipt that provides a full description. Be sure to find out if their insurance covers any damage to your piece while being repaired, redesigned or sized.

Again, in general, you will be in a stronger position to differentiate between a knowledgeable, reputable jeweler and one who isn't if you've shopped around first. Unless you are an expert, visit several firms, ask questions, examine merchandise carefully, and then you be the judge.

If You Want To File A Complaint

If any jeweler has misrepresented what they sold you, please contact the JEWELERS VIGILANCE COMMITTEE (JVC), 1185 Avenue of the Americas, Suite 2020, New York, New York 10036, (212) 869-9505. They can provide invaluable assistance to you, investigate your complaint, and take action against firms believed to be guilty of fraudulent activity in the jewelry industry.

To Sum Up

We hope you are now better informed about engagement and wedding rings and how to buy them. Use the information we provide here, but remember, it takes years of formal training and experience to become a true expert. For important purchases, always verify the facts with a qualified gemologist-appraiser.

PART SEVEN

IMPORTANT ADVICE
AFTER YOU BUY

CHAPTER 24

Choosing the Appraiser and Insurer

Why Is It Important to Get An Appraisal?

Whether you have bought a diamond or a colored gemstone ring, getting a professional appraisal and keeping it updated is critical. An appraisal is necessary for four reasons: to verify the facts about the jewelry you have purchased (especially important with the abundance of new synthetic materials and treatments); to obtain adequate insurance to protect against theft, loss, or damage; to establish adequate information to legally claim jewelry recovered by the police; and, if not recovered, to provide sufficient information to make sure that your jewelry is replaced with jewelry that actually is of "comparable quality," if that is what your insurance policy provides.

The need for appraisal services has increased greatly because of the high incidence of theft, and the sharp increases in the prices of diamonds and colored gems. It has become a necessity to have any fine gem properly appraised, particularly prior to making a purchase decision, given today's costs and the potential for loss if the gem is not accurately represented.

It is also important, given recent increases in gem prices, to update value estimations from old appraisals to ensure adequate coverage in the event of theft of gems that have been in your possession for several years or more. In addition, appraisals may be needed for inheritance taxes, gifts, or in the determination of your net worth.

❖ *How to Find a Reliable Appraiser*

The appraisal business has been booming over the past few years and many jewelry firms have begun to provide appraisal services. We must point out, however, that there are essentially no officially established guidelines for going into the "gem appraising" business. Anyone can represent themselves as an "appraiser." While there are many highly qualified professionals, there are also some who lack the expertise to offer these services. So it is essential to select an appraiser with care and diligence. Further, if the purpose of the appraisal is to verify the identity or genuineness of a gem, as well as its value, we recommend that you deal with someone who is in the business of gem identification and appraising and *not* primarily in the business of selling gems.

To assist you in finding a reliable gemologist-appraiser we have provided in the Appendix a list of internationally recognized gem-testing laboratories and gemologists, and a list of industry associations. In addition, the following suggestions should be helpful.

Obtain the names of several appraisers and then compare their credentials. To be a qualified gemologist-appraiser requires extensive formal training and experience. A preliminary check can be conducted by telephoning the appraisers and inquiring about their gemological credentials.

Some credentials to look for. The Gemological Institute of America and the Gemmological Association of Great Britain provide internationally recognized diplomas. GIA's highest award is G.G. (Graduate Gemologist) and the Gemmological Association of Great Britain awards the F.G.A. (Fellow of the Gemmological Association—and there are some who hold this honor "With Distinction"). Make sure the appraiser you select has one of these diplomas. Where possible, look for the title "Certified Gemologist Appraiser" (awarded by the American Gem Society), or "Master Gemologist Appraiser" (awarded by the American Society of Appraisers). These are currently the highest awards presented to American jewelry appraisers.

Check the appraiser's length of experience. In addition to formal training, to be reliable a gemologist-appraiser needs extensive experience in the handling of gems, use of the equipment necessary for accurate identification and evaluation, and activity in the marketplace. The appraiser should have at least several years' experience in a well-equipped laboratory. If the gem being appraised is a colored gem, the complexities are much greater and require more extensive experience. In order to qualify for CGA or MGA titles, the appraiser *must* have *at least* several years experience.

Ask where the appraisal will be conducted. An appraisal should normally be done in the presence of the customer, if possible. This is important in order to ensure that the same stone is returned to you and to protect *the appraiser* against charges of "switching." Recently we appraised an old platinum engagement ring that had over twenty years' filth compacted under the high, filigree-type box mounting typical of the early 1920s. After cleaning, which was difficult, the diamond showed a definite brown tint, easily seen by the client, which she had never noticed when the ring was dirty. She had just inherited the ring from her deceased mother-in-law, who had told her it had a *"blue white"* color. If she had not been present when this ring was being cleaned and appraised, it might have resulted in a lawsuit, for she would certainly have suspected a switch. This particular situation does not present itself often, but appraisers must always be careful not to chip or damage the item entrusted to them; and the customer must be equally alert to make sure that they do not. This can be very time consuming if several pieces are being appraised. It normally takes about ½ hour per item to get all of the specifications, and it can take much longer in some cases.

Appraisal Fees

This is a touchy and complex subject. As with any professional service, there should be a suitable charge. Fees should be conspicuously posted or offered readily on request so that the customer knows beforehand what to expect to pay for this service. Fees are essentially based on the expertise of appraisers and the time required of them, as well as secretarial work required to put the appraisal in written form—appraisals should be done in writing. While it used to be standard practice to base appraisal fees on a percentage of the appraised value, this practice is no longer acceptable. Today, all recognized appraisal associations in the United States recommend that fees be based on a flat hourly rate, or on a "per carat" charge for diamonds.

There is usually a minimum appraisal fee, regardless of value. The hourly rate charged by a professional, experienced gemologist-appraiser can range from $50 to $150, depending on the complexity of the work to be performed and the degree of expertise required. Find out beforehand what the hourly rate is and what the minimum fee will be.

For multiple-item appraisals, special arrangements are usually made. For appraisals containing many items, such as an estate appraisal, an hourly rate of $50 to $75 is normal. For certification or special gemological consulting requiring special expertise, rates can easily be $125–150 per hour. Extra services, such as photography, X-radiography, Gemprint, or spectroscopic examination of fancy colored diamonds, will require additional fees.

Be wary of appraisal services offering appraisals at very low rates, and of appraisers who continue to base their fee on a percentage of the "appraised valuation." The Internal Revenue Service, for example, will not accept appraisals performed by appraisers who charge a "percentage-based" fee.

Mr. Bonanno usually takes a photograph of the piece he is appraising (except for simple watches and simple rings). On the photograph he notes the approximate magnification, the date, and the owner's name, and he signs it using his personal embossing seal to make an impression over his name. This provides a means of identifying merchandise that may have been stolen, damaged, etc., and will also aid in duplicating the piece should the customer so desire. The photograph may also be used for the U.S. Customs Service should the customer be a world traveler.

With the information provided here, you will know how to evaluate the appraiser and make sure that accurate, complete documentation is provided.

❖ *A Word About Protecting Your Diamond with Gemprint*

Gemprint is a unique service that is available from many jewelers and appraisers. We recommend using it if the service is available in your community. While not totally foolproof (if anyone goes to the trouble of re-cutting the diamond, it may affect reliability), it is playing an increasingly important role in the recovery and return of lost and stolen diamonds.

Gemprint offers a means of identifying any diamond, even

stones already mounted in settings, by taking a photograph of the pattern of reflections created when a low-level laser beam hits the gem. Each diamond produces a unique pattern, which is documented on photographic film and, as with fingerprints, no two are ever alike. One could describe Gemprint as a diamond's "fingerprint."

The process takes only a few minutes. For a nominal cost ($35 to $50), two photographs are taken. One is given to the customer, accompanied by a numbered certificate of registration. The second is filed in the Gemprint Central Registry in Chicago. Gemprint sends the owner a confirmation of the registration, and a "notice of loss" form to hold for any future need.

If the stone is ever lost or stolen, the owner sends the notice-of-loss form to Gemprint, which immediately puts out a computerized alert that reaches police departments across the country. The police can then verify with the registry the identification of lost or stolen diamonds that have been recovered, so that the stone can be returned to its rightful owner.

As another safeguard, Gemprint also checks each new registration against its lost-and-stolen file before confirming and storing the registration. Gemprint can also be useful in situations where a diamond, or diamond jewelry, has been left for repair, cleaning, or resetting, to assure the owner that the right stone has been returned.

Some insurance companies today give an annual 10% off the premium paid on a floater policy insuring a diamond that has been Gemprinted. Check with your insurance company.

Gemprint is available in about 650 locations in the United States (jewelry stores, gem labs, dealers). You can obtain the name of the location nearest you by contacting Gemprint directly: Gemprint, Ltd., 1901 N. Naper Blvd., Naperville, IL 60540 (312) 505-1161.

❖ *Choosing an Insurer*

Once you have a complete appraisal, the next step is obtaining adequate insurance. Most people do not realize that insurers differ widely in what they offer regarding coverage and reimbursement or replacement. Many insurance companies will *not* reimburse the "full value" provided in the policy but, rather, exercise a "replacement" option—and will offer a sum in cash *less than* the amount for which the jewelry is insured, or offer to *replace it* for you. Therefore it is important to ask some very specific questions to determine the precise coverage offered. We recommend asking the insurer at least the following:

- *How do you satisfy claims?* Do you reimburse the insured amount in cash? If not, how is the amount of the cash settlement determined? Or do you replace the jewelry?
- *What involvement do I have in the replacement of an item?* What assurance do I have that the replacement will be of comparable quality and value?
- *What is your coverage on articles that cannot be replaced?*
- *Exactly what risks does my policy cover*—all risks? Mysterious disappearance? Am I covered in all geographic areas? At all times?
- *Are their any exemptions or exclusions?* What if the loss involves negligence?
- *What are the deductibles, if any?*
- *What documentation do you expect me to provide?*

Keep a "photo inventory" of all your jewelry. Simply lay it all out on a table and take a photo. Store the photo in a safe place, such as a bank safe deposit box. In case of theft or fire, a photo will be useful to help you remember what is missing and identify it, if recovered. It is also useful for insurance documentation.

CHAPTER 25

Caring for Your Engagement and Wedding Rings

You will most likely wear your engagement and wedding rings more than any other pieces of jewelry, so it is important to know how to care for and protect them. The following tips should help you in properly caring for your rings.

• *Try not to touch the stones in your rings* when putting them on or taking them off. Instead, take rings on and off by grasping the shank or metal portion that encircles the finger. Slipping rings on and off by grasping the metal shank rather than the stone will prevent a greasy buildup on the stone's surface, which greatly reduces the brilliance and sparkle of a stone.

• *To keep rings sparkling, get into the habit of "huffing" them.* This is a little trick we use to remove the dirt and oily film on the stone's surface (which occurs from incorrectly putting rings on and taking them off, or from occasionally "fingering" them—which most of us do without even realizing). Each time the stones are touched, a layer of oily film is applied to the top, and the stone's beauty is diminished. To restore its sparkle, just "huff" it. Simply hold the ring close to your mouth, "huff" on it with your breath—you'll see the stone fog up—and wipe it off with a soft, lint-free cloth, such as a handkerchief, scarf, or coat/blouse sleeve. You'll be amazed to see how much better jewelry can look simply by removing even the lightest oil film from the surface!

• *Don't take off rings and lay them on the side of the sink* unless you're sure the drain is closed. Also, never remove your rings to wash your hands when away from home (all-too-many have been forgotten . . . and lost).

• *Don't wear your ring while doing any type of rough work* such as house cleaning or gardening, or sports such as mountain climbing. Even diamonds can be chipped or broken by a hard blow in certain directions.

• *Avoid contact with chlorine,* the principal ingredient in many bleaches, household cleaners, and *swimming pool* disinfectants. Chlorine can cause pitting and discoloration to the mounting of your ring and to your gold or platinium wedding band.

• *Don't carelessly toss jewelry in a case.* Diamonds can scratch other gemstones very easily, and can also scratch each other. Ideally, to prevent scratching, diamond jewelry should be placed in a case with dividers or separate compartments, or each piece placed in a soft pouch or individually wrapped in tissues or a soft cloth.

• *Every 12–18 months have a reliable jeweler check each fine jewelry piece* to make sure the setting is secure, especially the prongs. If you ever feel (or hear) the stone moving in the setting, it's a warning that the prongs or bezel need tightening. Failure to repair this may result in loss or damage to the stone.

How to Clean Your Jewelry

Keeping your diamond and gemstone jewelry clean is essential if you want it to sparkle to its fullest. Film from lotions, powders, and your own skin oils will dull stones and reduce their brilliance. You will be amazed at how much a slight film can affect the brilliance—and color—of your gems.

It's easy to keep it clean. To clean your jewelry, wash with warm, sudsy water. This is perhaps the simplest and easiest way to clean any kind of jewelry. Prepare a small bowl of warm, sudsy water, using any kind of mild liquid detergent. Soak the piece for a few minutes and then brush gently with an eyebrow brush or soft toothbrush, keeping the piece submerged in the sudsy water. Rinse thoroughly under running water (make sure the drain is closed—some prefer to place jewelry in a wire strainer before placing under the running water) and pat dry with a soft lint-free cloth or paper towel.

To clean your diamonds only, make a solution of cold water and ammonia (half water/half ammonia) and soak your diamond in this solution for about 30 minutes. Lift it out and tap it gently from the sides and back and then brush it gently with a soft toothbrush. This technique is especially effective for diamond jewelry with a heavy buildup of oily dirt. It may take several "soaks" if the piece is very old and hasn't been cleaned for many years. Rinse and dry with a soft cloth or paper towel.

To clean your wedding band or any other gold jewelry without gemstones, rubbing with a soft chamois cloth will restore much of the luster. Tarnish can be removed with a solution of soap and water to which a few drops of ammonia have been added. Using a soft toothbrush, brush the jewelry with this solution, rinse with warm water and dry with a soft cloth. Grease can be removed by dipping in plain rubbing alcohol.

While more convenient, commercial jewelry cleaners are not necessarily more effective than the methods suggested above. *Never let gemstone jewelry soak in commercial cleaners for more than a few minutes.* Leaving stones such as emerald or amethyst in some commercial cleaners for any length of time can cause etching of the surface, which reduces the stone's luster.

We do not recommend ultrasonic cleaning for most gems and think it should be restricted to the cleaning of diamonds or gold jewelry only. Washing with warm, sudsy water is simple, effective, and safe for all jewelry.

❖ Store Jewelry Carefully

• *It is important to store your jewelry carefully, in a dry place.* Avoid extremes of temperature and humidity.

• *Keep gemstone jewelry, pearls, and gold and silver pieces separated* from each other to prevent scratching. Keep fine jewelry in soft pouches or wrapped in a soft cloth (or plastic "ziploc" type bags) to help protect it.

• *Don't overcrowd your jewelry box.* This can result in misplacing or losing pieces that might fall unnoticed from the case. Forcing jewelry into the box may cause damage, such as bending a fragile piece, or chipping a fragile stone.

PART EIGHT

APPENDICES

A Selected List of
Laboratories That Provide
Internationally Recognized Reports
of Genuineness and Quality

American Gemological
  Laboratory
580 Fifth Avenue, 12th floor
New York, NY 10036
(Services available to the jew-
  elry trade and to the public)

Colored Diamond Laboratory
  Services, Inc.
15 West 47th Street
New York, New York 10036
(Issuing reports on colored dia-
  monds only)

Gemmological Lab. Gubelin
Denkmalstrasse, 2
Ch-6006 Luzern, Switzerland
(Only to the jewelry trade)

GIA Gem Trade Laboratory
Gemological Institute of
  America
580 Fifth Avenue
New York, NY 10036
(Only to the jewelry trade)

GIA Gem Trade Laboratory
Gemological Institute of
  America
1660 Stewart Street
Santa Monica, CA 90404
(Only to the jewelry trade)

Hoge Raad voor Diamant
  (HRD)
Hoveniersstraat, 22
B-2018 Antwerp, Belgium

Schweizerische Stiftung fur
  Edelstein-Forschung (SSEF)
Lowenstrasse, 17
Ch-8001 Zurich, Switzerland

International List of Gem Testing Laboratories and Gemologists

The following has been compiled from the International Colored Gemstone Association membership, the American Gem Society, the Accredited Gemologist Association, and the American Society of Appraisers. We hope it will aid you in locating laboratories and gemologists to assist you with gem identification or appraisals.

An asterisk has been placed by labs we know to be accredited or recognized by a respected gem or jewelry industry association. CGA indicates a Certified Gemologist Appraiser is on staff. MGA indicates a Master Gemologist Appraiser is on staff.

For an up-to-date listing of CGAs in your area, contact the American Gem Society, 5901 West 3rd Street, Los Angeles, CA 90036-2898 (Tel. 213-936-4367). For MGA's, contact the American Society of Appraisers, Box 17265, Dulles International Airport, Washington, DC 20041 (Tel. 703-478-2228).

UNITED STATES

Alabama

*Jimmy Smith Jewelers
Southland Plaza Shopping
  Center
Decatur, AL 35602
(205) 353-2512
Jimmy Ray Smith (CGA)

*Mason Jewelers
3011 South Parkway
Huntsville, AL 35801
(205) 883-2150
Ronnie Robbins (CGA)
  and at
5901-73 University Drive
Madison Square Mall
Huntsville, AL 35806
(205) 830-5930
Emily White Ware (CGA)

*Mickleboro's of Montgomery
3003-C McGehee Road
Montgomery, AL 36111
(205) 281-6597
Amy J. Michaels (CGA)

*Ware Jewelers
111 So. College Street
Auburn, AL 36830
(205) 821-7375
Stanley Arington (CGA)
  and at
Village Mall
162 Opelika Road
Auburn, AL 36830
(205) 821-3122
Ronnie Ware (CGA)

Arizona

*Ambassador Diamond Brokers
4668 E. Speedway Blvd.
Tucson, AZ 85712
(602) 327-8800
Stewart M. Kuper (MGA)

*Caldwell Jewelry Corp.
7225 N. Oracle Rd.
Tucson, AZ 85704
(602) 742-3687
Brenda J. Caldwell (MGA)

*Dennis D. Naughton Jewelers
129 Park Central Mall
Phoenix, AZ 85013
(602) 264-2857
Net T. Burns (CGA)

*Grunewald & Adams Jewelers
Biltmore Fashion Park
2468 E. Camelback
Phoenix, AZ 85016
(602) 955-8450
Sandra Overland (CGA)

*Jim Anderson Jewelers
2112 N. Fourth Street
Flagstaff, AZ 86004
(602) 526-0074
James R. Anderson (CGA)

*Joseph M. Berning Jewelers
130 E. University Drive
Tempe, AZ 85281
(602) 967-8917
Patricia Berning (CGA)

*Marshall's Artistry in Gold,
  Inc.
4811 E. Grant Road, #113
Tucson, AZ 85712
(602) 325-9955
Richard G. Marshall (CGA)

*Michelle Hallier (MGA)
1250 East Missouri St.
Phoenix, AZ 85014
(602) 277-9780

*Molina Fine Jewelers
1250 E. Missouri St. #3
Phoenix, AZ 85014
(602) 265-5001
Alfredo J. Molina (MGA)

*Ouellet and Lynch
5743 W. St. Johns Road
Glendale, AZ 85308
(602) 264-3210
Craig A. Lynch (MGA)

*Paul Johnson Jewelers
1940 E. Camelback Road
Phoenix, AZ 85016
(602) 277-1421
Thomas Hergenroether (CGA)

*Paul Johnson Jewelers, Inc.
6900 E. Camelback Rd.
Scottsdale, AZ 85251
(602) 994-0133
Michael Holmes (CGA)

*Peterson's Jewelry
209 W. Gurley Street
Prescott, AZ 86301
(602) 445-3098
James Lamerson (CGA)

*Schmieder & Son Jewelers
Park Central Mall West
Phoenix, AZ 85013
(602) 264-4464
Carl Schmieder (CGA)

*Schmieder & Son Jewelers
10001 W. Bell Road
Sun City, AZ 85351
(602) 974-3627
Robert Delane Cloutier (CGA)

*Setterberg Jewelers
Campana Square
9885 West Bell Rd.
Sun City, AZ 85351
(602) 972-6130
Wendell Setterberg (CGA)

Arkansas

*Stanley Jewelers
3422 John F. Kennedy Blvd.
North Little Rock, AK 72116
(501) 753-1081
Loyd C. Stanley (CGA)

*Underwood's Jewelers
611 W. Dickson
Fayetteville, AK 72701
(501) 521-2000
William G. Underwood (CGA)

California

*A.L. Jacobs & Sons Jewelers
675 B. Street
San Diego, CA 92101
(619) 232-1418
Christopher Jacobs (CGA)

*The Altobelli Jewelers
4419 Lankershim Blvd.
North Hollywood, CA 91602
(818) 763-5151
Cos Altobelli (CGA)

*American Jewelry Co.
Oak Park Tower #500
3200 21st St. at Oak
Bakersfield, CA 93301
805-325-5023
Carl M. Saenger (CGA)

*Azevedo Jewelers and Gemologists
210 Post Street #321
San Francisco, CA 94108
(415) 781-0063
Kathleen Beaulieu (CGA)

*Balzan's Gemological Lab.
P.O. Box 6007
San Rafael, CA 94903
(415) 454-0925
Cortney G. Balzan (MGA)

*Barrett W. Reese-Goldsmith
499 No. Central Ave.
Upland, CA 91766
(714) 981-7902
Barrett W. Reese (CGA)

Brewsters
6052 Magnolia Avenue
Riverside, CA 92506
(714) 686-1979
Frank A. Wright

*Bubar's Jeweler
216 Santa Monica Place
Santa Monica, CA 90401
(213) 451-0727
Basil Marnoff (CGA)

*Cardinal Jewelers
1807-L Santa Rita Road
Pleasanton, CA 94566
(415) 462-6666
James A. Kuhn (CGA)

*Charles H. Barr Jewelers
1048 Irvine Avenue
Westcliff Plaza
Newport Beach, CA 92660
(714) 642-3310
Donna H. Blackman (CGA)

*Chase Jewelers, Inc.
20442 Redwood Road
Castro Valley, CA 94546
(415) 581-0632
Edward A. Chase (CGA)

*Currie & Underwood
3957 Goldfinch Street
San Diego, CA 92103
(619) 291-8850
Thom Sorensen Underwood
(MGA)

*Dudenhoeffer Fine Jewelry,
Ltd.
118 E. Main Street
El Cajon, CA 92020
(619) 588-9001
Roy Dudenhoeffer (CGA)

*Dudenhoeffer Fine Jewelry,
Ltd.
123 Horton Plaza
San Diego, CA 92101
(619) 236-0316

*European Gemological Laboratory
608 S. Hill Street, Ste. 1013
Los Angeles, CA 90014
(213) 623-8092
Thomas Tashey (MGA)

*Finley-Gracer
5112 E. Second Street
Long Beach, CA 90903
(213) 434-4429
Warren Finley (CGA)

*Frederic H. Rubel Jewelers
167 Central City Mall
San Bernardino, CA 92401
(714) 889-9565
Gary W. Rubel (CGA)

*Frederic H. Rubel Jewelers
560 Main Place
2800 N. Main Street
Santa Ana, CA 92701
(714) 558-9144
David A. Rubel (CGA)

*The Gem Connection
9227 Haven Avenue
Rancho Cucamonga, CA
 91730
(714) 941-4500
Ronald L. Base (MGA)

*Gem Profiles
416 West Santa Ana
Fresno, CA 93705
(209) 229-7361
Bob Praska

*George Carter Jessop & Co.
1025 Second Avenue
Westgate Mall
San Diego, CA 92101
(619) 234-4137
James C. Jessop (CGA)

*Gleim the Jeweler
119 Stanford Shopping Ctr.
Palo Alto, CA 94304
(415) 325-3533
David C. Loudy (CGA)

*Grebitus & Son Jewelers
Country Club Centre
3332 El Camino
Sacramento, CA 95821
(916) 487-7853
Robert Grebitus (CGA)

*Grebitus & Son Jewelers
511 L. Street
Sacramento, CA 95814
(916) 442-9081
J. Marlene White (CGA)

*G M E
1600 Howe Ave.
Sacramento, CA 95825
(916) 925-6711
Alison LeBaron (MGA)
G. Marilyn Thomas (MGA)

*Hammond's Jewelry, Inc.
16 N. Tower Square
Tulare, CA 93274
(209) 686-9224
Richard Hammond (CGA)

*The Hardware Store, Fine
 Jewelry
11621 Barrington Court
Los Angeles, CA 90049
(213) 472-2970
Gary M. Murray (CGA)

*Harlequin Jewelry Design
3158 Jefferson Street
Napa, CA 94558
(707) 255-2121
Mark London (CGA)

*Harwin Jewelers
110 S. Hope Avenue
Santa Barbara, CA 93105
(805) 682-8838
Joel S. Harwin (CGA)

*Houston Jewelers
4454C Van Nuys Blvd.
Sherman Oaks, CA 91423
(818) 783-1122
Richard Houston (CGA)

*Int'l Gemological Lab.
650 S. Hill St., Ste. 229
Los Angeles, CA 90014
(213) 688-7837
Andrew Y.K. Kim (MGA)

*J.C. Humphries Jewelers
1835 Newport Blvd. #D152
Costa Mesa, CA 92627
(714) 548-3401
Joseph C. Humphries (CGA)

Jack E. Rich Jewelers Inc.
338 Merchant Street
Vacaville, CA 95688
(707) 448-4808
Dale S. Rich (CGA)

*Jewels by Stacy
458 Morro Bay Blvd.
Morro Bay, CA 93442
(805) 772-1003
Nancy Frey Stacy (MGA)

*Johnson & Co. Jewelers
111 Stanford Shopping Ctr.
Palo Alto, CA 94304
(415) 321-0764
Steven Graham (CGA)

*Johnson Jewelers
16727 S. Bellflower Blvd.
Bellflower, CA 90706
(213) 867-4420
Russell Sowell (CGA)

*Lee Frank Mfg. Jewelers
2200 Shattuck Avenue
Berkeley, CA 94704
(415) 843-6410
Angie Dang (CGA)

*Lynn's Jewelry
2434 E. Main Street
Ventura, CA 93003
(805) 648-4544
Robert A. Lynn (CGA)

*Marshall Adams Gems
2364 N. Del Rosa Ave., #8
San Bernardino, CA 92404
(714) 883-8463
Marshall A. Adams (MGA)

*Montclair Jewelers
2083 Mountain Blvd.
Oakland, CA 94611
(415) 339-8547
David J. Coll (CGA)

*Morgan's Jewelers, Inc.
311 Del Amo Fashion Center
Torrance, CA 90503
(213) 542-5925
Marshall Varon (CGA)

*Shoemake's Jeweller/Gemmol-
   ogist
1323 J. St.
Modesto, CA 95454
(209) 577-3711
Otto R.Zimmerman (CGA)

*Sidney Mobell Fine Jewelry
141 Post Street
San Francisco, CA 94108
(415) 986-4747
Philip Chen (CGA)

*Sidney Mobell Fine Jewelry
Lobby Fairmont Hotel
San Francisco, CA 94106
(415) 421-4747

*Smith Jewelers
704 San Ramon Valley Blvd.
Danville, CA 94526
(415) 837-3191
Laurence James Smith (CGA)

*Morton Jewelers, Inc.
212 N. Santa Cruz Avenue
Los Gatos, CA 95030
(408) 395-3500
Sue Maron-Szuks (CGA)

*Nielsen Jewelers Inc.
1581 W. Main Street
Barstow, CA 92311
(619) 256-3333
Carl G. Nielsen (CGA)

*Norman Mahan Jewelers
2211 Larkspur Landing Circle
Larkspur, CA 94939
(415) 461-5333
Nancy Mahan-Weber (CGA)

*Robann's Jewelers
125 S. Palm Canyon Dr.
Palm Springs, CA 92262
(619) 325-9603
Roger Kerchman (CGA)

*San Diego Gemological Labo-
   ratory
3957 Goldfinch St.
San Diego, CA 92103
(619) 291-8852
Thom Underwood (MGA)

*Stucki Jewelers
148 Mill Street
Grass Valley, CA 95945
(916) 272-9618
George M. Delong (CGA)

*Timothy Fidge & Co.
27 Town & Country Village
Palo Alto, CA 94301
(415) 323-4653
Patricia Rickard (CGA)

*Troy & Company
527 South Lake Ave., #105
Pasadena, CA 91101
(818) 449-8414
Troy B. Steckenrider (CGA)

United States
  Gemological Services
14080 Yorba St., #237
Tustin, Ca. 92680
(714) 838-8747
David Ascher

*The Village Jeweler
1014-8 Westlake Blvd.
Westlake Village, CA 91361
(805) 497-4114
James W. Coote (CGA)

*Wickersham Jewelers
3320 Truxtun Avenue
Bakersfield, CA 93301
(805) 324-6521
John C. Abrams (CGA)

*Wight Jewelers
207 N. Euclid Avenue
Ontario, CA 91762
(714) 984-2745
P. Donald Riffe (CGA)

Colorado

*Merritt Sherer, Gemologist
Southmoor Park Center
6448 East Hampden Ave.
Denver, CO 80222
(303) 691-9414
Merritt Sherer (CGA)

*Molberg's Jewelers-Gemolo-
  gists Inc.
University Hills Shopping Ctr.
2700 S. Colorado Blvd.
Denver, CO 80222
(303) 757-8325
Leonard J. Molberg (CGA)

*Purvis Jewelers Inc.
9797 West Colfax Ave., #2G
Lakewood, CO 80215
(303) 233-2798
John Purvis III (CGA)

*Walters & Hogsett Fine
  Jewelers
2425 Canyon Blvd.
Boulder, CO 80302
(303) 449-2626
William Lacert (CGA)

*Zerbe Jewelers, Inc.
118 N. Tejon Street
Colorado Springs, CO 80903
(719) 635-3521
Charles J. Zerbe (CGA)

Connecticut

*Addessi Jewelry Store
207 Main Street
Danbury, CT 06810
(203) 744-2555
Doreen A. Guerrera (CGA)

*Craig's Jewelry Store
394 Main Street
Ridgefield, CT 06877
(203) 438-3701
William D. Craig (CGA)

*Lux Bond & Green
Somerset Square
Glastonbury, CT 06033
(203) 659-8510
Cynthia L. Konney (CGA)
  and at
15 Pratt Street
Hartford, CT 06103
(203) 278-3050
John A. Green (CGA)
  and at
46 La Salle Road
West Hartford, CT 06107
(203) 521-3015
Marc A. Green (CGA)

*M.B.A. Associates
99 Pratt Street
Hartford, CT 06103
(203) 527-6036
Neil H. Cohen (MGA)

*Michaels Jewelers
127 Bank Street
Waterbury, CT 06702
(203) 754-5154
Ernest Bader (CGA)

*Michael's Jewelers
926 Chapel St.
New Haven, CT 06510
(203) 865-6145

*Michaels Jewelers, Inc.
80 Main Street
Torrington, CT 06790
(203) 482-6553
Edward Bush (CGA)

*Neil Cohen Gemologist
99 Pratt Street
Hartford, CT 06103
(203) 247-1319
Neil Cohen (MGA)

Delaware

*Continental Jewelers
1732 Marsh Road
Graylyn Shopping Center
Wilmington, DE 19810
(302) 478-7190
Paul S. Cohen (CGA)

District of Columbia

(see "Maryland" and
  "Virginia")

Florida

*Antares & Co., Gems &
  Jewelry
5613 University Blvd., W.
Jacksonville, FL 32216
(904) 737-8316
B. Young McQueen (MGA)

*Bechtel Jewelers, Inc.
226 Datura Street
West Palm Beach, FL 33401
(407) 655-8255
Robert L. Bechtel (CGA)

*Burt's Jewelers
1706 N.E. Miami Gardens
  Drive
Miami, FL 33179
(305) 947-8386
Lloyd Aaron (MGA)

*Carroll's Jewelers, Inc.
915 E. Las Olas Blvd.
Ft. Lauderdale, FL 33301
(305) 463-3711
Robert B. Moorman Jr. (CGA)

*Gause & Son Oaks Mall
6663 Newberry Road
Gainesville, FL 32605
(904) 374-4417
Albert Seelbach (CGA)

*Gemological Lab Service
  Corporation
22 N. W. 1st Street, Ste. 101
Miami, FL 33128
(305) 371-6437
David M. Levison (MGA)

*Gemstone Corp. of America
7507 S. Trail
Sarasota, FL 34231
(813) 921-4214
Carol M. Daunt (MGA)
John J. Daunt III (MGA)

*Griner's Jewelry Haven, Inc.
850 Cypress Gardens Blvd.
Winter Haven, FL 33880
(813) 294-4100
Randall M. Griner (CGA)

*Harold Oppenheim (MGA)
633 N.E. 167th St., Rm.
  #1023
North Miami Beach, FL 33162
(305) 652-1319

*Indep. Gem Testing, Inc.
2455 E. Sunrise Blvd. #501
Fort Lauderdale, FL 33304
(305) 563-2901
William C. Horvath (MGA)

*J.B. Smith & Son Jewelers,
  Inc.
900 E. Atlantic Ave., Suite 21
Delray Beach, FL 33483
(407) 278-3346
James T. Smith (CGA)

Jaylyn Gemologists Goldsmiths
30 S.E. 4th Street
Boca Raton, FL 33432
(305) 391-0013
James O'Sullivan

*Jos. W. Tenhagen
Gemstones, Inc.
36 NE First Street, Suite 419
Miami, FL 33132
(305) 374-2411
Joseph Tenhagen (MGA)

*Kempf's Jewelers, Inc.
236 Fifth Avenue
Indialantic, FL 32903
(407) 724-5820
Gale M. Kempf (CGA)

*Lee Jewelry
1823 East Colonial Dr.
Orlando, FL 32803
(407) 896-2566
Robert A. Lee (CGA)

*Mayor's Jewelers, Inc.
283 Catalonia Avenue
Coral Gables, FL 33134
(305) 442-4233
Bruce Handler (CGA)

*Moon Jewelry Company
536 N. Monroe
Tallahassee, FL 32301
(804) 224-9000
Jeff Hofmeister (CGA)

*The Oak's Keepsake Diamond
Gallery
The Oaks Mall A-13
Gainesville, FL 32605
(904) 331-5337

*P.J. Abramson, Inc.
180 N. Park Ave., Suite 4D
Winter Park, FL 32789
(407) 644-3383
Pamela J. Abramson (MGA)

*Paul J. Schmitt Jeweler
765 Fifth Ave. S.
Naples, FL 33940
(813) 262-4251
Paul J. Schmitt (CGA)

*Paul J. Schmitt Jeweler
4321 Tamiami Trail
Naples, FL 33940
(813) 261-0600
James T. Merkley (CGA)

*Peter Bradley, Inc.
13499 US 41 S.E.
Fort Myers, FL 33907
(813) 482-7550
Peter F. Bradley (MGA)

*Roger Hunt & Son
Div. Maison D'Or, Inc.
232 S.W. 10th Street
Ocala, FL 32671
(904) 629-1105
Roger E. Hunt (CGA)

*Suncoast Accredited Gem.
Lab.
Bayshore Office Bldg.
6221 14th St. West, Suite 105
Bradenton, FL 34207
(813) 756-8787

*Wells Jewelers, Inc.
4452 Hendricks Avenue
Jacksonville, FL 32207
(904) 730-0111
Laurence Bodkin (CGA)

Georgia

*Ford, Gittings & Kane Inc.
312 Broad St.
Rome, GA 30161
(404) 291-8811
Jan J. Fergerson (CGA)

Hawaii

*Hallmark Jewelers
2242 Ala Moana Ctr.
Oahu, Honolulu
Hawaii, 96814
(808) 949-3982
Yoshimasa Ishihara (CGA)

Illinois

*Denney Jewelers
51 Central Park Plaza South
Jacksonville, IL 62650
(217) 245-4718
Shane S. Denney (CGA)

*Doerner Jewelers
9201 North Milwaukee Avenue
Niles, IL 60648
(312) 966-1341
Michael Doerner (CGA)

*Fey & Company Jewelers,
   Inc.
1156 Fox Valley Center
Aurora, IL 60505
(312) 851-8828
Edgar H. Fey III (CGA)

*Franz Jewelers, Ltd.
1220 Meadow Road
Northbrook, IL 60062
(312) 272-4100
Frank E. Pintz (CGA)

*Rand Jewelers, Inc.
2523A Waukegan Rd.
Bannockburn Green Shop. Ctr.
Bannockburn, IL 60015
(312) 948-9475
William E. Rand (CGA)

*Samuels Jewelers, Inc.
4500 16th Street
South Park Mall
Moline, IL 61265
(309) 762-9375
Corey James England (CGA)

*Stout and Lauer
1650 Wabash-The Yard
Springfield, IL 62704
(217) 793-3040
Deborah Lauer-Toelle (CGA)

Indiana

*Droste's Jewelry Shoppe, Inc.
4511 First Avenue
Evansville, IN 47710
(812) 422-4351
Gregory Scott Droste (CGA)

*Philip E. Nelson Jeweler, Inc.
22 E. Main Street
Brownsburg, IN 46112
(317) 852-2306
Jeffrey R. Nelson (CGA)

*Troxel Jewelers, Inc.
7980 Broadway
Merrillville, IN 46410
(219) 769-0770
Donald Troxel (CGA)

*Williams Jewelry Inc.
114 N. Walnut
Bloomington, IN 47408
(812) 339-2231
Mark A. Thoma (CGA)

Iowa

*Becker's Jewelers
123 West Monroe
Mt. Pleasant, IA 52641
(319) 385-3722
William D. Becker (CGA)

*Gunderson's Jewelers
Terra Center
600 Fourth St.
Sioux City, IA 51101
(712) 255-7229
Brian Gunderson (CGA)

*Josephs Jewelers
320 6th Ave.
Des Moines, IA 50309
(515) 283-1961
William J. Baum (CGA)

*Mark Ginsberg (MGA)
110 E. Washington St.
Iowa City, IA 52240
(319) 351-1700

*Samuels Jewelers, Inc.
320 W. Kimberly
Northpark Mall
Davenport, IA 52806
(319) 391-4362
Peggy K. Friederichs (CGA)

*Thorpe & Company Jewellers
501 4th Street
Sioux City, IA 51101
(712) 258-7501
Bruce C. Anderson (CGA)

Kansas

*Donaldson's Jewelers, Inc.
Seabrook Center
2001 S.W. Gage Blvd.
Topeka, KS 66604
(913) 273-5080
Tracie E. Forkner (CGA)

*Jewelry Arts, Inc.
8221 Corinth Square
Prairie Village, KS 66208
(913) 381-8444
Ryudy Giessenbier (CGA)

*Lavery's Jewelry
404 Delaware
Leavenworth, KS 66048
(913) 682-3182
Evelyn J. Chapman (CGA)

*Riley's Jewelry, Inc.
6116 Johnson Dr.
Mission, KS 66202
(913) 432-8484
William A. Riley (CGA)

Kentucky

*Bernard Lewis & Co.
313 Broadway
Paducah, KY 42001
(502) 442-0002
(800) 327-4056
Bernard G. Lewis (CGA)

*Brundage Jewelers
141 Chenoweth Lane
Louisville, KY 40207
(502) 895-7717
William E. Brundage (CGA)

*Cortland Hall Jewelers, Inc.
133 St. Matthews Avenue
Louisville, KY 40207
(502) 897-6024
Mark L. Redmon (CGA)

*Farmer's Jewelry
821 Euclid Avenue
Lexington, KY 40502
(606) 266-6241
William L. Farmer (CGA)

*Merkley Jewelers
400 Old East Vine
Lexington, KY 40507
(606) 254-1548
Kimberley S. Hall (CGA)

*Merkley-Kendrick Jewelers
  Inc.
138 Chenoweth Lane
Lousville, KY 40207
(502) 895-6124
Donald J. Merkley (CGA)

*Miller & Woodward, Inc.
115 West Short Street
Lexington, KY 40507
(606) 233-3001
Russell Pattie (CGA)

*Seng Jewelers
453 Fourth Avenue
Louisville, KY 40202
(502) 585-5109
Lee S. Davis (CGA)

Louisiana

*Champions Jewelers—
  Gemologists
1123 North Pine Street
Park Terrace Shopping Ctr.
De Ridder, LA 70634
(318) 463-7026
John Cunningham (CGA)

*Clarkes Jewelers, Inc.
3916 Youree Drive
Shreveport, LA 71105
(318) 865-5658
Gary L. Clarke (CGA)

*Simon Jeweller Gemmologist,
  Inc.
941 E. 70th Street
Shreveport, LA 71106
Horace Simon (CGA)

Maine

*Brown Goldsmiths & Co.,
  Inc.
One Mechanic Street
Freeport, ME 04032
(207) 865-4126
W. Stephen Brown (CGA)

*Etienne & Company
20 Main Street
Camden, ME 04843
(207) 236-9696
(800) 426-4367
Peter Theriault (CGA)

*J. Dostie Jeweler
4 Lisbon Street
Lewiston, ME 04240
(207) 782-7758
Linda Chamberlain (CGA)

Maryland

*Colonial Jewelry, Inc.
9 W. Patrick St., P.O. Box 674
Frederick, MD 21701
(301) 663-9252
Jeffrey I. Hurwitz (MGA)

*National Gem Appraising
  Lab.
8600 Fenton Street
Silver Spring, MD 20910
Antonio C. Bonanno (MGA)
Karen J. Ford (MGA)

*Tilghman Company
44 State Circle
Annapolis, MD 21401
(301) 268-7855
Thomas O. Tilghman (CGA)

Massachusetts

*Andrew Grant Diamond Center
144 Elm Street
Westfield, MA 01085
(413) 562-2432
Robert K. Grant (CGA)

*Appraisal Associates
7 Kent Street
Brookline Village, MA 02146
(617) 566-1339
Nancy A. Smith (MGA)

*Kenyon A. Carr, Jeweler
422 Main Street
Hyannis, MA 02601
(617) 775-1968
William F. Carr (CGA)

*La France Jeweler
763 Purchase Street
New Bedford, MA 02740
(508) 993-1137
Paul R. Rousseau (CGA)

*Romm & Co.
162 Main Street
Brockton, MA 02401
(508) 587-2533
Dean B. Learned (CGA)

*Scharfmans, Inc.
164 Worcester Center
Worcester, MA 01608
(508) 791-2211
(800) 451-7500
Nancy R. Rosenberg (CGA)

*Shreve, Crump & Low
330 Boylston Street
Boston, MA 02116
Joseph P. Pyne (CGA)

*Swanson Jeweler, Inc.
717 Massachusetts Ave.
Arlington, MA 02174
(617) 643-4209
Robert Swanson (CGA)

*Wyman Jewelers Inc.
18 Wyman Street
Stoughton, MA 02072
(617) 344-5000
Philip Minsky (CGA)

Michigan

*Birmingham Gemological
   Services
251 Merrill Street
Birmingham, MI 48011
(313) 644-8828
James Krol (MGA)

*Dobie Jewelers
14600 Lakeside Circle #205
Lakeside Mall
Sterling Heights, MI 48078
(313) 247-1730
Edmund P. Dery (CGA)
   and at
500 S. Washington St.
Royal Oak, MI 48067
(313) 545-8400
Joseph M. Cayuela (CGA)

*Everts Jewelers, Inc.
109 E. Broadway
Mount Pleasant, MI 48858
(517) 772-3141
Lawrence W. Everts (CGA)

*F.A. Earl Jewelers
156 E. Front Street
Traverse City, MI 49684
(616) 947-7602
Brad Shepler (CGA)

*Haffner Jewelers
3204 Rochester Rd.
Royal Oak, MI 48073
(313) 588-6622
David Williamson (MGA)

*J. F. Reusch Jewelers
427 E. Mitchell Street
Petoskey, MI 49770
(616) 347-2403
John F. Reusch (CGA)

*Jules R. Schubot Jewellers
3001 W. Big Beaver Rd., #112
Troy, MI 48084
(313) 649-1122
Brian T. Schubot (CGA)

*Losey's Fine Jewelry
133 East Main Street
Midland, MI 48640
(517) 631-1143
Roger E. Schmidt (CGA)

*Milkins Jewelers
13 Washington St.
Monroe, MI 48161
(313) 242-1023
Bruce A. Milkins (CGA)

*Mosher's Jewelers, Inc.
336 Huron Ave.
Port Huron, MI 48060
(313) 987-2768
William A. Mosher (CGA)

*Siegel Jewelers
Amway Grand Plaza Hotel
Pearl & Monroe
Grand Rapids, MI 49503
(616) 459-7263
B. Miller Siegel (CGA)
   and at:
28 Woodland Mall
3135 28th S.E.
Grand Rapids, MI 49508
(616) 949-7370
James W. Siegel (CGA)

Minnesota

*Bockstruck Jewelers
27 W. Fifth St.
St. Paul, MN 55102
(612) 222-1858
DeWayne Amundsen (CGA)

*Korst & Sons Jewelers
3901 W. 50th Street
Edina, MN 55424
(612) 926-0303
William Korst Jr. (CGA)

*R.F. Moeller Jeweler
2073 Ford Parkway
St. Paul, MN 55116
(612) 698-6321
Mark Moeller (CGA)

*Stadheim Jewelers
215 S. Broadway
Albert Lea, MN 56007
(507) 373-3440
Beth S. Ordalen (CGA)

Mississippi

*Way-Fil Jewelry
1123 W. Main Street
Tupelo, MS 38801
(601) 844-2427
Patricia A. Witt (CGA)

Missouri

Clayton Gemological Services,
Inc.
Bemiston Tower, Suite 800
231 South Bemiston
St. Louis, MO 63105-1914
(314) 862-4005
Therese S. Kienstra

*Elleard B. Heffern, Inc.
7777 Bonhomme Ave.
Suite 1800
St. Louis, MO 63105
(314) 863-8820
Christopher E. Heffern (CGA)

*Frank Gooden Co., Inc.
Gemlab
1110 Grand Avenue
Kansas City, MO 64106
(816) 421-0281
Ricki Kendall Gooden

*Tivol, Inc.
220 Nichols Rd.
Kansas City, MO 64112
(816) 531-5800
J. Michael Tracy (CGA)

Montana

*Blacks' Jewelers
211 Third Ave.-Box 869
Havre, MT 59501
(406) 265-2522
(800) 843-3564
Richard J. Growney (CGA)

*Chaussee Precious Gems &
Fine Jewelry
228 N. Higgins
Missoula, MT 59802
(406) 728-8639
Yvette I. Clevish (CGA)

*Crown Jewelry, Inc.
419 Central Ave.
Great Falls, MT 59401
(406) 453-5312
E.W. O'Neil (CGA)

*William Sargent, Jeweler
20 N. Main
Kalispell Center Mall
Kalispell, MT 59901
(406) 752-7464

Nebraska

*Karl's Jewelry
84 West 6th
Box 710
Fremont, NB 68025
(402) 721-1727
Karl Rasmussen IV (CGA)

*Michael's Jewlery of Fremont,
N.E. Inc.
540 N. Main Street
Fremont, NB 68025
(402) 721-7300
Dolores Dunker (CGA)

*Sartor-Hamann Jlrs.
3404 W. 13th
Grand Island, NB 68803
(308) 382-5850
Bennett Murphy, Jr. (CGA)
and at:
1150 "O" Street
Lincoln, NB 68508
(402) 226-2917
Robert H. Fixter (CGA)

Nevada

*Huntington Jewelers, Inc.
3661 S. Maryland Parkway
#19N
Las Vegas, NV 89109
(702) 732-1977
Richard C. Huntington (MGA)

New Hampshire

*A.E. Alie & Sons, Inc.
1 Market Street
Portsmouth, NH 03801
(603) 436-0531
Stephen R. Alie (CGA)

*Beacon Hill Jewelers, Inc.
42 Hanover St.
Manchester, NH 03101
(603) 627-7338
Judith Fineblit (CGA)

*Harrington's Jewelers
New London Shopping Center
New London, NH 03257
(603) 526-4440
Douglas J. Lantz (CGA)
and at:
33 Main St.
Newport, NH 03773
(603) 863-1662
Douglas J. Lantz (CGA)

*Sawyers Jewelry
Downtown Laconia Mall
Laconia, NH 03246
(603) 524-3309
Richard Beauregard (CGA)

New Jersey

*Earth Treasures
Circle Plaza Shopping Center
Eatontown, NJ 07724
(201) 542-5444
Paul Bischoff

*Hamilton Jewelers
2542 Brunswick Pike
Lawrenceville, NJ 08648
(609) 771-9400
Hank B. Siegel (CGA)

*The Jewel Shop
436 Main Street
Metuchen, NJ 08840
(201) 549-1490
Andrew H. Zagoren (CGA)

*Martin Jewelers
12 North Avenue West
Cranford, NJ 07016
(201) 276-6718
Ellen R. Ramer (CGA)
and at:
125 Quimby St.
Westfield, NJ 07090
(201) 232-6718
Davia Sue Freeman (CGA)

*Rose City Jewelers-
   Gemologists
Corner of Waverly & Main
   Streets
Madison, NJ 07940
(201) 377-2146
Joseph Falco Jr. (CGA)

*Simms Jewelers, Inc.
17 Mine Brook Road
Bernardsville, NJ 07924
(201) 766-4455
Arthur Sockolof (CGA)

New Mexico

*Butterfield Personal Service
   Jewelers
2411 San Pedro, N.E.
Albuquerque, NM 87110
(505) 884-5747
Larry D. Phillips (CGA)

*J.A. May Jewelers, Inc.
112 West Main Street
Farmington, NM 87401
(505) 325-5102
William D. McGraw (CGA)

*Larry D. Phillips (MGA)
801 Marie Park NE
Albuquerque, NJ 87123
(505) 884-5747

*Shelton Jewelers, Ltd.
7001 Montgomery Blvd., N.E.
Albuquerque, NM 87109
(505) 881-1013
Eric M. Shelton (CGA)

New York

*American Gemological Lab.
580 Fifth Avenue, Suite 1211
New York, NY 10036
(212) 704-0727
C.R. "Cap" Beesley (MGA)

*Castiglione Gem Jewelers Inc.
25 N. Main Street
Gloversville, NY 12078
(518) 725-1113
Louis J. Castiglione (CGA)

*Cornell Jewelers
Dutchess Mall, Rt. 9
Fishkill, NY 12524
(914) 896-8950
Thomas F. Kavanagh (CGA)
and at:
119 Newburgh Mall
1067 Union Avenue
Newburgh/Beacon, NY 12550
(914) 564-5100
Charles T. Kavanagh (CGA)

*Freedman Jewelers
345 New York Ave.
Huntington, NY 11743
(516) 423-2000
Eric M. Freedman (CGA)

*International Gemmological
  Institute
580 Fifth Avenue
New York, NY 10036
(212) 398-1700
David Weinstein (CGA)
Debra Henreckson (CGA)

*Lights Jewelers & Gemologists
Plattsburgh Plaza
Plattsburgh, NY 12901
(518) 561-6623
Andre Thomas Light (CGA)

*Lourdes Gemological Lab.
Rt. 6 & Hill Blvd.
Jefferson Valley, NY 10535
(914) 245-4676
Howard N. Biffer (MGA)

*Reyman Jewelers, Inc.
16 W. First Street
Mount Vernon, NY 10550
(914) 668-9281
Mark Reyman (CGA)

*Ruby & Sons Jewelers
6 Washington Avenue
Endicott, NY 13760
(607) 754-1212
Leonard Levine (CGA)

*Schneider's Jewelers, Inc.
290 Wall St.
Kingston, NY 12401
(914) 331-1888
Thomas W. Jacobi (CGA)

*T.H. Bolton Jeweler Inc.
16 East Main Street
Rochester, NY 14614
(716) 546-7074
E. Jean Bolton (CGA)

*Van Cott Fine Jewelry
Oakdale Mall
Johnson City, NY 13790
(607) 729-9108

*William Scheer Jewelers Inc.
3349 Monroe Ave., Pittsford
  Plaza
Rochester, NY 14618
(716) 381-3050
Jack Monchecourt (CGA)

North Carolina

*Arnold Jewelers
305 Overstreet Mall
Southern National Center
Charlotte, NC 28202
(704) 332-6727
Frank V. Taylor (CGA)

*Bailey's Fine Jewelry
117 Winstead Ave.
Rocky Mount, NC 27804
(919) 443-7676
(800) 338-7676
Clyde C. Bailey (CGA)

*Bisanar Jewelers
226 Union Square
Hickory, NC 28601
(704) 322-5090
J. Timothy Cline (CGA)

*Green's Jewelers
106 N. Main St.
Roxboro, NC 27573
(919) 599-8381
Sam B. Green (CGA)

*Henry J. Young's Diamonds
  and Fine Jewelry
257 N. Hills Mall
Raleigh, NC 27609
(919) 787-1422
Henry J. Young (CGA)

*Johnson's Jewelers, Inc.
309 Fayetteville St.
Raleigh, NC 27602
(919) 834-0713

*Karat Gold Corner, Inc.
1809 Pembroke Road
Greensboro, NC 27408
(919) 272-2325
Lorraine D. Dodds (CGA)

*McCormick Jewelers
9015-1 J.M. Keynes Drive
Charlotte, NC 28213
(704) 547-8446
James G. McCormick (CGA)
  and at:
3716 MacCorkle Ave. S.E.
Charleston, WV 25304
(304) 925-3435
James R. McCormick (CGA)

*NC Gem Lab
107 Hunter's Ridge Road
Chapel Hill, NC 27514
(919) 966-2227
William Benedick (MGA)

*Parker-Miller Jewelers
100 S. Main St.
Lexington, NC 27292
(704) 249-8174
Christopher L. Bramlett (CGA)

*T. William Benedict (MGA)
107 Hunter's Ridge Road
Chapel Hill, NC 27514
(919) 929-9179

*Wick & Greene Jewelers
121 Patton Ave.
Asheville, NC 28801
(704) 253-1805
Michael E. Greene (CGA)

Ohio

*Argo & Lehne Jewelers
20 So. Third St.
Columbus, OH 43215
(614) 228-6338
Shannon F. Patterson (CGA)

*David Baker Creative
  Jewelers, Inc.
37 West Bridge Street
Dublin, OH 43017
(614) 764-0068
David M. Baker (CGA)

*E.M. Smith Jewelers, Inc.
668 Central Ctr.
Chillicothe, OH 45601
(614) 774-1840
Robert J. Smith (CGA)

*Grassmuck & Lange Jewelers,
  Inc.
441 Vine Street
Carew Tower Arcade
Cincinnati, OH 45202
(513) 621-1898
William F. Grassmuck (CGA)

*Henry B. Ball, West
2291 W. Market St.
Pilgrim Square
Akron, OH 44313
(216) 867-9800
Mary Ball Gorman (CGA)
  and at:
5254 Dressler Rd. N.W.
Belden Village
Canton, OH 44718
(216) 499-3000
Robert A. Ball (CGA)

*Jack Siebert, Goldsmith &
   Jeweler
1623 W. Lane Ave. Ctr.
Columbus, OH 43221
(614) 486-4653
Jack Siebert (CGA)

*John Gasser & Son Jewelers
205 Third Street, N.W.
Canton, OH 44702
(216) 452-3204
Gerald D. Blevins (CGA)

*O'Bryant Jewelers & Gemolo-
   gists
101 E. Wayne Street
Maumee, OH 43537
(419) 893-9771
James P. O'Bryant (CGA)

*Raymond Brenner, Inc.
7081 West Blvd., Route 224
Youngstown, OH 44512
(216) 726-8816
Raymond Brenner Jr. (CGA)

*Thomas Jewelers, Inc.
409 S. Main St.
Findlay, OH 45840
(419) 422-3775
James L. Thomas (CGA)

*Wendel's
137 S. Broad Street
Lancaster, OH 43130
(614) 653-6402
Stuart Palestrant (CGA)

*Wm. Effler Jewelers
7618 Hamilton Ave.
Cincinnati, OH 45231
(513) 521-6654
Mark T. Andrus (CGA)

*Yeager Jewelers, Inc.
14814 Madison Ave.
Lakewood, OH 44107
(216) 521-6658
Jack Yeager (CGA)

Oklahoma

*B.C. Clark, Inc.
101 Park Avenue
Oklahoma City, OK 73102
(405) 232-8806
Paul C. Minton (CGA)

Oregon

*Deuell Jewelers, Inc.
1327 Main Street
Philomath, OR 97370
(503) 929-3422
JoAnne Hansen (CGA)

*Gayer Jewelers
300 E. Second Street
The Dalles, OR 97058
(503) 298-GEMS
Scott Gayer (CGA)

*The Gem Lab
20776 St. George Court
Bend, OR 97702
(503) 389-6790
Jim "Fritz" Ferguson

*Hart Jewelers
235 S.E. 6th Street
Grants Pass, OR 97526
(503) 476-5543
Thomas R. Hart Sr. (CGA)

Pennsylvania

*Bill Lieberum Fine Jewelers
   & Gemologists
Centre Pointe Place Shopping
   Ctr.
872 West Street Rd
Warminster, PA 18974
(215) 443-8000
William R. Lieberum (CGA)

*D.A. Palmieri Co., Inc.
666 Washington Road
Pittsburgh, PA 15228
(412) 344-0300
Susan G. Bower (MGA)
Donald Palmieri (MGA)

*D. Atlas & Co., Inc.
732 Sansom Street
Philadelphia, PA 19106
(215) 922-1926
Michael Jordan (MGA)
Edward R. Skinner Jr. (MGA)

*David Craig Jewelers, Ltd.
Summit Square Shopping Ctr.
Langhorne, PA 19047
(215) 968-8900
David C. Rotenberg (CGA)

*Futer Bros. Jewelers
Continental Square
York, PA 17401
(717) 845-2734
J.H. Eigenrauch III (CGA)

*Gemological Appraisal
   Associates, Inc.
666 Washington Road
Pittsburgh, PA 15228
(412) 344-5500
Donald Palmieri (MGA)

*John M. Roberts & Sons Co.
429-431 Wood Street
Pittsburgh, PA 15222
(412) 281-1651
Maureen F. O'Brien (CGA)

*Joseph A. Rosi Jewelers
4636 Jonestown Road
Harrisburg, PA 17109
(717) 652-8477
Joseph A. Rosi Jr. (CGA)

*M.A.B. Jewelers
1162 Baltimore Pike
Olde Sproul Village
Springfield, PA 19064
(215) 554-4656
Samuel S. Bruner (CGA)

*N.B. Levy's
120 Wyoming Ave.
Scranton, PA 18503
(717) 344-6187
Seymour H. Biederman (CGA)

*Yardley Jewelers
JBD Studio–2 So. Main Street
Yardley, PA 19067
(215) 493-1300
Jon Barry DiNola (CGA)

Rhode Island

*Tilden-Thurber Corp.
292 Westminster St.
Providence, RI 02903
(401) 421-8400
Robert Quinn (CGA)

South Carolina

*Cochran Jewelry Company of
   Greenville, Inc.
211 North Main Street
Greenville, SC 29601
(803) 233-3641
Walter S. Morris (CGA)

Tennessee

*Alexander & Co., Inc.
5050 Poplar, #634
Memphis, TN 38157
(901) 767-4367
William A. Mathis (MGA)

*Fischer Evans Jewelers
801 Market Street
Chattanooga, TN 37402
(615) 267-0901
Mrs. Taylor M. Watson (CGA)

*Helm's Jewelry
100 W. 7th Street
Columbia, TN 38401
(615) 388-7842
Debbie Nelson Wells (CGA)

*M.M.Schenck Jewelers, Inc.
3953 Hixson Pike
Chattanooga,TN 37415
(615) 877-4011
Mrs. Mary Schenck (CGA)

*Mackley & Co., Inc.
8906 Kingston Pike, Suite 214
Knoxville, TN 37923
(615) 693-3097
Joseph Mackley (MGA)
Emily White Ware (CGA)

*Sites Jewelers, Inc.
206 Franklin Street
Clarksville, TN 37040
(615) 648-0678
William C. Sites (CGA)

Texas

Ann Hawken Gem Laboratory
603 West 13th, Suite 312
Austin, TX 78701
(512) 288-3590
Ann Hawken

*Anna M. Miller (MGA)
P.O. Box 1844
Pearland, TX 77588
(713) 485-1606

*Antique Appraisal Service
P.O. Box 27903
Houston, TX 77227
(713) 665-8245
Christine W. York (MGA)

*Barnes Jewelry, Inc.
2611 Wolflin Village
Amarillo, TX 79109
(806) 355-9874
Vess Barnes Jr. (CGA)

*C. Kirk Root Design
6418 B Westside Drive
Austin, TX 78731
(512) 338-0360
Charles K. Root (MGA)

*Crowell Jewelers, Inc.
2417 West Park Row
Arlington, TX 76013
(817) 460-1962
C.G. Crowell, Jr. (CGA)

*Duncan & Boyd, Jewelers
113 West 8th Street
Amarillo, TX 79101
(806) 373-1067
Ronald Boyd (CGA)

*I. David Clark & Associates
305 21st St.
Galveston, TX 77551
(409) 762-3229
Irving D. Clark (CGA)

*Jewelry Forest
9100 N. Central/Park Lane
185 Caruth Plaza
Dallas, TX 75231
(214) 368-5352
Jerry Forrest (CGA)

*Lacy & Co.
River Oakes Shopping Village
3301 So. 14th
Abilene, TX 79605
(915) 695-4700
Ellen W. Lacy (CGA)

*Nowlin Jewelry, Inc.
145 Oyster Creek Dr.
Lake Jackson, TX 77566
(409) 297-7252
John F. Nowlin (CGA)

Utah

*John's Jewelry
3920 Washington Blvd.
Ogden, UT 84403
(801) 627-0440
John Christiansen (CGA)

*Robert L. Rosenblatt
2736 Commonwealth Ave.
Salt Lake City, UT 84109
(801) 364-3667

*Spectrum Gems
1615 S. Foothill Drive
Salt Lake City, UT 84108-2742
(801) 266-4579
Dana Lynn Richardson (MGA)

*Sutton's of Park City
Park City Resort Village
Park City, UT 84060
(801) 649-1187
Keith M. Sutton (CGA)

Virginia

Bonanno's Antiques
619 Caroline
Fredericksburg, VA 22401
(703) 373-3331
Kenneth Bonanno (FGA)

*Carreras, Ltd.
150 Sovran Plaza
Richmond, VA 23277
(804) 780-9191
Mark A. Smith (CGA)

*Cowardin Jewelers
Chesterfield Towne Center
Rt. 60 and Rt. 147
Richmond, VA 23235
(804) 794-4478
Ronald L. Cowardin (CGA)

*Everhart Jewelers, Inc.
6649 Old Dominion Dr.
McLean, VA 22101
(703) 821-3344
William R. Everhart II (CGA)

*Fauquier Gemological
  Laboratory
P.O. Box 525, Main Street
Marshall, VA 22115
(703) 364-1959
Jelks H. Cabaniss (MGA)

*Frank L. Moose Jeweler
207 1st St. S.W.
Roanoke, VA 24011
(703) 345-8881
F. Geoffrey Jennings (CGA)

*The Greenhouse
P.O. Box 525
Marshall, VA 22115
(703) 364-1959
Jelks Cabaniss (MGA)

*Hardy's Diamonds
4212 Virginia Beach Boulevard
Wayside Village, VA 23452
(804) 486-0469
George B. Hardy (CGA)

*Marvin D. Miller Gemologists
3050 Covington St.
Fairfax, VA 22031
(703) 280-2169
Marvin D. Miller (MGA)

*Schwarzchild Jewelers, Inc.
Broad at Second St.
Richmond, VA 23219
(804) 644-1941
B. Harton Wolf (CGA)

*Thomas P. Hartnett (MGA)
11344 Links Drive
Reston, VA 22090
(703) 437-7108

*Van Doren Jewelers
6025-D Burke Center Pkwy.
Burke, VA 22015
(703) 978-2211
Christian W. Lietwiler (MGA)

Washington

*Ben Bridge Jeweler
1101 Pike
Seattle, WA 98111
(206) 628-6879
Jane Ann Buescher (CGA)
  and at:
1119 Tocoma Mall
Tacoma, WA 98409
(206) 473-1227
Cathy Hall (CGA)

*Blessing's Jewelers
225 W. Meeker St.
Kent, WA 98032
(206) 852-3455
Leslie S. Thomas (CGA)

*Button Jewelers, Inc.
2 S. Wenatchee Ave.
Wenatchee, WA 98801
(509) 663-4654
Douglas D. Button (CGA)

*Carroll's Fine Jewelry
1427 Fourth Avenue
Seattle, WA 98101
(206) 622-9191
Patricia M. Droge (CGA)

*Fox's Gem Shop
1341 Fifth Ave.
Seattle, WA 98101
(206) 623-2528
Sandra L. Ordway (CGA)

*Gemological Training
  Corporation
1425 4th Avenue, Ste. 502
Seattle, WA 98101
(206) 625-0105
David W. Hall (MGA)

*Henry Gerards Jewelers, Inc.
W. 714 Main
River Park Square Skywalk
Spokane, WA 99201
(509) 456-8098
Janis Ann Gerards (CGA)

*Pavilion Gemological
   Laboratories
19415 Pacific Hwy. So., Ste.
   414
Seattle, WA 98188
(206) 824-9132
Joseph V. Paul (MGA)

*S.O. Hawkes & Son Jewelers
   Inc.
123 E. Yakima Ave.
Yakima, WA 98901
(509) 248-2248
Kathy Hawkes Smith (CGA)

West Virginia

*Calvin Broyles Jewelers
4833 McCorkle Ave. S.W.
Spring Hill, WV 25309
(304) 768-8821
Don C. Broyles (CGA)

*McCormick Jewelers, Inc.
3716 MacCorkle Ave. S.E.
Charleston, WV 25304
(304) 925-3435
James R. McCormick (CGA)

*R.D. Buttermore & Son
623 Market St.
Parkersburg, WV 26101
(304) 422-6401
R.D. Buttermore Jr. (CGA)

Wisconsin

*Gemstone Goldsmiths
100 Main Street
Stone Lake, WI 54876
(715) 865-2422
David R. Neilson (CGA)

*J. Vander Zanden & Sons
   Ltd.
217 N. Washington St.
Green Bay, WI 54305
(414) 432-3155
Peter Vander Zanden (CGA)

*Midwest Gem Lab of Wisc.,
   Inc.
1335 S. Moorland Rd.
Brookfield, WI 53005
(414) 784-9017
James S. Seaman (MGA)

*Rasmussen Jewelry
3119 Washington Ave.
Racine, WI 53405
(414) 633-9474
William E. Sustachek (CGA)

*Schwanke-Kasten Co.
324 E. Silver Spring Dr.
Milwaukee, WI 53217
(414) 964-1242
James E. Brown (CGA)

Wyoming

*Wiseman Jewelers
501 Ivinson Avenue
Laramie, WY 82070
(307) 745-5240
Scott Alan Wiseman (CGA)

Other Countries

Australia

ACT Institute of T.A.F.E.
Gemmology Dept.
P.O. Box 273
Civic Square
ACT, 2608 Australia
Tel. 451798

Australian Gemmologist
P.O. Box 35
South Yarra, Victoria 3141
Australia

*Gemm'l. Assoc. of
 Australia—

N.S.W. Div.
Box 1532 G.P.O.
Sydney, N.S.W.
2001 Australia

Queensland Div.
20 Rosslyn St.
East Brisbane, Queensland
Australia 4169
Tel. (07) 3915

S. Australia Div., Box 191
Adelaide, S. Australia 5001

Western Australia Div.
P.O. Box 355
Nedlands, West Australia

Austria

*Austrian Gemmological
 Research Institute (Erste
 Osterreichische
 Gemmologische
 Gesellschaft-EOGG)
Salesianergasse, 1
A-1030 Vienna, Austria
Tel. (222) 71168, Ext. 318 or
 260

Belgium

European Gem'l. Laboratory
Rijfstraat, 3
2018 Antwerp, Belgium
Tel. 233 82 94

Hoge Raad voor Diamant
 (HRD)
Hoveniersstraat, 22
B-2018 Antwerp, Belgium

Canada

Brodman Gem'l Lab., Inc.
1255 Phillips Square #1105
Montreal, Quebec, Canada
 H3B 3G1
Tel. (514) 866-4081

*De Goutiere Jewellers, Ltd.
2542 Estevan Avenue
Victoria, British Columbia
Canada V8R 2S7
(604) 592-3224
A. De Goutiere (CGA)

*Ernest Penner Inc.
53 Queen Street
St. Catherines, Ontario
Canada L2R 5G8
(416) 688-0579
Ernest Penner (CGA)

Gem Service Lab
Harold Weinstein Ltd.
55 Queen St. E. 1301
Toronto, Ontario, Canada
 M5C 1R6
Tel. 366-6518

*The Gold Shop
345 Quellette Avenue
Windsor, Ontario
Canada N9A 4J1
(519) 254-5166
Ian M. Henderson (CGA)

Kinnear d'Esterre Jewellers
168 Princess Street
Kingston, Ontario
Canada K7L 1B1
(613) 546-2261
Erling Alstrup (CGA)

*Nash Jewellers
182 Dundas Street
London, Ontario
Canada N6A 1G7
(519) 672-7780
John C. Nash (CGA)

England

British Museum (Natural
 History)
Dept. of Mineralogy
Cromwell Road
London SW7 5BD, England
Tel. (01) 938-9123

*The Gem Testing Laboratory
27 Greville Street

Saffron Hill Entrance
London EC1N8SU, England
(Not available to the public.
Identification/verification can
be requested by a jeweler or
gem dealer on behalf of customer).

*Sunderland Polytechnic
Gemmological Laboratory
Dept. of Applied Geology,
Benedict Bldg., St. George's
Way
Stockton Rd.
Sunderland, SR2 7BW,
England
Tel. (091) 567-9316

Huddlestone Gemmological
Consultants LTD
100 Hatton Garden, Suite 221
London EC1N 8NX, England
Tel. 01-404-5004

France

*European Gemological
Laboratory
9, Rue Buffault
75009 Paris, France
Tel. (1) 40-16-16-35

*Laboratoire Public De Con-
trole des Pierres Precieuses
de la Chambre De Com-
merce (C.C.I.P.)
2, Place De La Bourse
75002 Paris, France
Tel. 40268312

Germany

*Deutsches Diamant Institut
Poststrasse 1
Postfach 470
D-7530 Pforzheim, Germany
Tel. 07231/32211

*Deutsches Edelstein
Testinstitut (only gemstones)
Mainzerstrasse 34
D-6850 Idar-Oberstein,
Germany

*Deutsche Gemmologische
Gesellaschaft EV
Prof.-Schlossmacher-Strasse 1
D6580 Idar-Oberstein 2,
Germany
Tel. 6781/4-30-11

German Foundation of
Gemstone Research (DSEF)
Prof.-Schlossmacher-Str. 1
D-6850 Idar Oberstein,
Germany
Tel. 6781/4-30-13

Holland

*Nederlands Edelsteen
Laboratorium (only gem-
stones)
Hooglandse Kergracht 17
2312 HS Leiden, Nederland
Tel: (31) 071-143844

*Stichting Nederlands Diamant
Instituut (only diamonds)
Van de Spiegelstraat 3
Postbus 29818
NL-2502LV's-Gravenhage,
Nederland
Tel. 070-469607

Hong Kong

*Yang Mulia Gem Technologi-
cal Consultancy and Laboratories
1103, Blissful Bldg.
247 Des Voeux Road Central
Hong Kong
Tel. 5-8152705

India

Gem Identification Laboratory
372 Gopal Ji Ka Rasta
Jaipur 302003, India
Tel. 47528

Gem'l Inst. of India
29 Gurukul Chambers,
187 Mumbadevi Rd.
Bombay 400 002, India

Gem Testing Laboratory
Rajasthan Chamber
Mirza Ismail Rd.
Jaipur, India

Israel

Gem'l Inst. for Precious Stones
52 Bazalel St., 1st Floor
Ramat Gan 52521, Israel

*Nat'l Gem'l. Inst. of Israel
52 Bazalel St.
Ramat Gan 52521, Israel
Tel. 751-7102

Italy

Analisi Consulenze
  Gemmologiche
Via Tortrino, 5
15048 Valenza (Alessandria)
Italy
Tel. 0131-953161

Centro Analisi Gemmologiche
Viale Vicenza 4/D
15048 Valenze, Italy

*Cisgem-External Service for
  Precious Stones/Chamber of
  Commerce of Milan
Via Brisa/Via Ansperto, 5
20123 Milano, Italy
Tel. 02/85155499

Instituto Analisi
  Gemmologiche
Via Sassi, 44
15048 Valenza, Italy
Tel. 0131-946586

Instituto Gemmologico Italiano
Viale Gramsci, 228
20099 Sesto San Giovanni
Milano, Italy
Tel: (02) 2409354
  also at:
Via Appia Nuova, 52
00183 Roma, Italy
(06) 7575685

*Laboratorio Scientifico
Professionale di Controllo di
Diamanti, Pietre Preziose e
Perle della CONFEDORAFI
Via Ugo Foscolo 4
1-20121 Milano, Italy

Japan

Central Gem Lab
Taiyo Bldg. 15–17, 5 Chome,
Ueno, Taito-Ku
Tokyo 110, Japan
Tel. 03-836-3131

*CIBJO Institute of Japan
  (only diamonds)
Tokyo-Bihokaikan 1–24
Akashi-Cho
Chuo-Ku, Tokyo, Japan
Tel. 03-543-3821

Kenya

Mr. P. Dougan
P.O. Box 14173
Nairobi, Kenya

*Ruby Center of Kenya Ltd.
Fedha Towers, Second Floor
Muindi Mbingu Street
Nairobi, Kenya (East Africa)
Tel. 335261, 334299

Korea

Mi-Jo Gem Study Institute
244-39, Huam-dong
  Youngsan-ku
Seoul, Korea 140-190
Tel. 754-5075, 0642

Republic of South Africa

European Gemological
  Laboratory
Paulshop Bldg.
Corner Plein & Twist Streets
Johannesburg, South Africa
Tel. 29-9647

*Gem Education Center
508 Medical Arts Bldg.
220 Jeppe Street
Johannesburg, 2000, South Africa
Tel. 337-3457, 3458

Independent Coloured Stones
Lab.
5 Hengilcon Avenue
Blairgourie, Randburg
Transvaal,
Rep. of South Africa 2194
Tel. (011) 787-3326

Singapore

International Gemological Lab.
(S) Pte. Ltd.
402 Orchard Road
#03-07, Delfi Orchard
Singapore 0923
Tel. 732-7272/ 732-3636

Spain

*Instituto Gemologico Espanol
Victor Hugo, 1, 3e
Madrid-4, Spain

*Laboratorio Oficial de la
  Association Espanola de
  Gemologia AEG
Pseo. de Gracia 64 entr. 2a
Barcelona-7, Spain
Tel. 2 15 43 12

Sri Lanka

Gem'l Assoc. of Sri Lanka
Professional Center
275/75 Bauddhalokka Mawatha
Colombo 7, Sri Lanka

*Gemmology Laboratory
  Department of Mining &
  Minerals Engineering
University of Moratuwa,
Katubedde, Sri Lanka
Tel. Colombo 505353

Petrological Laboratory
Geological Survey Dept.
48, Sri Jinaratana Rd.
Colombo 2, Sri Lanka

Tel. 29014/15

State Gem Corporation
Gem Testing Laboratory
24, York Street
Colombo 1, Sri Lanka
Tel. 28701

State Gem Corporation
No. 92/4A, Templars Road
Mount Lavinia, Sri Lanka

Sweden

Swedish Inst. for Gem Testing
P.O. Box 3021
S-12703 Stockholm, Sweden

Rolf Krieger
Kungsgatan 32 VI
S 111 35 Stockholm, Sweden
Tel. 8/ 10-13-65

Switzerland

*Gemgrading
4, Rue Albert-Gos
1206 Geneva, Switzerland
Tel. (022) 46-60-61

*Gemmological Lab Gubelin
Denkmalstrasse, 2
Ch-6006 Luzern, Switzerland

*Gemmologie Laboratoire Service
  Rue de Bourg, 3
1003 Lausanne, Switzerland
Tel. (021) 20-49-77

*Schweizerische Stiftung
fur Edelstein-Forschung (SSEF)
  Lowenstrasse 17,
CH-8001 Zurich, Switzerland
Tel. 01/211 24 71

Thailand

*Asian Institute of
  Gemological Science
987 Silom Rd.
Rama Jewellery Bldg., 4th Floor
  Bangkok 10500, Thailand
Tel. 233-8388/9, 235-1254/5

Zimbabwe

Gem Education Centre of
Zimbabwe
Founders House
15 Gordon Avenue
Harare, Zimbabwe 707580

Associations
United States and Canada

Accredited Gemologists Assoc.
1615 South Foothill Drive
Salt Lake City, Utah 84108
(801) 581-9000 or 364-3667
Dana Richardson, Editor

American Gem Society
5901 West 3rd Street
Los Angeles, California 90036
(213) 936-4367
Tom Dorman, Exec. Director

American Gem Trade
Association
#181 World Trade Center
2050 Stemmons Expressway
Dallas, Texas 75207
(214) 742-4367, (800) 972-1162
Peggy Willett, Exec. Director
(For information about colored
gems and their availability.)

American Society of Appraisers
Box 17265
Washington, DC 20041
(703) 478-2228
Shirley Belz, PR Director

Appraisers Association of America
60 East 42nd St.
New York, NY 10165
(212) 867-9775
Victor Wiener, Exec. Director

Association Professionelle des
Gemmologists du Quebec
6079, Boul. Monk
Montreal, Quebec
Canada H4E 3H5
(514) 766-7327

Association of Women
Gemologists
P.O. Box 1844
Pearland, Texas 77588
(713) 485-1606
Anna Miller, Director

Canadian Gemmological
Assoc.
P.O. Box 1106, Station Q
Toronto, Ontario
Canada M4T 2P2
Warren Boyd
(416) 652-3137

Diamond Council of America
Inc.
9140 Ward Parkway
Kansas City, MO 64114
(816) 444-3500
Jerry Fogel, Executive Director

International Colored
Gemstone Association
22643 Strathern St.
West Hills, CA 91304
(818) 716-0489
Maureen Jones, Exec. Director
(For information about colored
gems and their availability.)

Jewelers of America, Inc.
1271 Avenue of the Americas
New York, New York 10020
(212) 489-0023
Michael D. Roman, Chairman
and Exec. Director

National Association of Jewelry
Appraisers
4210 North Brown Avenue
Suite "A"
Scottsdale, AZ 85251
(602) 941-8088
Richard E. Baron, Executive
Director

Associations: Other Countries

Austria

Bundesgremium Des Handels
  Mit Juwelen
P.O. Box 440
A-1045 Vienna
Austria
Karl M. Heldwein

Australia

Gemmological Association of
  Australia
P.O. Box 184
East Brisbane, Queensland
  4169
Australia

Gemmological Association of
  Australia
also at:
G.P.O. Box 5133 AA
Melbourne, 3001
Australia
Mr. Franz Thrupp

Australian Gem Ind. Assoc.
P.O. Box 104, Bondi Beach
New South Wales
Australia
Joy Clayton

Brazil

ABGM
Rue Barao de Itapetininga
No. 255–12 Andar
CEP 01042–Sau Paulo–SP
Brazil

Ajorio–Sindicato National
Do. Com. Atacadista de Pedras
  Preciosas
Av. Graca Aranha
19/40 Andar Sala 404
CEP 20031
Brazil

Associacao Brasileria de
  Gemologiae
Mineralogiae Rue Alvarez
  Machado
41,18000/801 501
Sao Paulo

IBGM
Rua Teixeira Da Silva, No.
  654
CEP 04002–Paraiso
Sao Paulo–SP
Brasil

Instituto Brasileiro de Gemas e
  Metais Precoisos
Av. Rio Branco
135 Sala 1018
CEP 20040
Brasil

Burma

Gem & Jade Corporation
86, Kala Aye Pagoda Road
P.O. Box 1397 Rangoon

Dubai

Institute of Goldsmithing &
  Jewellery
Sikat Al Khail Road
P.O. Box 11489
Dubai, U.A.E.

England

De Beers Consolidated Mines
  Ltd.
40 Holborn Viaduct
London ECIPIAJ

Gemmological Association of
  Great Britain
Saint Dunstan's House
Carey Lane
London, EC2V 8AB

Jewellery Information Centre
44 Fleet Street
London, ECA

Finland

Gemmological Society of
 Finland
P.O. Box 6287
Helsinki, Finland

France

French Diamond Association
7 Rue de Chatesudun
Paris 75009
France
Claude Varnier

Service Public Du Controle
2, Place de la Bourse
Paris 75002
France
Mr. Poirot

Syndicat des Maitres Artisans
 bijoutiers-joailliers
3, Rue Sainte-Elisabeth
Paris 75003
France

Association Francaise de
 Gemmologie
1 Rue Saint Georges
Paris 75009
France

Germany

Deutsch Gemmologische
 Gesellschaft EV
(German Gemmological
 Society)
Prof.-Schlossmacher-Str. 1
Postfach 122260
6580 Idar-Oberstein 2
West Germany

Diamant - und Edelsteinborse,
 Idar-Oberstein E.V.
Mainzer Str. 34
D-6580 Idar-Oberstein
West Germany

Hong Kong

The Gemmological Association
 of Hong Kong
TST P.O. Box 97711
Kowloon
Hong Kong

Hong Kong Gemmologists'
 Assoc.
P.O. Box 74170
Kowloon Central Post Office
Hong Kong

India

The All India Jewellers' Assoc.
19 Connaught Place
New Delhi
India

Andhra Pradesh Gold, Silver,
 Jewellery and Diamond
 Merchants Association
Secunderabad
India

Bangiya Swarna Silpi Samitee
162 Bipin Behari Ganguli
 Street
Calcutta 12
India

Bombay Jewellers Association
308 Sheikh Memon Street
Bombay 400 002

The Cultured & Natural Pearl
 Association
1st Agiary Lane, Dhanji Street
Bombay 400 003
India

Gem & Jewellery Information
Centre of India
A-95, Jana Colony
Journal House
Jaipur 302 004

Gujarat State Gold Dealers and
 Jewellers' Association
2339-2, Manek Chowk
Ahmedabad
India

Jewellers' Association
Nagarthpet
Bangalore 560 002
India

Tamil Nadu Jewellers
  Federation (also The Madras
  Jwlers. & Dia. Merch.
  Assoc.)
11/12 Car St.
Netaji Subhaschandra Road
Madras 600 001

Indonesia

L.G. Tampubolon
Indonesian Gemstone &
  Jewellery Assoc.
Jl. Teuku Umar 53
Jakarta 10310
Indonesia

Israel

Gemmological Association of
  Israel
1 Jabotinsky Street
Ramat-Gan
52520, Israel

Israel Precious Stones
  Exchange
Maccabi Building
1 Jabotinsky Street
Ramat-Gan 52520
Israel
Yehuda Kassif

Italy

CIBJO
Lungo Tevere Osali Anguillarh 9
  Roma 00153
Italy
Dr. Amirante

Instituto Gemmologico Italiane
Piazzale Gambrare, 7/8
20146 Milano, Italy

Japan

CIBJO of Japan
Chuo-Jiho Bldg. 3.1-3 Shintomi
  2 Chome, Chuo-ku, Tokyo
Japan

Gemmological Association of
  All Japan
Tokyo Biho Kaikan
24 Akashi-chu, Chuo-ku,
  Tokyo 104 Japan

Kenya

Kenya Gemstone Dealers Assoc.
  P.O. Box 47928
Nairobi
Kenya
Dr. N.R. Barot

Malaysia

Malaysian Institute of
  Gemmological Sciences
Lot 3, 76-3, 78 3rd Floor
Wisma Stephens
Jalan Caja Chulma
Kuala Lempur

Netherlands

CIBJO-International
  Confederation of Jewellery,
  Silverware, Diamonds, Pearls
  and Stones
Van de Spiegelstratte #3
P.O. Box 29818
The Hague, Netherlands
2502LV
Dr. Bernard W. Buenk,
  President

Pakistan

All Pakistan Gem Merch. &
  Jwlrs. Association
1st Floor, Gems & Jewellery
  Trade Centre
Blenken Street
Saddar Karachi-3
Pakistan

Singapore

Singapore Gemologist Society
3, Lengkok Marak
Singapore-1024

South Africa

Gem'l Assoc. of South Africa
P.O. Box 4216
Johannesburg 2000
South Africa
A. Thomas

Sri Lanka

Gemmologists Association of
   Sri Lanka
Professional Centre, 275-76
Baudhaloka Mawatha
Colombo-7
Sri Lanka

Sweden

Swedish Association of
   Gemmologists
Birger Jarlsgatan 88
S-114 20 Stockholm
Sweden
Ake Gewers

Swedish Geological Society
c/o SGU, Box 670
S-751 28 Uppsala
Sweden

Switzerland

The Swiss Society of
   Gemmology
Kanagase 6,
Biel, Switzerland

Scheweizerische
Gemmologische
Gesellschaft
St. Gallen, Switzerland

Swiss Gem Trade Association
Nuschelerstr. 44
8001 Zurich
Switzerland
Dr. Christoph Kerez

Thailand

Asian Institute of
   Gemmological Sciences
987 Silom Road
Rama Jewellery Building, 4th
   Floor
Bangkok 10500, Thailand

Thai Gems and Jewelry Assoc.
33/85 Surawongse Road
17th Floor
Bangkok 10500
Thailand
and
942/152 Charn Issara Tower
15th Floor
Rama 4 Road, Bangkok 10500
Thailand

Zambia

Zambia Gemstone & Precious
   Metal Association
P.O. Box 31099, Room 17
Luangwa House
Cairo Road, Lusaka
Zambia

Zimbabwe

Gem Education Centre of
   Zimbabwe
Founders House
15 Gordon Avenue
Harare, Zimbabwe 707580
Lesley Faye Marsh, F.G.A.

Selected Readings

Arem, Joel E. *Color Encyclopedia of Gemstones.* Second Edition. New York: Van Nostrand Reinhold, 1987.
  Excellent color photography makes this book interesting for anyone.

Bruton, E. *Diamonds.* 2nd Edition. London: Northwood, 1978.
  An excellent, encyclopedic, well-illustrated book, good for both amateur and professional gemologist.

Federman, David. *Modern Jeweler's Consumer Guide to Colored Gemstones.* New York: Van Nostrand Reinhold, 1989.
  Provides fascinating historical lore about each gemstone, information about supply and demand, and such gemological basics as hardness, durability, and color enhancement.

Kunz, G.F. *The Curious Lore of Precious Stones.* Reprinted 1972, with *The Magic of Jewels and Charms.* New York: Dover Publications.
  An Illustrated guide to the history and powers of gemstones. Includes information about birthstones, gemstone properties and therapy.

———. *Rings For the Finger.* Unabridged republication of 1917 edition. New York: Dover Publications. 1973.
  Fascinating for young and old; for the historical romantic.

Levi, Karen, ed. *The Power of Love: Six Centuries of Diamond Betrothal Rings.* London: The Diamond Information Centre, 1988.
  Wonderful photographs and fascinating historical anecdotes tracing diamond betrothal rings from the middle ages to the present.

Matlins, Antoinette and Antonio. C. Bonanno,. *Jewelry & Gems: The Buying Guide.* Second Edition. So. Woodstock, Vermont: GemStone Press, 1989.
  A great complement to *Engagement & Wedding Rings* (written by the same authors), this book covers a broader range of gemstones and provides useful price guides on colored stones and pearls.

———. *Gem Identification Made Easy: A Hands-On Guide to More Confident Buying & Selling.* So. Woodstock: GemStone Press, 1989. The only book of its kind that explains in non-technical terms how to *identify* diamonds and colored gems and to separate them from imitations and "look-alikes," by using several easy-to-use instruments. The companion book to the authors' earlier titles.

Schumann, W. *Gemstones of the World.* Translated by E. Stern. New York: Sterling Publishing Co., 1977.
  This book has superior color plates of all of the gem families and their different varieties and for this reason would be valuable to anyone interested in gems.

Zucker, Benjamin. *Gems and Jewels: A Connoisseur's Guide.* New York: Thames and Hudson, Inc., 1984.
A lavishly illustrated book on the history and use of principal gems and "great" gemstones of the world, giving fascinating historical facts and mythological tidbits as well as many examples of the jeweler's art from widely differing cultures.

The Anniversary Gift List

Anniversary	Suggested Gift
1	Gold Jewelry
2	Garnet
3	Pearl
4	Blue Topaz
5	Sapphire
6	Amethyst
7	Onyx
8	Tourmaline
9	Lapis Lazuli
10	Diamond Jewelry
11	Turquoise
12	Jade
13	Citrine
14	Opal
15	Ruby
16	Peridot
17	Watches
18	Cat's Eye
19	Aquamarine
20	Emerald
21	Iolite
22	Spinel
23	Imperial Topaz
24	Tanzanite
25	Silver Jubilee
30	Pearl Jubilee
35	Emerald
40	Ruby
45	Sapphire
50	Golden Jubilee
55	Alexandrite
60	Diamond Jubilee

This anniversary gift list was compiled and recently adopted by representatives of six jewelry industry organizations: AGTA, Jewelers of America, The American Gem Society, the Gemological Institute of America, the Jewelry Industry Council, and the Cultured Pearl Association.

INDEX

A WORKSHEET TO HELP YOU SELECT YOUR RINGS

Ring sizes	Wedding band width
Bride's _____	Bride's _____ millimeters
Groom's _____	Groom's _____ millimeters

Jewelry Store: _____

Address: _____

Phone No.: _____

Store representative's name: _____

Price of ring: $_____

Description of ring:

Setting   (Check appropriate descriptions)

    Metal: □ 14k □ 18k □ 22k □ yellow gold □ white gold
             □ platinum □ platinum iridium

    Custom-made: □ yes   □ no

    Is this a designer ring?   □ yes   □ no

    If yes, name of designer? _____

Identity of main stone: _____

    Weight: _____   **Shape:** _____

    Dimensions (millimeters): _____ X _____ X _____

Additional Information (including answers to questions in Chapter 22):

_____

_____

_____

For Diamonds —

Is the stone accompanied by a diamond grading report?*

    If so: **Issued by:** _____ **Date:**_____

    Color grade (circle one)

    D E F G H I J K L M N O P Q R S T U V W X Y Z

    Clarity (Flaw) grade (circle one)

    FL IF VVS_1 VVS_2 VS_1 VS_2 SI_1 SI_2 I_1 I_2 I_3

For Colored Gems —

Is the stone accompanied by a colored gemstone report?*

    If so: **Issued by:** _____ **Date:**_____

    Color grading data

    (hue/tone/saturation): _____

Clarity grade (circle one)   FL   VVS/LI   VS/LI   SI/MI   I/HI

*Ask for a copy of the report to take with you
(See Chapters 8 and 13)

Jewelry Store: _____

Address: _____

Phone No.: _____

Store representative's name: _____

Price of ring: $_____

Description of ring:

Setting (Check appropriate descriptions)

    Metal: ☐ 14k ☐ 18k ☐ 22k ☐ yellow gold ☐ white gold

               ☐ platinum ☐ platinum iridium

    Custom-made: ☐ yes ☐ no

    Is this a designer ring? ☐ yes ☐ no

    If yes, name of designer? _____

Identity of main stone: _____

    Weight: _____   **Shape:** _____

    Dimensions (millimeters): _____ X _____ X _____

Additional Information (including answers to questions in Chapter 22):

_____

_____

_____

For Diamonds —

Is the stone accompanied by a diamond grading report?*

    If so: **Issued by:** _____ **Date:**_____

    Color grade (circle one)

    D E F G H I J K L M N O P Q R S T U V W X Y Z

    Clarity (Flaw) grade (circle one)

    FL IF VVS_1 VVS_2 VS_1 VS_2 SI_1 SI_2 I_1 I_2 I_3

For Colored Gems —

Is the stone accompanied by a colored gemstone report?*

    If so: **Issued by:** _____ **Date:**_____

    Color grading data

    (hue/tone/saturation): _____

Clarity grade (circle one)   FL   VVS/LI   VS/LI   SI/MI   I/HI

*Ask for a copy of the report to take with you

(See Chapters 8 and 13)

Jewelry Store: _____

Address: _____

Phone No.: _____

Store representative's name: _____

Price of ring: $_____

Description of ring:

Setting   (Check appropriate descriptions)

      Metal: ☐ 14k ☐ 18k ☐ 22k ☐ yellow gold ☐ white gold
                 ☐ platinum   ☐ platinum iridium

      Custom-made: ☐ yes   ☐ no

      Is this a designer ring?   ☐ yes   ☐ no

      If yes, name of designer?   _____

Identity of main stone: _____

    Weight: _____   **Shape:** _____

    Dimensions (millimeters): _____ X _____ X _____

Additional Information (including answers to questions in Chapter 22):

_____

_____

_____

For Diamonds —

Is the stone accompanied by a diamond grading report?*

    If so: **Issued by:** _____ **Date:**_____

    Color grade (circle one)

    D E F G H I J K L M N O P Q R S T U V W X Y Z

    Clarity (Flaw) grade (circle one)

    FL IF VVS_1 VVS_2 VS_1 VS_2 SI_1 SI_2 I_1 I_2 I_3

For Colored Gems —

Is the stone accompanied by a colored gemstone report?*

    If so: **Issued by:** _____ **Date:**_____

    Color grading data

    (hue/tone/saturation): _____

Clarity grade (circle one) FL   VVS/LI   VS/LI   SI/MI   I/HI

*Ask for a copy of the report to take with you
(See Chapters 8 and 13)

Jewelry Store: _____

Address: _____

Phone No.: _____

Store representative's name: _____

Price of ring: $_____

Description of ring:

Setting   (Check appropriate descriptions)

Metal: ☐ 14k ☐ 18k ☐ 22k ☐ yellow gold ☐ white gold
☐ platinum ☐ platinum iridium

Custom-made: ☐ yes ☐ no

Is this a designer ring?   ☐ yes ☐ no

If yes, name of designer?   _____

Identity of main stone: _____

Weight: _____   **Shape:**   _____

Dimensions (millimeters):   _____ X _____ X _____

Additional Information (including answers to questions in Chapter 22):

_____

_____

_____

For Diamonds —

Is the stone accompanied by a diamond grading report?*

If so: **Issued by:** _____ **Date:**_____

Color grade (circle one)

D E F G H I J K L M N O P Q R S T U V W X Y Z

Clarity (Flaw) grade (circle one)

FL IF VVS_1 VVS_2 VS_1 VS_2 SI_1 SI_2 I_1 I_2 I_3

For Colored Gems —

Is the stone accompanied by a colored gemstone report?*

If so: **Issued by:** _____ **Date:**_____

Color grading data

(hue/tone/saturation): _____

Clarity grade (circle one)   FL   VVS/LI   VS/LI   SI/MI   I/HI

*Ask for a copy of the report to take with you
(See Chapters 8 and 13)

Please send me _____ copies of ENGAGEMENT & WEDDING RINGS at $14.95* plus $2.50 postage and handling each.

☐ Check enclosed for $ _____ (make checks payable to: "GemStone Press")

☐ Charge to my credit card ☐ Visa ☐ Mastercard ☐ American Express

Name on card _____

Credit Card # _____ Expiration date _____

Signature _____ Telephone # _____

Please send book(s) to:

Name _____

Street _____

City/State _____ Zip _____

Phone or mail orders to: GemStone Press, P.O. Box 276, So. Woodstock, VT 05071 (802) 457-4000
FOR TOLL FREE CREDIT CARD ORDERS CALL 1-800-962-4544   FAX (802) 457-4004
QUOTES ON QUANTITY ORDERS AVAILABLE   *Price subject to change

Cut Along Dashed Line

Please send me, at no charge, a copy of *"AFTER YOU BUY: TIPS ON GEM & JEWELRY CARE & PROTECTION,"* and add my name to your *free* mailing list to receive important consumer-alert bulletins, money-saving tips, and information about jewelry and other gem and jewelry books:

My
Name _____

Street _____

City/State _____ Zip _____

Send to:
GemStone Press, P.O. Box 276, So. Woodstock, Vt. 05071

For additional copies of
AFTER YOU BUY: TIPS ON GEM & JEWELRY CARE & PROTECTION
Send $3.00 and a large stamped, self addressed envelope
for each copy to:
GemStone Press, P.O. Box 276, So. Woodstock, Vt. 05071

NOW YOU CAN HAVE THE "PROFESSIONAL'S ADVANTAGE"!
With Your OWN Jeweler's LOUPE
The Essential "TOOL OF THE TRADE"!

Personally selected by the authors, this valuable jeweler's aid is *now available to the consumer* from GemStone Press. And GemStone Press includes, FREE, a copy of "The Professional's Advantage: How To Use The Loupe And What To Look For," a $3.50 value. Written with the engaged couple in mind, you can now HAVE MORE FUN WHILE SHOPPING, AND MAKE YOUR CHOICE WITH GREATER CONFIDENCE. This is not just a magnifying glass. It is specially made to be used to examine jewelry. It will help you to —

- *Enjoy* the inner beauty of the gem as well as the outer beauty
- *Protect yourself* — see scratches, chips, or cracks that reduce the value of a stone or make it vulnerable to greater damage
- *Prevent loss* — spot weak prongs that may break and cause the stone to fall from the setting.
- *Avoid bad cutting*, poor proportioning and poor symmetry
- *Identify the telltale signs* of glass or imitations

. . . And much more, as revealed in "The Professional's Advantage"!

You'll love it. You'll enjoy looking at the rings up close — it makes this special experience even more exciting. And sometimes, as one of our readers recently wrote:

"Just having the loupe and looking like I knew how to use it changed the way I was treated."

Cut Along Dashed Line

GEMSTONE PRESS
Helping Consumers and the Gem Trade Increase Their Understanding, Appreciation And Enjoyment of Jewelry, Gems and Gemology

An international source for books and other items designed to help people in the gem trade and consumers learn more about jewelry, gems and gemology.

GemStone Press books are easy to read, easy to use. Designed for the person who does not have a scientific or technical background, titles include:

◆**Jewelry & Gems: The Buying Guide** — How to buy diamonds, pearls, precious and other popular gems with confidence and knowledge. More than just a buying guide . . . Know what you want, know what you're buying, save money and avoid costly mistakes.

> *"An essential resource for the gem buyer . . ."*
> —Art & Antiques

> *"Restores the magic! This book is going to entertain and enlighten all its readers and save some from heartbreak."*
> —Paul Harvey, Paul Harvey News

> *"The 'unofficial bible' for the gem investor."*
> —The Robb Report

◆**Gem Identification Made Easy: A Hands-On Guide to More Confident Buying & Selling** — Learn how to use the "tools of the trade." This book makes gem identification fun and interesting rather than "tedious" — even for those without a scientific inclination!

> *"The book you can't do without"*
> —Rapaport Diamond Report

> *"Useful . . . for the professional and not intimidating for the amateur."*
> —Diamond Insight

◆**Engagement & Wedding Rings: The Definitive Buying Guide For People In Love** —Tells everything you need to know to design, select, buy and enjoy . . . to truly experience the wonder and excitement that should be part of it, part of creating that "perfect ring."

*Available from your bookstore
or directly from the Publisher by using the coupons
on the pages that follow.*

GemStone Press also assists its readers by offering **jeweler's loupes, color filters and other instruments** to help identify and enjoy gems. Call us for more information.

GEMSTONE PRESS
P.O. BOX 276, SO. WOODSTOCK, VT 05071
TEL: (802) 457-4000 ◆ FAX: (802) 457-4004
TOLL FREE CREDIT CARD ORDERS CALL (800) 962-4544